Not As
the Crow Flies

Racquet-tailed Drongo, Injipara, India

Not As the Crow Flies

Terry Shortt

McClelland and Stewart Limited

To Audrey,
Valiant Companion at Home
and in the Field

The Canadian Publishers
McClelland and Stewart Limited
25 Hollinger Road, Toronto

Printed and bound in Canada by
T. H. Best Printing Company Limited, Don Mills, Ontario

Contents

Introduction

I was eleven years old. The big double-barrelled Liege twelve-gauge shotgun kicked violently and the thunderous explosion rocketed through the woods. Up near the top of the tall slender poplar the crow swayed for a second, then plummeted straight to the ground. I walked over to survey my victim with a sensation of righteous pride—had I not with skill stalked and brought retribution to the black ravager who had plundered the robin's nest that I had been watching for a week?

The dead crow lay on its back, its long wings partly open. I picked it up by the feet and turned it over. I was instantly impressed by the firm, glossy feathers of its back and wings. As I turned it in my hands the sheen of its plumage changed colour, now blue, now green, then bronze. The clean shining feathers and the magnificent symmetry of their arrangement came as a revelation. The bird smelled of the woods: clean, fresh and feathery. It was a moment of rapturous discovery—a crow was beautiful! I thought it the most gorgeously perfect thing I had ever seen.

It was, perhaps, when I tried to paint a picture of my crow that there originated the desire to be a painter of birds or at least a naturalist by vocation. But progress toward this goal was to be obscure and circuitous. It was not as the crow flies. Winnipeg offered no opportunity for such interests in the 1920s and when I reached the age of fifteen, I turned to art school and commercial art.

The next few years seemed interminable. I had built up a goading daydream of beholding and painting wildlife in far off corners of the earth—South America, Asia and above all Africa. The break came in

1930 when I was offered a position as "assistant" in the Royal Ontario Museum of Zoology in Toronto. Without asking exactly what being an assistant entailed, I accepted the job. As it turned out I found myself involved in taxidermy, sign writing, moulding and casting, carpentry, wall painting and even sweeping floors. But also there was opportunity to participate in field work, to study animals and to illustrate a few zoological publications.

In 1936 I was made, nominally, a member of the newly formed Department of Birds, but the Museum work force was not ample enough to allow me to devote all of my time to ornithology. I still divided my time between bird study and the preparation of exhibition materials. My partiality toward recording the aesthetic and artistic aspects of birds remained, both in the Museum and on expeditions, my avocation. Perhaps because of that my enthusiasm never cooled. Over the years I have made thousands of sketches of birds, recording their postures, perched and in flight, at ease and in action, and above all their portraits, the unique physiognamies of individual species—the beautiful, the bizarre and the grotesque, the ferocious, the mild and even the vacuous—the many faces of birds.

In 1948 I was able to organize and head up the Life Sciences Department of Art and Exhibits. This department, which has undergone several changes of appellation, is the one with which I have been associated ever since. Its scope was such that I was able to realize my ambition to observe and sketch the creatures of exotic lands.

In all I participated in more than two "baker's dozens" of field expeditions, from the arctic to the tropics. It is of events, places, creatures and people encountered on these excursions that I write about here. I have, I hope, looked at animals through an artist's eyes and seen them in terms of my own imagination and interpretation and not within the limits of what I have been taught.

I have never striven to be an impartial student of nature—I would rather be part of it.

ONE

Northern Canada Expeditions

Beelzebub, the unneighbourly Moose

Mud, Muskeg and Mosquitoes

My initial introduction to natural history was as a boy on the long grass prairie, along the edges of wheatlands, in the poplar and oak "bluffs" and about the prairie sloughs. In the late '20s with the acquisition of an old *Reo* car, my brother Angus and I began to explore farther afield. We made our acquaintance with the taiga, the vast needleleaf evergreen forest of spruce and tamarack—the spruce-moose biome. We worked mostly in the Brokenhead River region east of Winnipeg, with excursions farther afield to Gimli, Elk Island in Lake Winnipeg and once up on the "Muskeg Special" railway as far as Ochre River.

After joining the Royal Ontario Museum I made many trips into the taiga; to southern Algoma in 1931, Lake St. Martin in the Interlaken of Manitoba in 1934, to North Bay in 1935, Thunder Bay and Kenora in 1937 and 1947, Moosonee in 1939, Fort Albany in 1942 and to Lake Athabaska in 1945.

There is a singularity, a universality to this vast area that stretches from the Atlantic to the western mountains and I have found it expedient to lump together accounts of expeditions to the taiga conducted over a twenty-year period under one chapter heading. It was also convenient to include Ontario's "Southern Arctic" in this section.

The taiga, or needleleaf evergreen forest, encircles the globe in a wide belt around the northern hemisphere—roughly, between 45°

and 65° north latitude. (Patches and fingers of it extend far to the north and south of these latitudes; for example, north to Great Bear Lake and beyond the Arctic Circle in the Mackenzie River basin, and south into California and Colorado—even down the western cordillera of Mexico.) It is generally a region of deep snow, severe cold, and clear nights in winter; of high humidex, muskeg, mosquitoes, and biting flies, and short, cool, quiet nights in summer.

Next to the polar tundra, the taiga is the least variable of the major biological zones. Its general aspect in northern Alberta, Newfoundland, Finland or central Siberia is much the same, with only slight differences in the fauna. Because the northern hemisphere contains two thirds of the continental land-masses, much of the earth's surface—from Alaska to Newfoundland and from Norway to Kamchatka—is, or was, covered by boreal forests. These forests, then, of spruce, larch and tamarack, fir and pine, form one enormous, homogeneous zone around the world. The flora—and the fauna —may be considered impoverished in terms of the number of different *kinds* of plants and animals in comparison with southern and tropical forests; its relatively few species, however, exist in astonishing numbers. And, as indicated above, most forms of taiga life are circumpolar. Moose, ermine, grosbeaks, crossbills, kinglets, tits, wolverine, red fox, three-toed and spotted woodpeckers, hawk owls, martin, lynx, otter, waxwings, grey jays, and shrikes exist either as identical or closely-related species in both northern North America and northern Eurasia. In North America the avifauna is, to a large extent however, composed of the forest thrushes, wood warblers, and many species of finches peculiar to the New World. The juncos, (members of the finch family) are found in abundance from coast to coast. There are probably more of these in Canada than there are of all the species of several families in all the tropical regions put together.

Summer on the taiga is unique. It is aromatic, for one thing. The hot sun brings out the smell of spruce, fir, tamarack, and pine. There is a scent peculiar to the green needles of each, another to the resins, and still another to the carpet of dead needles toasting in the heat. The day-time sounds tend to be a bit monotonous: the weak twitterings and lispings of the wood warblers; the wooden *zib-zib-zib* of juncos; the rattling, harsh cries of woodpeckers; the thin, weak songs of chickadees, kinglets, and creepers; the whine of too many mosquitoes. In pine forests, add the sound of mandibular crunching by Pine Sawyer larvae.

But in the evening?—in the evening the finest songs in the world are heard: the flutings of the forest thrushes; the whistling of the Whitethroated Sparrow; the tinkling, water-drop song of a Saw-Whet Owl; and, too rarely, the enriching song of a Timber Wolf. Then night falls. Such quiet is found elsewhere only in winter. The call of a Hermit or Greycheeked Thrush occasionally breaks the silence. Since frogs breed in the spring, their amatory trilling and piping is soon stilled. Silence—and frequent, brilliant displays of northern lights: cold, hostile—a time to roost, to huddle, to sleep.

For some, the uniformity of the taiga may be tedious: seemingly endless conformist spruce forests broken only where nature or man, by lightning, fire or axe, has eliminated them. Yet, new burns are a delight to behold. Acre upon acre of radiant, mauve-pink fireweed—as conformist as the spruce with its uniform shape —stands against the stark, charcoal-coated stumps of burned trees. Old burns, too, break the monotony. They are populated by young, pale green poplars, permitted to grow in the taiga only because the death of the tall spruce has allowed the sunlight they need.

Taiga—vast, monotonous, invigorating, tedious, exciting, lonely—a naturalist's delight or nightmare, where little can happen except getting lost, being trapped in quaking bog, or being eaten alive by biting, sucking insects.

Cape Henrietta Maria

When I joined the Museum staff in 1930 there was talk of an expedition to Moosonee at the head of steel on James Bay. In those days this was the "far north". It became my ambition to be included in this field party. The trip finally materialized in 1939 and with Lester Snyder and Douglas B. Deeks I undertook to do the job. It was a big let-down. The glamour soon faded in wet muskeg, mud, mosquitoes, cold rainy weather and a meagre fauna.

But I had established myself as one of the Museum's northern collectors and in 1942 with C.E. Hope I was assigned the task of making a bird survey of the region about the mouth of the Albany River one hundred miles farther north on the bay. The trip was negotiated both ways in a big sponson freighter canoe. Once again the experience was little short of nightmarish: drenchings in salt water, impassable ice fields (until the wind changed), storm-bound on shore by fog, high winds, violent storms and even a blizzard. We ran out of food and had to snare rabbits. One bitterly cold night I awoke to find that my head had slipped off my bedroll and that my hair was frozen to the ground!

After that experience I was thoroughly disenchanted by the great sodden, muskeggy west coast plain of James Bay. But when an expedition was formed to investigate the fauna of the Cape Henrietta Maria region at the northern tip of the bay in 1948, guess who volunteered? It turned out to be one of the most pleasant and rewarding of all my field trips. The physical aspect of the terrain resembled the high Arctic tundra with its waterfowl and shorebirds which had captured my affection years before.

14

It was a large and congenial party of six that arrived at Moosonee to negotiate the transportation of bodies and equipment to Moose Island at the mouth of the Moose River —which was accomplished thanks to a fleet of freighter canoes piloted by Swampy Cree Indians. When we were finally settled at Moose Factory on the island, we met our bush pilot, George Charity, who was to fly us in to the Cape. George, who always looked as though he needed a good night's sleep, was a quiet, cheerful man. It was his job to land us on the water, close to shore, despite very real possibilities of sudden squalls, ice fog, and ice-choked shorelines. Three trips would be necessary to fly in all our gear and party.

We were delayed a day by weather, and then finally the first load left. George returned the next morning reporting that the advance party had got ashore safely—though wettishly—a few miles below the Cape. The second load also arrived safely. Wyn Watson and I had been left to look after the tag ends and accompany the remainder of the gear. When our turn arrived, the Norseman—a light airplane used in bush-flying throughout the North—was loaded to the gills. The morning was clear with little wind. But take-off was difficult because of the short strip, and we cleared the tops of the spruce trees with so little to spare that I could smell the spruce gum. The first half of the flight went smoothly. We stopped at Albany and at Attawapiskat, the half-way point, for refuelling. The region from Attawapiskat to Cape Henrietta Maria was totally uninhabited. All we saw were the James Bay ice fields, blankets of ice fog, gams of white whales, and herds of seals among the ice pans.

As we approached the Cape, the air became turbulent. "We'll be coming in under the overcast. It may be a bit bumpy. Hang on tight. If we flip, tuck in your chin." As George was given to understatement, I was sure that it was going to be damned bumpy. I looked around; there was nothing to hang on to. I decided that if things looked bad I would draw up my knees, hold the top of my head with both hands, press my elbows against my ribs, go limp, and hope for the best. Our landing was, however, uneventful. George set the plane down on the rough water, we bounced lightly once, and taxied in to our eager colleagues. Like a well-drilled team, they charged down the gravelly beach, grabbed the wings and, nearly waist-deep

15

in the icy water, held the plane off shore. Our gear was soon piled on land under a protective tarp.

We all clutched the wings and steered George around to his requested take-off position. He gunned the engine, took off, made one circle, dipped his wings, and flew south, barely a hundred feet above the water. We wouldn't see another human being for more than a month.

It was the most auspicious beginning to a field trip that I'd ever had. All I had to do was set up my "safari bed" and lay out my eiderdown. The tents were already neatly and squarely set up, complete with mosquito bars. The work tables were ready with tools laid out. And the cook tent being in good order, a hot dinner was about ready for "come and get it, before we throw it to the pigs."

The first evening in camp was electrifying: Smith's Longspurs, Stilt Sandpipers, Dunlin, Old Squaws, Ptarmigan, and Northern Phalaropes in abundance. There were also Polar Bear and wolf tracks on the beach. My enthusiasm was mounting. Much that we found would be new to the scientific world because Cape Henrietta Maria hadn't been subjected to a biological investigation of any significance. Everything we found would be new knowledge or corroboration of superficial observation.

The Cape takes in the entire treeless area bordered for about fifty miles (eighty kilometres) by Hudson Bay on the north and for an equal distance by James Bay on the east. The world's southernmost patch of Arctic, it is uninhabited except for occasional groups of Indians hunting geese in the autumn and trapping fox in the winter. The terrain is exceedingly flat, broken only by several sand dunes, relics of old shorelines that rise six to eight feet above the plain. The whole area, in the geologically recent past, was below sea level. The greater part of the Cape is grass tundra, by far the richest, faunally, of all Arctic associations. In the number of animals an acre, it rivals that of any of the earth's biomes (communities of plants and animals, the make-up of which is determined by the soil and climatic conditions). The grass tundra is interrupted by slightly higher ridges or bars of gravelly, disintegrated limestone. These areas are usually barren though lichens, mosses, and recumbent flowering plants persist. Such areas are often referred to as desert tundra, and support only impoverished fauna.

16

Along the banks of creeks and streams, and around the margins of the numerous "snowpools", there is a sparse growth of shrubs. Varieties of the willow predominate, which, in particularly favourable situations, reach a height of four to six feet. Boggy places on the edges of fresh-water pools favour stunted Dwarf Birch. A few Black Spruce and Tamarack grow singly, rarely reaching a height of more than three feet. This area, then, has the physical aspect and climate of true Arctic tundra although it lies at 55° north latitude—about the same as Newcastle or Belfast. This is owing to its peninsular character and to the fact that the mouth of James Bay traps the southward-drifting ice fields of Hudson Bay. During the summer months, when Hudson Bay is relatively free of ice, there are still vast ice-packs in the northern part of James Bay. The Cape is almost continually chilled by the prevailing north and east winds that sweep across the ice. The mean temperature recorded by our expedition for July and the first two weeks of August was just under 45°F. (21°C.)

Frequently enshrouded in chilling ice fog, which creates grotesque mirages of stunted spruce trees, it is weird, lonely, cold country to work in. In the fog, these spruce trees rise up out of the gloom like misshapen spires only to collapse, dwarf, and fold in upon themselves as one draws closer. Then they dissolve into innocuous, half-starved, aged little trees, gnarled and twisted by wind and abrasive, blowing snow. Onshore winds and tide often bring in an almost solid mass of floes that trundle across the beach to run aground within a hundred yards of our tents. When this happens, the nights are indeed cold. With the next tide and an offshore wind, the big pans are hauled out to float freely once more. As they "waddle" across rippled sand, they leave tracks as if some titanic vehicle had driven into the water.

Yet, this country suits me. I enjoy the melancholy wilderness of bleak, inclement places—if they are wilderness. I always feel at home on limitless grasslands, on moors and fens, on a high plateau, on a cliff-rimmed coast with the crash of breakers and the shrill cries of sea birds in my ears.

My colleagues, too, enjoyed Cape Henrietta Maria—and not only its climate and physical environment, but also the unexpected. Once, after a long morning in the field, Cliff and I were trudging wearily across the tundra, discussing the birds that we had seen and collected.

17

We had penetrated deep into barren lands, and were now heading back toward camp, leg-weary, and tired of battling mosquitoes. We climbed the last of the series of ancient dunes that paralleled the shore on which we were camping. When we reached its crest and our camp came into view, we realized that something was amiss. Other members of our party were launching the canoe to bring us across the creek that lay between us and the tents. They were also waving and shouting excitedly. Fatigue was forgotten as we hurried across the last few hundred yards. We heard the ominous words, "Polar Bear".

Dalton Muir had found the nest and eggs of a Pintail about a quarter of a mile south of camp. It was in a particularly pleasing setting, partially shielded by a thin clump of tall, coarse grass with wheat-like plumes. Dalton had set up his camera with remote control, erected a small burlap hide, and had settled down to wait. He had taken some pictures of the duck on her nest, had run out of film, and had gone back to camp to reload. He spent some time talking to Wyn Watson, who was going over his insect collection of the morning, and Lew Walden, who had run his small-mammal trapline.

Dalton was appalled at what he saw when he returned to his lookout fifteen minutes later. His hide had been crushed and scattered. The camera and tripod were strewn about, the duck's eggs were gone, and the brooding bird's feathers were everywhere. The sand all around was pockmarked with the huge pugs, or paw prints, of a Polar Bear. Had Dalton not run out of film, he would have been crouched in the cramped little hide with little or no chance of escape.

With binoculars, we examined the cache of specimens that had been set up on the beach under a tarpaulin ready for George Charity and his plane. The bear had been at that too.

"He'll probably be back," I said, "and it will be the camp next time. He'll smell the cook tent. If he comes at night, we're in trouble."

We were a hundred and twenty miles (193 km.) to the nearest help at Attawapiskat and another two hundred miles (320 km.) to a doctor at Moose Factory. Our only means of transportation was a frail canoe intended for use on the creeks and rivers of the Cape. It certainly wouldn't be adequate to get a bear-mauled museum collector to a

18

doctor. I broke open the gun box and took out two heavy rifles.

"Come on, Lew," I said. "It's too bad, but we've got to track him down and shoot him. We just can't take the risk of his coming back." At that moment, Wyn reported that the bear was on the shore near the water's edge, just north of our camp.

"Most beautiful sight I've ever seen," he said, and indeed the eurhythmical cadence of its swinging walk, for all its bulk, was a sight to behold. Lew and I, followed by Dalton with tripod and camera, set off after the great white trouble-maker. The wind was in our favour, and the shore was paralleled by a ten-foot sand dune. We stayed on the landward side of this, climbing to its crest occasionally to see where the bear was. It was making good time, its big feet hardly sinking in the hard-packed sand of the beach; we were floundering through loose sand and marshy areas. At last we got to within seventy-five yards and crossed the dune onto the beach directly behind it. All we could see were its great buttocks waddling along; we were still impressed by the gracefulness of its walk. We had to follow it another fifty yards before it turned sideways and afforded a practical shot.

"Just one burst of movie before you shoot," Dalton said quietly.

As it was about to enter the water, we shot it. The hunter's story ends there. And the museum collector's begins. Museum collectors don't kill indiscriminately; every time we do kill, we make a great deal of work for ourselves. A Polar Bear specimen from Ontario was important to the mammal department. We skinned for the rest of the day: there's more to preparing a specimen for a museum than there is to getting a rug for the family room. Each digit of the paws—eyelids, ears, lips, nose must be skinned out and scraped absolutely clean. We carried back the heavy hide, the skull, and one haunch at ten o'clock—just as the sun was setting. Most of the next day was taken up with scraping off the thick layer of oily fat that clung to the skin and in some further cleaning of the skull. By this time we were slippery with grease and smelled like the bear cage at the zoo. The collector's story ends there.

And the cook's begins. The haunch that we brought back was butchered and boiled with dehydrated carrots and onions. We looked forward to this change in our diet of dried and tinned meat. It turned out to be the most unpalatable stew we'd ever eaten—and it was days before the cook tent lost its unpleasant odour. Old *Thalarctos* had indeed caused us a lot of trouble. Yet, when the hide was salted and packed away, we felt sorry that we had been forced to kill this magnificent animal.

The Unneighbourly Moose

The Timber Wolf, the now rare and much vilified Wolverine, and the Canada Lynx are seldom aggressive. Stories of attack by these animals are either the result of a last-ditch offensive by a cornered animal or they are apocryphal. I've had more trouble with deer —White-Tailed and Mule bucks especially. I've seen a person gored by a Sika, too. But an animal that I respect is the Moose.

I was on a collecting expedition in a tamarack-black spruce bog—moose country—not far from Abitibi Canyon. I was walking in rubber hip-boots in the bog where the sphagnum moss was deep and spongy. At every step, I sank almost to the knee; it was tiring. To rest, I frequently straddled a little tamarack and leaned back. (This takes practice if you're not to be dumped on your backside in the water-filled sphagnum!) On one of these rests, I became aware of a moose coming toward me. I kept still, thinking that he would stop as soon as he saw me. He kept coming, however, walking slowly, deliberately. It struck me as odd, too, that he had his head low, swinging it from side to side in a very purposeful manner. I suddenly realized that he had seen me as soon as I had seen him—that he hadn't changed his pace or his actions—that he was looking right at me —and that he was now only about forty feet away! (Unfortunately —from a scientific point of view—my instinct for self-preservation prevented me from finding out just what he had in mind.) I swung upright—the tamarack didn't dump me—grabbed my shotgun, and fired a load of heavy shot just over his head from less than thirty feet. Some of the shot must have penetrated his small velvety antlers. He swerved, and, with fantastic leg action, churned off through the bush. I couldn't help but admire—and envy—the speed and ease with which he strode over the muskeg.

On another occasion, Lester Snyder, a curator of birds at R.O.M., and I were on a collecting trip near Kenora, Ontario. We had rented a cabin in a little marsh bordering Wabigoon Lake. When I returned from the first day's collecting, I met our backyard—and frontyard—neighbour: a most odious-looking moose. It was the season of the year when moose antlers are still in velvet. This one had started to rub some of his velvet off. The furry skin was hanging in shreds and tatters from his less-than-imposing set of antlers. He had a bulbous, pendulous nose stuck on a thin face—indeed his head proportions closely resembled those of a cow moose. His coat was mangy, moth-eaten. He seemed uncommonly knock-kneed and had the swayback of an old draft-horse.

Normally it would have been most agreeable to have a moose in the yard—especially as it wasn't my yard. But not this moose: he had been sucking at our laundry! When I arrived, he was working over one of my best khaki bush-shirts. There were frothy saliva spots all over it as it hung limply from the line by one clothes-pinned shoulder. Other articles—socks, trousers, underwear—had been pulled down and trampled in the grass which, fortunately, hadn't been cut for some time.

Presuming to know the reactions of a moose, I advanced quickly, shouting colourful expletives. He didn't move a muscle, except to slowly turn his repulsive deformed head and look at me over his mangy shoulder. This caused his eyes to roll, and a big half-halo of white appeared above the near one—adding to his already repelling demeanour. I was surprised by this unmoose-like reaction. I continued, however, to advance and shout. He turned slowly, half faced me, and showed that baleful white crescent above his eyes. I then realized that he was not only irritable and getting angry: he looked psychopathic. He started for me. I turned and dashed through the copse and around the cabin. As I slammed the door behind me, I saw him through the window. He was coming after me, not running, not

21

even walking quickly—just purposefully. He came into the front-yard and stood there.

How to warn Lester? That bloody great hippogriff—which I dubbed Beelzebub—was still there. I slipped quietly out the back door, ran quickly to the thicket for protection, and then got out into the field beyond. In a few minutes, Lester appeared.

"We've got a belligerent moose in the yard. He's dangerous."

"Oh come now, Shortt," he laughed. "Who's afraid of a moose?"

"Well, you'll see," I replied, half hoping that Beelzebub hadn't gone. "I'll sneak up to see if he's there." From the copse, there was no sign of him in either the front or the backyard. I motioned to Lester to follow me. When I was about half-way to the cabin, Lester yelled, "Look out!" I turned and just made it back to the woods in time. Beelzebub had charged out from the other side of the cabin. He stopped at the edge of bushes, pawed the ground, snorted, rolled his dreadful eyes, and rocked his shaggy antlers. It appeared that he had chased me far enough away from "his yard"—and he had convinced Lester that he was no ordinary moose.

Much later that day, we regained our rights of residence. Beelzebub wandered down to the marsh, and I retrieved my clothes. For the duration of our stay, however, Beelzebub determined which door we should use. Whenever we went out into the yard, he charged—not full tilt—but with spleenful, squint-eyed deliberation and authority. He seldom followed us far. If he heard us when we left by either door, he would lumber around after us; he always gave up the chase, however, when we reached the copse. I guess you could add laziness to his other vices.

I challenged him a couple of times. One time, after a tiring day, I decided that I'd had enough of hiding in the copse, sneaking around the field, dashing for the door. As I emerged, headed for the back door, I yelled epithets at Beelzebub and threw a golf ball-sized stone at him, which hit his side with a hollow thud. Another caromed off his antlers. Yet another missed altogether as by now I was running backward like a trapped quarterback. He came for me faster than ever before.

I just made it to the front door.

Another time we were short of water. Even though Lester suggested that we wait until Beelzebub left for the marsh, I was determined to go to the pump. On the back porch, there was a pile of uncut, six-foot lengths of firewood. I set off for the pump with a stick and a pail.

"I'm going out to get some water, and if he comes after me, I'll break this club over his ugly head."

"I'll hold the door open," said Lester, chuckling.

I got to the pump. Beelzebub looked over. I put the stick down and began to pump. The water wouldn't come—it needed a prime. Eventually it began to flow, and I forgot about the moose.

"Here he comes," shouted the doorkeeper. In my excitement, I kicked my stick into the watery mud. Beelzebub was coming fast. I ran. He wasn't a dozen paces behind me when I shot through the doorway—without the water. Lester slammed the door—and laughed! Feeling cheated, Beelzebub came up to the window, shook his scruffy antlers, rolled his whitelunatic eyes, and wandered back to stand in *his* garden.

Beelzebub forced one final indignity upon us in addition to his having severely limited dignified exits and entrances, laundry chores, and water fetching. When we were ready to leave, we hired a truck to take us and our belongings to the railway station. The driver backed right up to the front door—fortunately there weren't any steps —while we loaded our possessions. (The driver, having seen Beelzebub, stayed in the cab.) We then climbed into the back, and didn't dare get out to join the driver in the cab until we were fifty yards down the road.

Beware the friendly moose!

Muskeg or "Quick! Three Beers"

Muskeg, from the Cree word *muskak,* meaning *swamp,* is a Canadian word. It is generally understood to mean an organic brown-to-black mixture of water and dead vegetation that is covered with a carpet of sphagnum. It can be quite deep. Permafrost forms the base; a layer of vegetation (saturated moss, peat, and silt) too solidly frozen to decompose. This layer, which may be yards thick, sticky as gum, and slippery as axle grease, is insulated by living moss. As much of our country is covered by it, the word at least—if not the real thing—is familiar to most Canadians. Until the forties, few Americans knew the word. From 1942 to 1945, however, ten thousand of them learned—first-hand—about muskeg as they built the Alaska Highway. From Fort St. John, B.C. to Fairbanks, Alaska, 1,670 miles of road was laid, much of it over muskeg. The number of trucks, tractors, and bulldozers—and Americans —that sank out of sight in it, is unknown.

Muskeg country—land of tens of thousands of lakes, some of which are invisible. They have a "ground cover" of sphagnum, crowberry, Labrador tea, and grasses that has trapped some soil on which alders, low-bush cranberry, willows, and even small spruce trees grow. Many muskeg lakes, however, consist of some still, deep, open water surrounded by a rim-anchored, floating mat—a mat of dense, intertwined plants that can often support the weight of a man. A similar phenomenon occurs farther south, but the plants of the water—Water Hyacinth, Water Lettuce, arrowheads, Pickerelweed—are usually quite distinct from those growing on solid ground. The vegetation on frozen muck and over water in muskeg, however, is the

24

same so that it is difficult to tell where one leaves off and the other begins.

The muskeg's "quaking bogs" provide clearings where the sunlight can beat down through the dark forest. These openings attract animals—such as muskrats—that don't like the dark forest of the surrounding taiga. Also, the open water of these areas lure waterfowl: Ringnecked Duck, Sora and Virginia rails, marsh wrens, coot.

To collect these and other specimens that are almost unattainable elsewhere, I often explored these quaking bogs. They are frightening, at first; I walked over them very gingerly. Experience enabled me to enjoy the sensation of walking on their buoyant surfaces. I gradually lost my fear—but seldom my respect. Man is not well designed for walking on muskeg: as he walks, all his weight is shifted from one central point to another. Only crossing a bog on a pogo stick would make him more vulnerable! A moose, on the other hand, with at least six times the weight of a man, distributes his mass in a more efficient way. If he steps on a thin spot and plunges through, he has a relatively small proportion of his body weight on that leg. He also has three other widely-spaced supports to take the load while he pulls out the one in trouble. But not man. When one leg goes through, the other one is too closely attached to be of any use, even if it too hasn't gone through. Man has only one advantage: he can spread his arms. When walking over this treacherous landscape, I never wore hipwaders; when worn with belt harness, they could be lethal if they filled with water. I usually wore sneakers and got my feet wet.

Just north of Chipewyan, on Lake Athabasca in northern Alberta, there are several small bog lakes—very fruitful collecting grounds. One hot July day, I returned to a familiar one, which covered about ten acres. It had a small patch of open water in the centre, and I had been out to the margin several times. This was a good place to collect specimens of Canvasback, Ruddy Duck, Horned Grebe, Virginia Rail, Sora Rail, and Wilson's Phalarope. In this vegetation-choked lakelet, I had seen Shorteared Owls and I had heard Longbilled Marsh Wrens. The trees around this lake, bathed in sunlight because of the open water, were luxuriantly foliated—lusher, greener than their forest counterparts. They were therefore inhabited by birds not found in the dark interior of the usual taiga, or boreal forest. The augmented food supply of caddis flies, May flies, chironomids, and mosquitoes accounted for the numbers of Western Wood Pewees, Olivesided Flycatchers, Eastern Kingbirds, Blackcapped Warblers, Yellowthroats, Redwings, Swamp Sparrows, Sharptailed Sparrows, and Le Conte's Sparrows that frequented the grass, the alders or the mixed spruce and poplars on the margins.

As I emerged from the forest at the edge of the bog lake, I heard the unmistakeable call of the Yellow Rail: *kek kek, kek kek kek.* I had found this species on the south side of Lake Athabasca, but doubted that it had ever been found on the north side. I set off over the trembling surface. The Yellow Rail is an expert at hiding and skulking; they are almost impossible to flush without a swift dog —the most reluctant of all rails to take wing—at least this is the opinion of many ornithologists. I think that this is truer when they are not on their nesting territory.

I learned a technique for collecting Yellow Rails when I was on a collecting expedition at Kabiskabikau on James Bay. I chased one of this species back and forth across a grassy marsh until I was exasperated. Then I realized that it always seemed to return to one of three or four locations, and it dawned on me that I was chasing not one but three or four birds. As I got near to one, it would go quiet and another, about fifty yards away, would become vocal. Thus, I stood as nearly on the site of the last call as possible, wondering if it might call again if I kept still. In about five minutes, the soft-winged little bird rose from the grass within ten feet of me and fluttered away. Using this "waiting-out-witting" technique, I've collected about fifteen rails in a dozen parts of Canada. But it's sometimes difficult to have the patience in mosquito country!

Back to the north shore of Lake Athabasca. It was a beautiful day—sunny, warm, breezy. I was in no particular hurry to get to the rail's area: I had confidence in my technique. From the edge of the forest came one of the truly characteristic sounds of the north: the whistled *Quick! three beers* of the Olivesided Flycatcher. Warm, at peace, and confident I stepped out onto the quaking bog. It brought out in me the small-boy's excitement that lurks in every man. It was an exceptionally thick carpet, and it kept bouncing me up and down as it undulated for fifty feet or more in every direction. I felt as though I was on a spongy trampoline and started to make it billow even more.

Then I went through.

From exhilaration to despair in one short stride. I was now up to my armpits with my head and outspread arms buried in wet, yielding sphagnum. I felt around with my feet, but there was nothing there but cold water.

"Don't panic," I said to myself, aloud.

Quick! three beers, whistled the Flycatcher.

Luckily I had hung onto my shotgun. I worked it around so that I could grip the ends of the barrels with one hand and the stock with the other. I pressed the gun deep into the sphagnum as far in front of me as possible. Although it wasn't getting me out, it prevented my sinking and gave me time to think. There was no possibility of help arriving. I suddenly realized that my weight was submerging the surrounding sphagnum—it was soaking up water like a sponge. I would soon be drowned in the middle of that large mossy saucer.

I drew a deep breath, lifted the gun, and lunged forward all at the same time. I had gained a few inches; part of my chest now rested on the moss. I did the same again; I gained a few more inches. But the matting was sinking and my face was only just above a pool of water that was oozing up over the moss. I could see that the interlocking fibres were giving way. If I struggled I might break through. And if I went under that dense matting it would be almost impossible for me to break through to the surface again. Not to struggle, however, meant being lowered—slowly and relentlessly—so that the water covered my head.

"It must be awfully dark under there. If I go through, nobody will ever find me," I thought.

Quick! three beers, jeered the Flycatcher.

I took another deep breath and lunged. The gun caught on the thin twigs of a small shrub. I tested its strength: it held. I lunged again and got far enough to be able to jack-knife myself over the treacherous carpet, and get hold of some stronger limbs of the shrub. I was now able to pull myself—on my belly—out onto stronger matting. I was still lying in three or four inches of water, but I was out of the hole.

"You're a damn fool. You know better than to dare the bog," I gasped.

Quick! three beers, shrieked the Flycatcher.

I crawled to safety—slowly. I emptied my shoes, my pockets, my

27

gun barrels. I threw away my sodden shells, wads of cotton, paper, and my sandwich. I was through for the day.

Kek kek, kek kek kek cried the rail.

"To hell with you!" I shouted.

Quick! three beers, whooped the Flycatcher.

TWO

The Nascopie
Expedition

Yellowbilled Loons, Somerset Island—with Longtailed Jaegers in background

Outfit 269

The first Hudson's Bay Company supply ship entered Canadian Arctic waters in 1670. And was later referred to as "Outfit Number One". The voyage of the *Nascopie* in 1938 was therefore known officially as "Outfit 269"—the 269th consecutive year of vessels serving the remote "factories" of the eastern Arctic. The party aboard for these annual trips usually included R.C.M.P. replacements, clergy, a doctor, a dentist, a postmaster, a journalist, and two or three scientists. The last group varied from year to year. Nineteen thirty-eight was my lucky year: a biologist/ornithologist was invited—and I was chosen.

In nearly three months, the Hudson's Bay Company icebreaker would travel 12,000 miles to carry supplies to the outposts, taking in relief personnel, bringing others out, and looking after 1001 matters that require attention when contact with the outside world is only once in a year. To be included in such an expedition was—as far as I was concerned—a marvellous piece of good fortune. In addition to the many experiences that I was to have, I came out with a collection that P.A. Taverner, Dominion Ornithologist, described as "the finest so far brought out of the Arctic by one man in one year."

Outfit 269 of "The Governor and Company of Adventurers of England trading into Hudson Bay" left Montreal on July 9, 1938. A cacophony signalled our departure: a blast of the *Nascopie*'s powerful fog horn; sirens, fog horns, and bells of every other ship and boat in the harbour; the honking of cars and trucks all over the dock area; and even nearby factory whistles. This send-off was a great salute to this

31

battered old icebreaker embarking on her annual voyage to the remote, lonely posts of Canada's Eastern Arctic.

I spent the first hour or so watching the skyline of Montreal slip by, then enjoying the scenery of the St. Lawrence River. At the same time, my mind was whirling with myriads of flashes of anticipated sights and experiences. How could I ever absorb all the sensations that I would encounter between Montreal and *ultima thule*—a place actually named Thule—fewer than a thousand miles from the North Pole! Not to mention the return trip.

Occasionally, an artist was included in these expeditions. Frederick Horsman Varley was on this one—and he was my cabin mate. The company of this delightfully witty, pithily philosophical artist provided yet another dimension to an already exciting experience for a twenty-seven-year-old bird collector. On meeting, it crossed my mind that this craggy-faced man might not appreciate the kind of work I was planning. I didn't have to worry: two "doubles", ordered and consumed within minutes of meeting, established an easy rapport. For the rest of the voyage, I put up with drying paintings, sketches propped up on my bunk, brushes soaking in the wash basin, tubes of paint on everything (including the floor), and smears of the same on most of my possessions. Varley, in turn, put up with racks of drying bird skins, sawdust, cotton batting, and stray feathers. Once—without warning—we struck an ice field: imagine the condition of the Varley-Shortt cabin! I picked feathers and batting from his oil paintings, and he helped me to reshape my precious bird skins, and smooth the disarrayed feathers. Thus, I came to know Varley as a philosopher, humourist, and warm-hearted human being.

During this trip we learned much from each other concerning painting and sketching. As I frequently had to make sketches in cold weather, I wore a heavy woollen sock on my sketching hand. The brush or pencil was forced through the weave of the toe and its barrel held in the bare hand giving better control. At the same time, it provided a mitt that was warmer than a glove. Fred did much of his painting on this trip with his hand in my sock. Intending to paint only in oils, which he soon found refused to dry in the cold humid air, Varley brought no water colours or water-colour brushes or fine quality paper. As I had a goodly supply, we shared. Before the voyage was over, however, we were reduced to writing paper, ruled notebooks, and brown wrapping paper. Varley was driven by the stark, towering immensities of hyperborean landscapes and the natural grace of the Eskimos.

One night, when the going had been particularly difficult, we put on an art show. It was probably the first one ever put on in the Arctic—and viewed by Eskimos. One particularly exquisite water-colour of the mountain behind the Arctic Bay post at the mouth of Admiralty inlet on Baffin Island was "hung" in this show. He had worked on it while it was actually snowing. Great, soft, moisture-laden flakes water-marked the washes during painting. The effect added immeasurably to the mood of the painting. Such was the prowess and awareness of Varley.

The "bull pen" was a large room lined with bunks and reserved for R.C.M.P. and Hudson's Bay Company personnel. It was the social centre of the *Nascopie*. Varley and I seldom missed an opportunity to visit the bull pen. Here one heard tales from conversation-starved men who had been having adventures and experiences to pale any fiction, tales of long dog-sled journeys, of hair-raising pursuits of ruffians under the six-month night, of Eskimo heroism. On some nights there would be a sing-song. Every evening was different as the company changed almost daily: eager men disembarked to do their stint; jubilant men began their furloughs. Just visualize a room full of R.C.M.P. personnel, H.B.C. factors, whalers, explorers, visitors from the posts where we anchored for the night. One cannot buy that sort of entertainment. One cannot help but be broadened by such an experience.

An occasional visitor to the bull pen was Bishop Clabaut—a megalithic man with a back as straight and as flat as an oaken door—who dwarfed all around him. His size was accentuated by his long black cassock, a black peaked cap, and an enormous black spade beard. I remember Varley's words when he first saw him: "My God! Look at that back. It should be on four legs!" Clabaut wore a cross that was so big that it was referred to as "the *Nascopie*'s spare anchor". The chain on which it was suspended would have tethered an Eskimo dog. His pipe, with its teacup-sized bowl, held enough tobacco for him to give every Eskimo man, woman, and child at a smaller post a

33

drag or two before returning it to his own mouth for a satisfying puff. His sense of humour, his laugh, and his appetite were proportionately as great as everything else about the man.

Archibald Fleming was the Anglican bishop of the Arctic. He and Clabaut carried on a running feud throughout the voyage. Fleming was, however, no match for his Roman counterpart. He played the game according to the rules of cricket; Clabaut played according to the rules of the hard North. Knowing the position of most northern Indians and Eskimos vis-à-vis organized religion, few paid much attention to the friendly feuding of these clerics.

The events of our three-day stop-over at Cape Dorset on Baffin Island were religiously enlightening. The delay afforded Clabaut and Fleming a fine opportunity to bolster the work of their resident missionaries. "Bun feeds" were arranged. Clabaut gave his the first night. Nearly all the Eskimos in the area attended, participating joyfully in eating ship's biscuits, butter, strawberry jam, drinking gallons of tea, and "converting" to the Roman Church. On the second night, Fleming threw a wingding with more hardtack, butter, and tea. It was equally well attended and the number of "converts" to Anglicanism most gratifying. The third night was not as successful: the Lutheran missionary was short of butter! In spite of this, however, attendance was quite high and the number of "converts" to Lutheranism encouraging. I chided one Eskimo whom I had seen at all three affairs. He asked me which denomination I belonged to, and I told him I was an Anglican. He looked at me slyly and said, "I'm three times as good as you; I'm a Roman Catholic, a Lutheran, *and* an Anglican!"

One evening, as tall tales were being told, the *Nascopie* suddenly shuddered and rocked. It seemed to be climbing up as if to stand on its stern. It had encountered another ice field and was ramming its way through. Drinks went flying, objects bounced across the floor, some people fell, some clung to the bunks, the lights dimmed and flickered. The ship had ridden up onto the edge of the ice pack so that its sharp prow and weight would break it. In a moment, there was a sharp, rending crack and the ship settled to an even keel as the ice parted and opened up a lead. There was little sleep to be had that night, however, as the *Nascopie* rammed and battled ice all night —and through the next day. It would hit the giant floes, shudder to a

34

stop, reverse engines, and charge again and again until it split them.

The *Nascopie* was a great ship; it—with its captain, Tom Smellie—deserves a special place in Canadian history. It was an acrobat; it rolled and pitched and tossed like a yacht. No other contemporaneous ship could have done what it did on nearly thirty voyages through the ice to the high Arctic. In 1937, this ship achieved, with the *Aklavik* coming from the west, the first successful negotiation of the Northwest Passage. It carried "Outfit 270" in 1939. For the next three years, it carried fertilizer between North Carolina and Halifax. In 1943, it was restored to the task of supplying the Arctic posts—a task at which it was without equal. In 1947, it sank on the reefs off Cape Dorset on Baffin Island: a fitting end for a great ship. It will always be remembered by those who travelled to the bleak and barren, benevolent and beautiful Arctic in the security of its ugly but sturdy bulk.

I Heal Quickly

On August 19, the *Nascopie* left Port Burwell on Killinek Island at the northern tip of the Labrador peninsula. We sailed almost due north for five days through Davis Strait and Baffin Bay. Sleet storms, rough water, blizzards, and days of thick fog in waters infested with gigantic icebergs from the glaciers of Greenland highlighted this segment of the trip. A primitive form of radar—sudden coldness of the air—would indicate that yet another iceberg was being approached. On the fifth day, we steamed past Melville Bay and Cape York in Greenland. Captain Smellie didn't go in too close: all along the coast floated hundreds of enormous icebergs. Behind them were

35

the great glaciers of Greenland—the spawning ground for the ice masses that are the scourge of the Atlantic shipping-lanes.

At last we could see Thule mountain and were soon sailing into Thule harbour. I was anxious to get on with the collecting of birds. It was no use asking the Major, the officer-in-charge: he would immediately say no. So, I found the first mate, a big Glasgow Scot, with whom I had established an excellent relationship.

To my query concerning immigration and customs and their permitting me to take a gun ashore, he reflected, "They won't let ye carry the gun in. But," he added, with a broad grin, "can ye no conceal it? Once ye get ashore, nobody is going to follow ye. The Danish officer will be too busy here—and I'll have some rum for him aboard ship."

I had a pair of baggy, fleece-lined ski pants and a parka. As we approached the landing, I strapped the gun barrels to my right leg, the stock to my waist, pulled on the ski pants, and went on deck. The first mate was supervising the loading of the scows and landing parties. I limped along the deck—the gun barrels (30-inch, 12-gauge) didn't allow much knee action. The big Scot saw me and burst into laughter.

"C'mon bird-snatcher wi' the gimpy knee. Ye go in on the first boat."

I started down the ship's ladder.

"Careful of that bad knee," he bellowed, scarlet with laughter. Descending a vertical ladder on the side of a ship that is wallowing in rough water, and jumping into a whaleboat is never easy for the landlubber. For a person with a "stiff" leg, it was a . . . . But I made it. The Major, a couple of Mounties, Fred Varley, one or two others, and the first mate boarded the boat and we cast off. The first mate knew the Major's quirks; he looked at him and then turned to me: "At least the Major won't have to worry about ye straying too far from the post this time. Ye'll no be doin' any nimble stepping with that limp!" If the gun hadn't been strapped to my leg, I'd at least have hit him with it.

When we reached the landing, the first mate helped me ashore and solicitously walked me up the beach, past the Danish police, and up to the settlement—laughing all the while.

"They'll soon all be too busy to notice ye've disappeared. Good luck!" he thundered, giving me an unnecessarily hard slap on the back.

Thule is dominated by Thule mountain—a strange prominence that looks like a sugar loaf with the top third cut off and replaced by a flattish, vertical-sided cap. I wandered out into the Greenland countryside. It was good to be on land after five days at sea in Davis Strait and Baffin Bay. Although I bagged only a few birds, the investigation of the base of this vast glacial mountain was a never-to-be-forgotten experience. It was nearly midnight when I re-strapped the gun inside my clothing and started back.

To get to the landing, I had to pass through the Eskimo village. The costumes of these happy Greenlanders were most interesting. The men wore lightweight, blue, cloth kuletuks, or atigis, (a sort of pull-on parka; white bearskin pants) and kamiks (a type of knee-length, waterproof boot made of sealskin). The dainty women, with shining raven hair pulled back into a kind of pony-tail, wore cotton blouses of colourful plaids and checks, white neck-pieces, hip-length boots made of white polar-bear hide with the fur on the inside and a fringe of the long hair protruding at the top. Their pants were even more intriguing. They were made of the long, soft, snowy-white fur of the Arctic Fox with insets, suggestively inserted fore and aft, of the dark, grey-brown fur of the Blue Fox. The beauty of their finely modelled faces was heightened by rosy cheeks.

I stopped to talk to two of these women. By means of gestures, smiles, and grimaces, we had a kind of communication. We had a smoke together, and I indicated that I had been to the base of Thule mountain. They took pity on a poor, "lame" white man who had walked so far. They offered me tea by saying the word and raising imaginary cups to their lips. I was invited to their tupek, a sort of rounded sealskin-roofed summer house of sod. (Some tupeks are just tents made of skin.) The doorway was small—although they were only five feet tall, they had to stoop to enter. With my "stiff" leg, it was quite difficult to get inside. The interior was extremely neat and tidy. I was then invited to sit on one of the low stools. Under the circumstances, I preferred to stand, insisting that they sit, which they misinterpreted as politeness. (They giggled and tried to conceal their amusement by covering nose and mouth with a hand: they were not used to this treatment.) My cup, a thick, white porcelain mug, was scalded before the tea was poured into it. The tea itself was hot, strong, and refreshing. After some delightful verbal and non-verbal communication, I thanked my hostesses, took my leave, and hobbled down to the landing.

The climb down the ladder had been difficult; getting up to the deck, however, was worse. The sea was now exceedingly rough, and it was quite a feat to leap from the rocking whaleboat to the ship's ladder—stiff-legged! When I finally made it to the deck, the Major suggested that I'd better get to bed and have the doctor bandage my knee. Little did he realize that the cure was to remove the "bandage". A few minutes alone in my cabin and my knee was restored.

As usual, I looked out of the porthole as soon as I got up the next morning. The ocean was glossy calm, but there was something abnormal about it. The sea was a glowing pinkish orange. I called Fred; neither of us had ever seen anything like it. We rushed to the main deck to find out. The sea was filled with tiny creatures about an inch and a half long, each with two small truncated "wings" that were beating rapidly as they flew through the water. There were billions—literally billions of them. They flapped along like small-winged aquatic butterflies. The water was coloured as far as we could see. Here and there among these creatures were shorter, jet-black ones. It was a polka-dot ocean—orange with black "polkas"!

Pteropod molluscs. I had to capture some. I raced to my cabin to get my dip net. When I returned, the first mate was at the rail.

"Whale food," he said. "We're likely to see some big whalebone whales today."

He kindly removed a section of the railing so that I could go down the ship's ladder to scoop some up. I scrambled nimbly down, and from the lowest rung I crouched down and started to scoop.

"Beware of that hurt sore knee of yours," blared the first mate with a diabolical burst of laughter. "Dinna aggravate it!"

In the excitement, I had forgotten all about my "hurt knee". I was clinging to the ladder like a monkey. The net was small and had only a thin, straight, wire handle that bent easily. The ship was rolling, and, on some sweeps, I even missed the water. Even though the little gastropods were packed in, I seldom managed more than one or two in a scoop. (There were perhaps three hundred to a cubic foot swimming just under the surface of the water.) Each time that I did get some, it was difficult to get them into a jar. I had to stand up, cling to the ladder with my elbow, unscrew the jar lid, dump the molluscs in, put the lid back on, get the jar back into my pants pocket, and squat down again to prepare for another sweep. This required plenty of knee action!

Eventually, I had about twenty of the orange and three or four black gastropods. I climbed back up the ladder.

"You've made a most remarkable recovery," said the Major, as I climbed back on deck. "I thought when I saw you come aboard last night that you'd be in bed for a couple of days with that leg."

"I massaged it well. It sort of snaps back into place. It feels fine now. I heal quickly!" I'm sure that he suspected that his leg was being pulled.

In the quiet of my cabin, I was able to examine the strange little molluscs. The "wings", or fins, were broad and squarish at the ends—as are the forewings of a butterfly. They had a small, transparent, sinistral shell (a shell having the whorl raising from right to left) provided with a delicate, glassy operculum, or lid. They had no eyes, but two tiny tentacles stuck out from the front of the head.

When the *Nascopie* raised anchor and sailed out of Thule harbour, we steamed through an immense orange shoal for more than an hour. As the first mate predicted, we saw two huge Humpback Whales and the "spouts" of others in the distance.

A Damn Fool—Eskimo?

The run at the Northwest Passage began when the *Nascopie* turned Cape Crauford, which is situated at the mouth of Admiralty Inlet. We then headed west through Lancaster Sound. Although there were a great many floes that required ramming, there were open leads and the ship made good time through the sound. We then turned south into Prince Regent Inlet. It was choked with bergs and pack ice. Some of the bergs were half a mile long and several hundred feet high. The whole spectacle was white, sky blue, and turquoise with dark cobalt water showing through in small irregularly-shaped patches between the masses of ice. It was a magnificent sight.

The ship would charge full-steam at the pack, split it, and open up a lead of perhaps fifty yards. It then shuddered to a halt. The engines were reversed, the ship backed off, and then it lunged forward again. Thirty yards. Sometimes it made a hundred yards; at other times it came to a dead stop without any progress whatever. There were times of open water and times when the ice split easily in front of the sharp, heavy prow opening a crack of some three hundred yards. But mostly it was a matter of ramming through twenty miles (thirty-two kilometres) of ice. The prow would often ride up on the ice, which would then split under the weight of the ship.

Few of us realized the danger. If we could have viewed the scene from a helicopter—the tiny *Nascopie* in that vast ice-field—our confidence might have been shaken. We would then have been able to see that many of the icebergs were ten times the length of our ship. On board, chaos frequently reigned. Everything not carefully fastened down went flying. Varley and I packed all our fragile belongings into suitcases and stowed them under the lower bunk. Even then they slid all over the place. Other things we put in our beds, pulled the bedclothes over them, and tucked the edges of the blankets under the mattresses. Being in the ship was worst when a chunk of ice, broken by the prow, roared back under the ship and was drawn into the screw where it lodged: the whole ship vibrated and rattled, and the engines stopped dead. This happened several times—once when the ship was charging the ice at better than eight knots. Reversing the engines dislodged the ice and the *Nascopie* charged again. Until we got used to it—as used to being vibrated from head to toe as one ever gets—this was a terrifying experience.

That night, we slept on the floor!

The next morning, we were steaming past Creswell Bay, with the rugged coast of Somerset Island highlighted pale-red by the morning sun. I was excited by the birds that criss-crossed the water between ship and shore.

The Major called "assembly number twenty"—the twentieth briefing that consisted mainly of a now-familiar enumeration of the dangers of the Arctic. As the rapport between the Major and me was tenuous, and as I was the one most likely to stray from the Hudson's Bay Co. post, he, as usual, directed his warning words to me. As usual, I ignored him.

The briefing over, I headed for the first mate. As he was in charge of the landing parties, I knew that he would get me ashore to do my job. He not only saw that I got ashore first, he told me exactly how long we would be in port. Again, he was often able to direct me as how to get away from the posts quickly and inconspicuously. As everything within a mile of habitation had been killed off by either the dogs or the people, there was no use hunting until I got well free of such influence.

When the last floe was cracked, we entered open water. In front of us lay Fort Ross, established on Somerset Island in 1937. Much earlier—by the use of binoculars—we had seen the masts of the *Aklavik,* which was riding anchor at this trading post. When first sighted, a cheer had been raised by our crew. For the second consecutive year, the Northwest Passage had been attained by the rendezvous of the *Nascopie* and the *Aklavik* in Bellot Strait.

Bellot Strait separates Somerset Island and Boothia Peninsula. The former is an island of about nine thousand square miles (23,300 km²). Until the establishment of Fort Ross, it was uninhabited —Eskimo trappers even had to be "imported" from Baffin Island to supply furs for the trading post. When I was there, it was, biologically speaking, one of the least known islands of the Canadian Arctic. I was, therefore, eager to go ashore even though I would have only one day.

With the help of the first mate, I soon put some distance between me and the post, and started to explore. The region was less barren than I had expected. There must have been some good soil as there was a rich growth of grasses including extensive stands of the beautiful Arctic Cottongrass—thousands upon thousands of waving, snowy-white silken tufts. I concentrated on snow-melt ponds as there is likely to be a greater assemblage of wildlife where there is water. An Arctic Fox, looking quite scruffy in his summer coat, trotted along beside me for several hundred yards, not more than fifty feet away. He'd probably never seen a human before; he didn't know what brutes men can be. I talked to him—but thinking it might be kinder if I chased him.

I came upon a tarn, rock-rimmed and barren looking. On this pool floated two large birds: loons. This was much farther north than the Common Loon had ever been recorded, and its racial status in any part of the Arctic was uncertain. I had to get one. I carefully sneaked around to a place on the margin of the tarn that was heavily fortified by boulders. As loons have an intense curiosity about any unidentified moving object, I took out a white handkerchief and started to wave it. This action was irresistible to them; they swam closer and closer. As I slid the gun barrel around the edge of a boulder, I got my first good look at them. I could hardly believe my eyes! Their big bills, instead of being black, were as if carved from fresh walrus ivory. Here was a pair of the rare, little-known Yellow-billed Loon far to the east of their recorded range. Even as I recognized them, one took alarm and dove, leaping almost clear of the water as it did so. The other started to follow, but my shot caught it in mid-dive. It emerged belly up.

I waded out, thankful that I had worn hip waders as the tarn was melt water, snow from last winter that had run into the bowl-like depression. Even after the full Arctic summer, it was still frigid. I towed the loon ashore as it must have weighed over ten pounds. It was like a big Common Loon but with a great upswept ivory-coloured bill. There were other differences, too. The sheen of its head and neck were violet, not green. The white stripes on its neck were fewer and coarser. This was also true of all the white spottings of the back, flanks, and rump. It was the largest loon that I had ever seen, a substantially more robust bird than the familiar Common Loon.

I decided to walk back along the beach, which was rough and gravelly. I saw nothing alive save a few Glaucous Gulls, Thayer's Gulls, and some Ringed Seals out on the ice. The straits were dotted with ice pans and small icebergs. All along the shore were blocks of grounded ice, many of which looked like gigantic mushrooms.

As I approached the towering cliffs, I saw that they were splattered in several places, each below a ledge, with streaks and splashes of white. These areas had large plots of brilliant orange lichen around them. The ledges were the favourite perches of some large birds. In

42

this harsh land, lichens thrive when fertilized by the droppings of birds. I hurried toward the cliff. Four big falcons were flying about its face. When they perched, I looked at them through the binoculars. There was a big female Peregrine Falcon, her smaller mate, and two fully grown immatures. It was the male that excited me: he was paler than any Peregrine I had ever seen and his "moustache" streak was thin and sharp. As it was beyond the bird's known range it would be an ornithological discovery; I had to get him. I fired, and was aghast as the bird flew erratically out over Bellot Strait. It flew about a hundred yards, collapsed, and fell into the ice-pocked water.

To collect the bird had been my unpleasant duty in the first place. To kill it and lose it was inexcusable. No time to get a boat from the station: I'd never find the bird again. It was too far out and the water too cold for me to swim. Then I saw an ice block gently swaying as it half-floated, half-beached itself. It was just a bit bigger than a card table. I took off my hunting coat already weighted down with specimens, and ran to the shore. As a wave lifted the big block, I gave it a slight push with one hand. It floated free. Again I was glad of my hip waders: I was able to "walk" the ice pan out into deeper water. Then I climbed aboard and, using the gun stock, started to paddle. It was easier than I had expected. In less than ten minutes I had scooped the big falcon out of the water and laid it on my block in front of me. I examined it. It was a paler and more extensively white Peregrine than any I had ever seen.

When I eventually looked up, a chill ran up my spine: I was now much farther out than when I had retrieved the specimen. I had drifted right by a big stranded iceberg. Ebb tide! No wonder I had made it out so easily.

"Can I get back?" I thought in alarm.

No need to turn my craft. I just turned myself around and began to paddle with all the strength and fury that I could muster. At first, I no more than held my own. Then I gained a few feet on the stranded iceberg, which I used as my fixed point. It seemed like hours before I had it behind me. My arms ached. My chest had a sharp band of pain across it from armpit to armpit. My knees, even in rubber boots and heavy pants, were freezing—yet, ribbons of perspiration trickled down my face and back. I didn't dare to stop to wipe it off; I just shook my head and blew it off my lips and the end of my nose.

Gradually, the shore seemed closer. I glanced back to look at my marker; in doing so, my eyes caught sight of the rear of my block. Trouble. My violent paddling had sent streams of water over the ice surface behind me. It was now honeycombed—melting away behind me. I forgot the pain, gritted my teeth, and dug in.

The struggle ended with unexpected suddenness. I reached shallow water where the tidal pull was much reduced. As the Peregrine and I neared shore, in thankfulness and to take a deep breath, I looked up. There, on top of the cliff, were two figures watching me.

A few minutes ago, I would have welcomed their attention. Now safe, I wanted only to get to shore unnoticed. I quickly took out my binoculars from under my shirt. The Major and a journalist, Mrs. Grange. . . .

"Confined to the ship for the rest of the voyage."

"Headlines: Zoologist Confined to Ship for Foolish Capers."

"Ontario Museum Man Disciplined for Disobeying Major's Orders."

"Displeasure of Museum Director."

Such thoughts occurred in rapid succession as I paddled the remaining distance. It took another ten minutes before I reached the shore. By then the two observers had vanished.

"Hurrying back to the ship to prepare the papers for a court martial, and to prepare the latest news from the *Nascopie*," I thought.

I gathered together my specimens. In addition to the loon and the Peregrine, I had taken a Longtailed Jaegar, a Thayer's Gull, some Lapland Longspurs, Horned Larks, and Snow Buntings. All these I wanted for painting as well as for specimens for the Museum. But what about Pond Inlet, River Clyde, and Pangnirtung—the stops still to be made on the rugged eastern coast of Baffin Island. I resigned myself to seeing these fabulous places from my porthole. Thus, in spite of having made what was one of the best day's collections of the trip, I was cheerless as I left the whaleboat and scrambled up the ship's ladder to the deck.

In the privacy of our cabin, I confided in Fred Varley. We discussed many ploys. Short of the Major falling overboard and Mrs. Grange losing her memory, there seemed to be no way out. That evening, a memo came around announcing "assembly number 21" for 10:00 a.m. the next day.

44

That morning, Varley and I arrived a few minutes early. I hoped that we might get it over before the rest got there. The Major was talking to a few people already assembled. He interrupted himself to welcome us.

"Good morning. Glad you're on time. I was just telling them about a crazy thing that Mrs. Grange and I saw yesterday. There was an Eskimo out in Bellot Strait paddling a block of ice."

"An Eskimo?" I said, stunned, incredulous.

"Riding on a block of ice," said Varley in mock surprise. "Whatever for?"

"Who knows?" replied the Major. "He was kneeling on it, right out there in all that floating ice—and with the tide running out. But he had made it almost in to shore when we left."

Varley laughed out loud: "What a preposterous thing to do. I thought Eskimos had more sense than white men."

"If he had a paddle," put in Nichols, the geologist, "what had become of his boat? Shouldn't you have gone down and found out? You should have notified the Captain. He'd have sent out a whaleboat to retrieve the Eskimo's boat. A man's boat is a substantial part of his wealth." "Shut up, Nichols," I thought.

"I wasn't going to climb down that cliff for any damn fool Eskimo. If he was so stupid as to go out there, he deserved to lose his boat."

"There were netchek (Ringed Seal) out there," I said quietly, thinking that total silence on my part might make me conspicuous. "The 'damn fool' may have been hunting."

The Major looked uncomfortable. "Let's get on with the agenda. Our next stop will be at Pond Inlet. It's wild, rugged country. Dangerous to venture far; so, I want you all to stay close to the post."

Fred was looking right at me, that big, wide-mouthed pixie grin on his face, daring me to look at him. I didn't, and the "assembly" finally ended.

"Come on," said Fred. "The least we can do is celebrate the safety of that damn fool Eskimo!"

Greenland Eskimos

THREE

The Klondike Expedition

Great Grey Owl

Queen of the Klondike

In 1944, I was involved in a zoological survey of the country opened up by the Alaska Highway. This highway was still being modified as portions of it sank into the muskeg or disappeared under rock slides. It was not easily travelled.

Dr. C. H. Douglas Clarke of the Department of Mines and Resources, a game warden, and I met in Edmonton and picked up two army trucks. We drove the length of the highway in Canada, making camps at Kluane Lake, Dezadeash Lake, Snag, and on the Haines Road, a feeder line from Haines, Alaska to a point on the Alaska Highway near Bear Lake, west of Whitehorse. Early in the autumn, we travelled to Dawson City and the Klondike.

At the turn of the century Dawson City had a population of ten thousand. Some claim that with tent camps and itinerant miners the number of inhabitants swelled to nearly twenty-five thousand. In 1944, it is doubtful if there were eight hundred. Dawson City was by then virtually a ghost town.

Doug and I made the trip from Whitehorse on the old stern-wheeler, *Whitehorse,* across Lake Laberge, down the river then known as the Lewes River, past Carmacks and Fort Selkirk, through the Five Finger rapids, down the Yukon River, past the post of Stewart River, and so to Dawson City. The trip was fascinating: Indian villages, with the children shouting and laughing, running along the river trails—racing the paddlewheeler; stops at remote woodpiles to load fuel; and shouted greetings from lonely trappers on the banks. There was the deep layer of volcanic ash like a white ribbon below the topsoil on the steep, towering cutbanks.

Dawson City was like a haunted house. Many of the old buildings

49

were sagging and rickety. The ones with enormous "false fronts" presented a mask to the world, concealing a tiny shop behind. Their windows were boarded up; their paint—where there was any left —was peeling; their signs were barely visible from weathering. A ripsnorting town, headquarters of the greatest and most desperate gold-rush in history, had virtually died. It depressed me.

I rose early the next morning and made my way down to the lobby of the Royal Alexandra Hotel into which we had checked the previous day. There had been an ice-jam on the Yukon River just below Dawson City. The waterfront and the main streets had been flooded causing muddy water to rise to a height of four feet in the lobby of the hotel. Although most signs of it had been cleaned up, there was still a high-water mark around the walls. On one wall hung two paintings of life-sized nudes of the approved dimensions of the late nineteenth century. Unlike some of the buildings, these girls had no need of "false fronts"! One was preparing to bathe out-of-doors; she stood gracefully poised with one toe testing the temperature of the pool. By coincidence, the flood waters had risen up the wall to reach and immerse only this toe. When I commented on this, the proprietor, Sam Broughton, his white moustache quivering, said, tenderly, "She never looked so natural as she did then, what with her reflection in the water and all."

Just then, a tall, stately woman descended the stairs. She was smartly turned out in a grey flannel suit with matching hat and a white ruffle-fronted blouse. Her figure was trim enough to be the envy of many young women in their twenties. She entered the foyer, greeted Sam cheerfully, and looked me over. She smiled: "Young man, I'm Kate Rockwell Matson and I always take a stroll before breakfast. This morning you're going to escort me; please introduce yourself."

Before I go into a new part of the country, I research it as thoroughly as possible, concentrating on the botany, fauna, climate, topography, history, and people. I was, therefore, familiar with such names as "Soapy" Smith, "Skookum" Jim, "Tagish" Charlie, "Klondike Mike", and George Carmack. And I certainly knew that I was now being fingered by the incomparable "Klondike Kate".

"I'm honoured, Mrs. Matson. I'm Terry Shortt. May I offer you my arm?"

"Thank you. I knew I hadn't made a mistake," she said.

But, in a way, I had. Most of the residents of Dawson City dated back to the gold-rush days: many had suffered the ravages of accidents, frostbite, and time. They had known Kate when she was the beauty of the day—she was now sixty-eight. Many of these old-timers had been in love with her, and still nursed a kind of wistful, nostalgic devotion to the memory of the most popular of all the dance-hall girls of the early nineteen-hundreds.

As we strode along the weathered, undulating wooden sidewalk of Front Street, I felt uncomfortable. I received disapproving looks from those hunched in chairs and on benches on the verandahs and steps along the street. They had come to the Klondike fifty years ago—in 1897 and 1898. They formed a kind of fraternal and benevolent society known as the YOOPS (Yukon Order of Pioneers). This acronym and the odd radio were among the few concessions that these sourdoughs had made to the twentieth century. They did not approve of a young cheechako squiring their Kate in their town.

It was almost unbelievable—and sad—how out of touch many of these old-timers were. One day, for example an old man hobbled into the lobby of the hotel and sat down on the fringed, black-leather settee.

"What's the music, Sam?" he asked

"What music?"

"The music from upstairs."

"That's no music, you damned old fool," said Sam, kindly, "It's the vacuum cleaner."

"What's a vacuum cleaner?" asked the puzzled sourdough. Sam explained, carefully and affectionately.

"Isn't that wonderful," said the old man, quietly. "And it sounds kind of pretty, too."

Another day, Dawson City was buzzed by an army plane. It came in with full throttle after a dive, not fifty feet above the buildings at about 400 m.p.h. (800 km.p.h.). The noise was shattering. All the YOOPS in the lobby limped, staggered, lurched, and hobbled out into the street. All they saw was the plane leaping skyward at the end of its sweep, climbing and diminishing rapidly in size.

"I'll bet ye he's doing sixty!" acknowledged one old-timer.

The years had twisted the boardwalk so that it tipped as much as a foot from side to side. I found it disconcerting at times, but it didn't bother Kate; she had walked it hundreds of times. We strolled the length of Front Street and down a roller-coaster side street as far as the "Governors" residence, a rococo old building. As we passed the "Red Feather Saloon", the "Nugget Dance Hall", the "Dawson City" and the "Occidental" hotels, the "Floradora Dance Hall", and the "Opera House"—all frame buildings, their windows boarded up and their paint peeling, and signs barely visible from the effects of sun, snow, rain, wind, and age—Kate reminisced. At the Savoy Auditorium, one of the few buildings that had not been burned and rebuilt, she said, "This is where I put on my first performance in Dawson." We paused. "I remember Christmas 1900. The miners crowned me 'Queen of the Yukon'. They placed a tiara on my head with tiny lighted candles on it. I was billed 'The Prettiest Dancer under the Northern Lights!' "

At another point she stopped. "This is where my theatre was before it burned down. I bought it and called it 'The Orpheum'. After the fire, I had the ashes sifted and retrieved quite a nice little poke of gold. The miners were very careless about their dust and spilled it everywhere, especially in the bars," she laughed. "Some people had the sawdust-sifting concessions in the bars. They sometimes made two or three hundred dollars in a morning.

"I used to roller-skate along this sidewalk," said Kate. "But it was in better repair in those days. The 'good' women of Dawson were scandalized. It didn't take much to shock them. The miners cheered."

Kate was witty, at times racy, but always generous, warm-hearted, and courageous. She talked freely of the days when she was a "percentage girl", getting a share of the profits from the drinks that she encouraged the miners to buy. The profits were high as the enamoured sourdough always bought her a drink for each one he himself had—and Kate always drank cold tea!

"I think more gold nuggets passed through my hands than anyone else ever handled," she said, "and I mean 'passed through' them," she added, laughing.

We stopped to look at a vegetable garden. I was amazed at the robust plants growing away up here above latitude 64° N. Especially impressive were the cabbages, big as pumpkins and so solid that they rang like watermelons when "thunked" with a forefinger.

"Most people can't believe that we grow good vegetables in the Yukon," said Kate. "It's the long hours of sunlight. They're growing twenty hours a day in midsummer."

She talked about her present husband, the "silent Swede", Johnny Matson. "Yonny" had a camp far back in the bush, and, at seventy-eight, was still panning for gold and trapping for furs. As a young miner in 1900, Matson had fallen in love with the "Queen of the Klondike". It was, however, thirty-three years later, when Kate Rockwell was down on her luck, that Johnny Matson proposed marriage. They were married in Vancouver in 1933 and honeymooned in Dawson City. Kate then returned to Oregon and Johnny into the bush. (Johnny's trip to Vancouver to get married was the only time in forty years that he went "out".) I gathered from what Kate said that they saw each other only every couple of years. Even then it seemed that it was for only a few days in Dawson when Kate relieved Johnny of the bother of disposing of his poke and his furs.

We stopped before a store on Front Street. The elderly proprietor nodded and spoke to Kate, who introduced us. Ed Rickard, (who claimed to be the brother of "Tex" Rickard, boxing promoter of Jack Dempsey's fights) was in the process of cleaning up his store after the flood. I was sure that this would keep him quite busy for many months. Although it was not very big, the store was packed with hoardings, booty, and loot of the early days of the gold rush, dance-hall posters; brass bar-rails; brandy, whiskey, and wine glasses; "Wanted" and "Reward" posters; an old, hand printing-press; sluice pans; long-handled shovels; "chamois" gold-dust pokes; and hundreds of memorabilia. But Ed didn't sell any of it; he stored it like a pack rat. He even rented other buildings for the overflow and bought others just to get their contents. He was preserving the Klondike!

Although a visitor from New York had left Ed's store empty-handed as Ed would let none of his "treasures" go at any price, a colleague and I fared well. Our friendship with Kate and the fact that we were able to identify the species in his collection of stuffed birds softened him up. One day he surreptitiously gave both Doug and me eight liqueur stem-glasses and an equal number of jiggers from the "Malemute Bar". As he gave them to us, he looked at us with a roguish sidelong glance and said, "I never give anything away. I'm going to charge you each fifty cents."

During our stay in Dawson City, we made a number of trips to Klondike City, Wounded Moose, and Hunker Summit. Klondike City across the river from Dawson City was even more dilapidated. It was a ruin. The only readable sign was "Restaurant". The creeks and rivers of the surrounding country were blighted. Many were virtually eliminated as huge dredges with their endless chains of buckets hoisted the earth and gravel up to be washed and screened. Their tailings filled the river beds with hideous, long, sinuous, cross-ribbed mounds of gravelly muck. Powerful hydraulic hoses washed away the hillsides, uprooting shrubs, trees, and grass. It seemed like senseless vandalism and it is unlikely that anything will ever grow there again.

The higher country of Hunker Summit verged on the timber line, but it wasn't barren. Though it was only the end of August, autumn colour cloaked the scene in majesty. The hillsides were covered with Dwarf, or Arctic, Birch blazing a bright, rich red; rows and scattered clumps of dark spruce and orange-golden aspens relieved this luxuriant red. It wasn't the brilliant riot of colour of the eastern beech-maple hardwood bush, but it was tasteful. The artist used a limited palette of well-chosen hues.

The highlight of this part of our trip, however, wasn't the scenery. Klondike Kate, who died in 1957, was the last of the great gold-rush entertainers—Cad Wilson, Golden Gut Flossie, The Texas Filly, Spanish Dolores, The Oregon Mare, and Nellie the Pig had all predeceased her. She outlasted, outwitted, outshone them all.

Dance-hall girl? Entertainer? Gold-digger? Prostitute? Percentage girl? Call her what you will, but no one could fail to admire and like Kate Rockwell, "Queen of the Klondike".

You H'eat ze H'owl?

Doug and I were exploring the Flat Creek-Wounded Moose region of the Klondike. He had to make a report on the moose population, which local hunters reported to be on the decline "owing to the depredation of wolves". We had travelled since early morning, mostly walking behind a horse-drawn wagon, driven by an irascible chap named Fournier, who possessed the foulest tongue of anyone I've ever met.

By mid-morning, it had started to snow—heavy, wet snow that soaked through our coats, pants, and boots. At one point we came to a stream the bridge over which had been washed out. We had to stop, cut spruce trees, and build a new bridge, often up to our knees in icy water. (We were soaked anyway so it didn't really matter.) Whatever one thought of Fournier, he had to be admired for his skill with a big double-bitted axe. He could fell a tree, lop off its limbs, cut key notches at just the right places, and hike it into position on our "bridge" without ever laying a hand on it. Having neither Fournier's woodsman's skill nor his "language" skill, Doug and I had to wrestle our rough-barked, cold, wet logs into place with our bare hands in relative silence.

We came upon an old shack in mid-afternoon. It was to be our shelter for the night. Doug and Fournier went on, but I stayed behind: got a fire going in the old potbelly stove, took off my wet clothes, put on dry ones, and got to work on my specimens. Fournier's old dog, a large nondescript animal of varied ancestry, had eyed first his master, his friend the horse, then me and the stove. The stove won. He heaved a weary sigh and stretched himself out on the floor beside it. I was tempted to join him.

55

To work on my collection I moved the battered old table over to a window. The oilcloth was ancient, stained yellowish-brown with layers of soup and stew, and so worn at the creases that it resembled a fly screen. I wiped the cobwebs, grime, and dead flies off the window. Even then it was fogged, cracked, and rimy with condensation; little light entered the room. Now that I was warm and comfortable, I was able to admire the view—a semi-cleared area ringed with a spruce woods all quilted with a heavy layer of new-fallen snow. Few things in nature are more pleasing to the eye.

As I finished one bird skin, I glanced through my misty window: there, on top of a four-foot spruce perched a huge owl. Its long tail was wagging up and down; the upward motion was jerky and rapid until the tail plane was at right angles to the bird's back. Then it was lowered slowly to a normal position for an owl's tail—then jerked up again. I had seen only the Hawk Owl indulge in such behaviour; this bird, however, was far too big for a Hawk Owl—or was the filmy glass playing tricks on me? I almost kicked over the table, startled the dozing dog, pulled on my boots, grabbed the gun, and ran out the door. When I got round the shack, the owl was gone.

I was sure that I had glimpsed a Great Grey Owl, though it had behaved in a manner undescribed in any ornithological literature that I knew of. But then, how many Great Greys have been studied in the wild? In all my travels, I'd never met one to really study. At Lost River near Yakutat, I had flushed one from its perch in a Sitka Spruce forest. But I got only a fleeting glimpse of its large, dark form, its long tail, and its huge, broad wings. A few nights later, on that same expedition, I had heard a single, low, reverberating *hoo-oo-oo,* a full tone lower than any Horned Owl's call I'd ever heard. That had been my total experience with this magnificent owl.

The Great Grey had become one of Canada's rarer birds. Although it appears to be larger than a Great Horned or a Snowy Owl, the bird itself is notably small bodied. Its apparent dimensions are produced by the remarkably copious, lax plumage. Its beak and feet are relatively slight and weak compared with other big owls. Its food is therefore quite small mammals and birds, and not infrequently carrion, which, at one time, resulted in its decreased numbers owing to the indiscriminate use of strychnine-poisoned bait set out for wolves. This practice, which should be outlawed, seriously decimated the numbers of many of the fur country's most interesting animals: Raven, Wolverine, Fisher, Golden Eagle, Canada Jay, as well as the Great Grey Owl.

I was most anxious to get a Great Grey in order to sketch and record it; so, with the old dog at my heels, I ploughed through the deep, wet snow hoping it might reappear. After a while, I gave up. Then, as I approached the cabin, a big bird appeared, flying about six feet above the snow. It was the unmistakeable swift deliberate flight of a Hawk Owl. As the Museum had no specimen so far north, I shot it.

As I made colour notes and took measurements of this owl, I was wondering how I could have mistaken this fifteen-inch bird with a wing spread of less than three feet for a thirty-inch Great Grey whose wingspan would be greater than five feet. I figured I must be a bit bushed. As these thoughts occupied my mind, again I glanced through my window to the tiny spruceling. My jaw dropped. A re-run! A great owl sat on top of the same spruce, facing the same way, and jerking its tail up over its back—as it had before. Again, I grabbed my gun and scrambled for the door.

There was no cover, nothing from behind which I could sneak up on the owl; so, I did what had proven successful on other stalks. Before rounding the corner of the cabin into full view of the owl, I rose up as tall as I could and raised my arms over my head. As I slowly approached, in a direct line, I gradually lowered my arms and bent my body so that my "height" remained the same to the owl. When I got within range, I was hunched over with knees bent in a most uncomfortable—and probably absurd-looking—position. Just as I stopped and raised my gun, the big owl—it *was* a Great Grey —launched itself off the spruce, dropped almost to ground level, and glided off directly behind the tree. In desperation I fired the heavy charge right through the dense limbs of the little evergreen. The owl did a cartwheel in the air and dropped. The shot electrified the old dog; he charged at the owl, who was now standing upright in the snow. I was horrified—he might maul the owl before I got there. I dropped the gun and raced after the dog. I needn't have hurried. Just as my old companion lunged at the owl, the Great Grey fell on his back and lashed out with its needle-sharp talons. One foot caught the sensitive flesh of the dog's nose. There was a terrified yelp, a wild head-shaking; the dog broke loose, and, with his tail between his legs, ran to me and crouched down, cowering, his nose streaming red in the snow.

By the time I reached the owl, he was standing again. I walked round behind him; only the big head with its small yellow eyes swivelled after me. With a quick swoop I pinioned the huge wings to the body and lifted the unprotesting bird from the ground. I was amazed at its lightness, and my hands easily encompassed its girth. It was at this point that I realized that my feet were cold; I was in my bare feet! In the excitement, I had forgotten my rubber boots, and in the mad rush over the snow-covered muskeg after the dog, I had run right out of my socks.

I took the owl into the shack, consoled the poor old dog, picked up my gun and socks, and warmed my feet. I now spent an ecstatic hour sketching one of the most exciting birds I've ever seen. No other species has a face comparable to that of the Great Grey. The huge facial disks were shaded with dark brown and pale grey rings in peculiarly effective asymmetrical regularity. These rings were concentric to each small, pale yellow eye, excepting those above the eyes, which meet in almost straight lines resembling furrows of perplexity and giving the owl an expression of perpetual anxiety. The greenish-yellow beak was nearly buried in the dense feathers of the facial disks. Seen from the side, the face is almost flat, the profile of the head being an almost perfect quarter circle. The total effect of the great facial disks is that of a platter. To northern trappers this bird is therefore known as "plate face", an example of the complete appropriateness that so often lends charm to the colloquial.

The wings were not only longer than those of the Great Horned, but much broader—enormous, soft, rounded airfoils. Each flight feather was at least two and a quarter inches wide. (When I shot this fine bird, one pellet had "ticked" the right wing and broken the humerus.) When I finished sketching and examining this beautiful creature I rolled him, regretfully, in a heavy jacket and chloroformed him.

Toward dark, Doug and Fournier came in, cold, wet, and weary.

"More moose tracks and browse up there than you can shake a stick at," Doug growled. Fournier spotted the Great Grey. A look of incredulity spread across his face.

"You h'eat ze h'owl?" he exclaimed.

An explanation of museum collecting seemed superfluous; so, I simply said, "Yes, boiled with onions."

The Optimist *and the Hubbard glacier*

FOUR

The Alaska Expedition

*The large, dark Song Sparrow of the Yakutat Bay
region, compared with the typical eastern Song Sparrow*

Yakutat

Bear-hunting in southern Alaska in 1936: realizing the possibilities vis-a-vis the Museum's collections, I was invited to join this particular expedition. Yakutat Bay region—isolated by the high St. Elias, Fairweather, and associated mountain ranges and by vast glaciers —was one of the least explored areas of the northwest. It was known to contain several distinct kinds of birds and mammals. Thus, I was able to persuade the Museum's authorities to let me accept the invitation.

It was a motley crew that arrived in Yakutat in early May —Jack Fletcher: ex-Mountie, ex-trapper, future American army major; Doug Deeks: Torontonian, sportsman; Bud Roos: photographer, who would have preferred to have spent his summer in Muskoka; and me: an oddball who couldn't wait to zero in on the strange and unfamiliar fauna. By May 24, we had collected our gear—tents, guns, cameras, sleeping bags, and food—and loaded it aboard George Nelson's fishing boat, *Optimist*.

We explored the head of Yakutat Bay first—a deep, wide-mouthed, funnel-shaped bay that penetrated far into the heart of the mountains to the north. We chugged out past Khantaak, Dolgoi, Otmeloi, Kriwoi, Krutoi and Fitzgerald! The bay's head, blocked by a semi-circle of big glaciers, turns sharply upon itself and extends back almost to the sea in Russell Fiord, bordered on each side by high mountain walls. It was bitterly cold. The shores were still largely snow-covered: in places, in the form of snowslides; in others, dappled and splattered with a patchwork of snow and bare rocks.

With binoculars, we could see scores of game trails across the snowslides. At Eleanor Cove, we saw several Black Bears and two enormous black Timber Wolves. Birdlife was not abundant, but we did see Arctic and Redthroated Loons, Pelagic Cormorants, Marbled Murrelets, Pigeon Guillemots, Ravens, Bald Eagles, and small stag parties of Harlequin Ducks. I heard Fox Sparrows and Water Pipits singing, as well as the occasional cackle of a cock Willow Ptarmigan. We soon came in sight of the glaciers of Disenchantment Bay —glaciers that only a few hundred years ago had blocked the entrance to Russell Fiord. A Spanish navigator, Malaspina, thought he'd found the Northwest Passage—until he saw the glacier: hence the original name, Bahia Desencanto. Many large floating blocks of ice made progress slower. At dusk, George dropped anchor in the shelter of Haenke Island.

Low-hanging clouds and ice fog screened the mountains and the glacial wall from view. We crawled into our sleeping bags, wearing most of our clothes. We still shivered through the night. Periodically there were sounds like distant thunder; George said that they were from the Hubbard glacier. This thunder (the roars of falling ice), the dank chill of the air, and anticipation of tomorrow's sights made sleep fitful. We were up at dawn. It was overcast, but bright enough for us to see across the bay to three glaciers. The Turner was quite an extensive discharging glacier whereas the Haenke and the Miller were much smaller ones.

Even as breakfast was being prepared, George had weighed anchor and we were threading our way through drifting icebergs. He said that the sun would soon break through for a short time; so, the cameras were made ready for we were anxious to film the Hubbard glacier in sunlight—a fleeting commodity in mountain-glacier country. We soon turned the cape at the head of Disenchantment Bay, and before us lay the great Hubbard glacier. A wall of sparkling ice, five miles (eight kilometres) wide and between two and three hundred feet (seventy-five to a hundred metres) high—a majestic spectacle. The water in front of the glacier was so choked with ice that it tested George's navigational skills to get the *Optimist* in close. There were frequent explosions followed by a downpour of masses of ice and clouds of spray.

George manoeuvered the *Optimist* in as close as he dared. He cut the engines to reduce the vibrations for filming. It seemed that we were right under the cleft, snaggle-toothed, toppling, staggering front of the great glacier. The sun was shining full on it and the camera was recording it all.

Suddenly there was an ear-splitting thunderclap. A gigantic ice-column—the exposed portion of which was as tall as a twenty-storey building—broke away from the front of the glacier, leaned forward, righted itself, and slid almost vertically into the water. For a moment we saw nothing but a vast fountain of spray. Then the wave hit the *Optimist* broadside . . . she almost heeled over. (By sheer luck, we saved the camera.) Chunks of floating ice, bobbing like apples at a Hallowe'en "ducking", bounced and scraped against the ship. But the terrifying part was yet to come. The big iceberg—free from its century-old bind—plummeted deep into the water. It was aimed in the general direction of the *Optimist* when it disappeared. Was it going to come up right under the boat? After a few moments of past-life-flashing suspense, it emerged—*beyond* the *Optimist*. It surfaced slowly, majestically, like the breaching of a leviathan, lifting its nose at least fifty feet into the air. Water pouring off it in white sheets, it subsided and floated out into the bay driving a colossal wave in front of it.

Then George swore. (There is a time and place for cussing. I resent hearing good cuss words cheapened and degraded by inappropriate or too frequent usage.) His vocabulary was rich and strong, but not repulsive. It was at once a total summing up of the situation, a rebuke to our corporate stupidity, a repudiation of human intelligence, yet a strange kind of benediction and absolution. Its effect was to make any other comment, discussion or recrimination superfluous; it was accompanied by precipitate action. The *Optimist*'s engines coughed and sputtered into life; in minutes we were chugging through pan ice toward Osier Island. When we were safely into open water, we looked back at the now slowly drifting iceberg. Looking at the hazy cloud that was now rising from it, I said, by way of consolation, "That's water vapour. Our big friend is already starting to melt. By this time tomorrow, at least some of his ugly bulk will have been carried as moisture in the onshore wind and will have been deposited as snow back up where he came from. In a month, he'll be back up at the end of that icy queue, and he won't be back out here for at least a hundred years."

Islands fascinate me, especially uninhabited ones. Khantaak Island in Yakutat Bay was no exception. Rocky shores and a dense covering of needleleaf evergreens looked inviting to this naturalist. The forest on the other side of water always looks greener! As I wandered along the shores of Yakutat Bay, I cast wistful glances at Khantaak, wondering what marvellous birds it might harbour: falcons, owls, shorebirds, terns. I persuaded George to take me across, drop me off, and return for me in three days.

My packsack bulging with food, collecting materials, and a change of clothing, we chugged across the bay, my anticipation high. I could see gulls, Black Oystercatchers, shorebirds, and Pigeon Guillemots flying about the rocky shores. My enthusiasm was somewhat dampened by the heavy surf that was running—it would make landing difficult. The boat was anchored some distance offshore, and we took to the dory. George faced the bow and rowed from a standing position, as close to shore as possible.

"You're going to get wet," said George, matter-of-factly.

I removed all my clothing, except briefs and boots, shouldered my pack, held my sheathed gun high over my head, and went over the side. The water was waist deep—and cold. I just made it to shore before the next comber, or roller, came in; nevertheless it broke on my heels and showered me with icy spray. George had already turned the dory around, and I waved my thanks to him, somewhat ruefully. I climbed up over the boulders out of reach of the spray, emptied my boots, and wrung out my underwear. The wind off the glaciers and ice fields of Disenchantment Bay covered me with goose pimples —and the mosquitoes covered the goose pimples!

I quickly pulled on dry clothing, including a heavy mackinaw, shouldered my pack, picked up my gun, and set off to explore in the now waning light. As well as looking for specimens, I kept an eye out for a sheltered spot in which to spend the night. I looked forward to listening to the night sounds—a rewarding adventure I forced on myself on every field trip. I had gone only a few yards along the shore when, under the shelter of big Sitka Spruce, I saw a house. What a disappointment! Was no place uninhabited by man? As I got closer, however, I realized that it had long since been abandoned. It was not as high as a man, it sagged badly on its rotten logs. A five or six-foot spruce tree grew out of its sod roof. It was open at one end, but had no door or window. I went in on my hands and knees. I took only a quick look as my flashlight batteries were almost dead. I had noticed a mud floor, however, a mouldy ceiling that came almost to the ground at the sides, and a musty smell. No one had used it for many years. I felt better. It was now my shelter. I covered the holes in the roof with spruce boughs; scraped the litter from the floor and covered it with boughs. This gave me a bed and a spruce-scented deodorant all in one. A place to cache my pack, a place to sleep—a base camp.

Burdened with only binoculars and gun, I set off to explore a bit before dark. There were plenty of birds, but, disappointingly, none that weren't also found on the mainland. The big Yakutat version of the Song Sparrow was common. Half as big again as that of the south and east, it is a saturated, dark sooty brown. Its song, however, is the same as that heard in the gardens and shrub hedges of farm woodlots in Ontario. The even darker Fox Sparrows were tame and in good numbers. A Blackcapped Warbler sang from some willows near the shore, as did an Orangecrowned Warbler from somewhere up in the dark Sitka Spruce. Along the shore, Surfbirds and Rock Sandpipers sat in clusters on the boulders. A Black Turnstone flew by, calling noisily. A few Shortbilled Gulls and a Glaucouswinged Gull perched on a barnacle-covered rocky spit. But all these were already in the collection.

In the shadows of the forest, it was getting quite dark, which made walking the rocky shore dangerous. So, back to base camp, get a fire going, have some tea, and plan on an early start in the morning. I gathered an armful of wood, looking forward to the warmth and cheer of a campfire. Then I heard the call of the Great Horned Owl. Here was a bird worthwhile. I knew of no example of this species from the isolated Yakutat region, where a number of species were known to differ in colour and form from their counterparts even in adjacent parts of Alaska. Darkness had now come in the forest, and there was no visibility from ground level up to about twenty feet. Above that, however, there was some light in the sky silhouetting the crowns and upper reaches of the trees. I hoped to be able to see the owl against this background. He was no more than a hundred yards away. I had covered about half of this distance when I came to an opening in the forest—an opening in that there were no big trees, just a tangle of willows and alders matted with young spruce and Devil's Clubs.

As I started across this clearing, I tripped over something and fell to my knees. As I did so, I was aware of a whispering sound. Something big and hard and heavy grazed my back and struck me on the shoulder. I went down on my face, thoroughly frightened. I was just righting myself when it struck again. As I went down this time, I twisted myself and rolled so that I landed on my back. I felt that I was struggling for my life; I intended to fight. My gun was gone; in the darkness I didn't know where. What "it" was, I had no idea: a bear? a wolverine? a man? In fleeting seconds, I thought of many possibilities—of the flashlight in my pocket. (The sudden brilliance of a light has deterred many wild animals from attacking.) I got it out eventually and fumbled for "hours" for the switch. The feeble beam stabbed upward to reveal a head with an enormous eagle beak and outspread wings so expansive that the tips were lost in the darkness. The great hanging feet were barely visible in the penumbra of the beam.

Although my heart was still pounding, I was no longer terrified. I knew something was not right—no eagle attacks you, not in the dark, anyway. As my eyes became more adjusted I began to see that my "eagle" looked very old and tired, and that he had no eyes. His wings looked suspiciously like driftwood. On closer examination, I discovered that it was completely wooden, and suspended by a thong or wire from a T-shaped stake. As I shone the flashlight, I saw that there were other wooden markers all about me. I had literally stumbled into an old Tlingit graveyard, a shaman's graveyard. The shamans (mystery men or priests), were buried in the ground, and over their graves were erected images, or figures, of wood: eight-foot bears, large herons, frogs, ravens—or eagles.

I found my gun as my flashlight gave out. Picking up some firewood, I made my way to the mud hut, cheered by the prospect of a roaring fire and hot tea. As I neared my hut, I was trying to recall all that I had read about Tlingit burial customs. It was the rule for the common people to be burned and their ashes put into a totem pole, in a small box fastened to the top of a post or in a "dead house", a small, roofed structure—*a small, roofed structure*! My base camp—it was a *dead house*. My first impulse was to flee. A roaring fire, however, a billycan of tea, and some grub restored a more sensible frame of mind and cheerful outlook. Nevertheless, dancing flames throwing weird, moving patches of light and shade on the trunks and foliage of the

68

nearby spruce and hemlocks frequently caused me to start. Eventually, I doused the fire, crawled into my "dead house", and lay down on my spruce-bough bed, covering myself with my mackinaw. Sleep didn't come easily. I fancied that I detected the smell of death. Perhaps I did. Physical exhaustion eventually overcame fancy, and I slept as soundly as the dead.

I awoke to a damp, grey, misty morning; beads of moisture hung from every leaf and limb. Not being a Boy Scout, I had no dry mouse's nest in my pocket to get a fire started. A thick, condensing mist penetrates more effectively than a rainstorm. After much effort and a quick review of my cussing vocabulary, I got some living spruce branches afire, and the fierce heat of burning resin ignited the damp logs. Before I finished my hot breakfast, however, it was raining in earnest. The "dead house" now became a sanctuary. I had come to Khantaak, however, to do scientific collecting; so, as the rain did not seem to be abating, I decided to leave the spirits' hut. I put some strips of jerky, or *charqui,* of Pacific Salmon in my pocket, put on a light, waterproof poncho over my mackinaw, and set out determined to make wonderful ornithological discoveries.

I went down to the rocky point where I had seen the shorebirds and gulls the night before. A Wandering Tattler flew off uttering its loud, whistling cry. Otherwise I saw nothing but steady rain. I spent the whole morning and most of the afternoon wandering about the rocky point, then into the woods, then back along the shore. I did come across a few other birds: Oregon Juncos, a Goldencrowned Kinglet, some Steller's Jays, an Osprey, a long flight of Pelagic Cormorants in single file, low over the water. I collected a few specimens, all of which I could have taken in comfort on the mainland. At last I sat down on some shore rocks, partially sheltered by overhanging spruces, and munched disconsolately on the jerky. Then I noticed my boots: the toes looked like great yellow chrysanthemums. The leather of each one was shredded into a hundred petals, the work of the razor-sharp barnacles that almost completely covered the rocks—the same barnacles that I had been blessing for the wonderful "grip" that they provided on the otherwise treacherously slippery boulders. The soles, too, were in shreds. Once again I packed it up. This and the steady rain were too much; I made my way back to what was now my beloved little "dead house". I had just enough time to prepare my few specimens, get a fire going, and prepare a frugal meal before dark. Then I crawled into my little house, promising myself that tomorrow would be different.

It was indeed different. Dawn brought a downpour. The battered little "dead house" served me well, and I was developing a real affection for it. It provided most welcome shelter, and, with a smudge at the door, it protected me from mosquitoes. Yes, it would have been easy for me to sit in my Khantaak home, but I wanted to see the other end of the island. Owing to the shredded condition of my boots, I decided to work mostly through the forest. The trees at this end were much taller forming a dense canopy overhead. Little light penetrated to the forest floor, which was covered with moss so deep and spongy that I often sank up to my knees. When I reached the shore at the far end, I was exhausted. I had collected a Chestnut-backed Chickadee, a Western Flycatcher, and a violet Green Swallow—a most imposing bag! As my boots were already ruined, I decided to walk back along the barnacle-encrusted shore.

I was cheered somewhat by the acquisition of a Pigeon Guillemot, a bird I had wanted to sketch. The rain, however, still came down in earnest.

When I reached the mud hut, I took stock. A paltry dozen specimens—all but the guillemot obtainable right at our Yakutat camp. Both shins rubbed raw, excoriated, as only fallen Sitka Spruce can do; my best boots ruined; good meals missed; all my clothes damp to wet—and George not due until tomorrow. I decided to spend the last morning close to my "dead house" and examine the shamans' graveyard. As for birds, the likelihood of finding something of value was as great right here as at the far reaches of the island: the Horned Owl was probably perched on a tree within a hundred yards right now.

A familiar sound plucked me out of my philosophical mood. George. It took me only moments to load my packsack and dash to the shore. George was coming in with the dory; I was soon scrambling aboard.

"I was around this way and wondered if you'd finished with your work," George lied.

We were soon aboard the *Optimist,* and George appointed me cook. There was a roaring fire in the stove, the pan was ready, and big, thick salmon steaks lay on the counter. When they were ready, I took them topside. The sky was clear, and, although it was getting dark at sea level, the vast icy crest of Mount St. Elias was a blazing pinkish-orange, trailing a long snow plume from its summit. What a pleasant sequel to my island adventure.

As we entered the harbour of Yakutat, we were suddenly aware that the sea had become luminescent. Its surface was broken everywhere by patches of radiance as millions of one-celled animals floating or swimming near the surface were being stimulated to glow at any disturbance of the water. At the bow of the boat, in its wake, and at the shallow peaks, were eerie, glowing pools of light. It was the finest display of bioluminescense that I have ever seen.

If I hadn't gone to Khantaak, I wouldn't have known my now fondly-remembered "dead house"; I'd never have seen an old Tlingit graveyard; I'd never have experienced Mount St. Elias at sunset or the bioluminescent extravaganza of Yakutat Bay. These easily offset my ornithological disappointments.

Red Blackflies
on the Situk

"Little critters" cause many collectors of museum specimens the most trouble. And the members of the blackfly group are the worst, in my experience. These small, vicious flies are hump-backed, hence their other name: "buffalo gnats". They occur wherever there is running water, and, like mosquitoes, range from the Arctic to the Tropics. The anti-coagulant enzymes in their saliva destroy corpuscles in the blood; prolonged exposure to their painful bites can and has caused death. They have two constant characteristics: they are abroad only in the day-time, and they suffer from claustrophobia. They seldom follow a person indoors—even the shelter of a tent is sufficient to discourage them.

My worst experience occured on this Alaskan expedition. We had established a base camp at the mouth of the Situk River, a few miles southeast of Yakutat. Jack Fletcher and I decided to paddle up the river to Situk Lake. Jack was interested in bear and I thought that the lake might be the home of some waterfowl that had not yet been collected in the region. With the help of a Tlingit guide, the canoe trip up river was negotiated without great difficulty. Twice we saw Black Bears and once a Grizzly. That evening, I wandered off along the lake shore. I collected two Barrow's Goldeneyes, which I later prepared by the light of a roaring fire under the shelter of some tall Sitka Spruce. We opened a tin of butter and had fried duck, hardtack, and tea for supper.

The moon was nearly full and was mirrored in a long, radiant path across the gently rippled surface of the lake. We dragged some logs of driftwood over to the fire, propped our backs against them, and sat up through the night. Other than the long, wavering howls of the Timber Wolves up on the shoulder of Mt. Tebenkoff, the night was still. We watched a moose, silhouetted against moon reflection, as it fed in shallow water near the far shore of the lake. Twice the luminous area of the water was ruffled by the wake of muskrats. An inquisitive marten emerged from the trees and trotted out on shore to investigate the firelight. The peacefulness demanded that we speak in low voices, almost in whispers.

On the trip up, I had heard birds that I wanted to collect for sketching and as museum specimens: American Dippers, Varied Thrushes, Pine Grosbeaks, Fox Sparrows, Steller's Jays, Oregon Juncos. Some of these were of geographic races peculiar to southeastern Alaska, and indeed some peculiar to the Yakutat Bay region itself. Jack and the guide decided that next day they would drift down river to achieve a silent approach to bears. Thus, I would leave at dawn on foot, and they would leave in the afternoon in order to have as much twilight time on the river as possible. By so doing, I would be far below them by mid-day and my shots would not interfere with their efforts.

After a breakfast of bully beef, hardtack, and tea, I set off into the forest close to the river. This was a primeval needleleaf rain forest

72

composed of Western Hemlock, Sitka Spruce, Yellow Cypress, and large Western Cedar. The crown of the forest hung about eighty feet above my head. There was an underbrush of blueberry, alders, and Devil's Club; the forest floor was carpeted with a deep, lush growth of mosses. The walking was quite good as I found numerous bear trails through the woods, often paralleling the river and only a few yards from its bank. Frequently these trails led out onto gravel bars that were favoured fishing sites of the bears. These locations gave me an opportunity to scan the river. (Recent bear-tracks in the muddy areas indicated that Big Brown Bears, and Black and Grizzly bears had been here as we dozed and whispered on the lakeshore during the night.)

By noon, I had been hiking steadily for more than six hours, and the collecting had been very satisfactory. I had, wrapped carefully and tucked away in my jacket, a Varied Thrush, a Pine Grosbeak, a Steller's Jay, the big dark Yakutat form of the Fox Sparrow, an equally large and dark Song Sparrow, Orangecrowned and Black-capped Warblers, a Chestnutbacked Chickadee, and a very handsome specimen of the small Northwestern Crow.

The crow was the most exciting capture. Not only was it a member of my favourite bird family, but up until now it had been considered to be merely a geographic race of the American Crow. I was sure that it wasn't. They were quite common in the village of Yakutat, acting as part of the garbage-disposal squad along with the Ravens and Glaucouswinged Gulls. Facially they resembled the Raven rather than the large crow of the east, especially in the way in which the feathers of the forehead and throat were raised—out of curiosity or indecision. When they flew, their wing strokes were so rapid and shallow that they bore little similarity to the bigger bird. The call, too, was different: high-pitched and nasal. I was, therefore, anxious to make some sketches of it; so, I started to travel faster and stop less frequently to hunt.

I had covered perhaps ten or more miles (about sixteen kilometres) when I spotted a huge Bald Eagle perched on the top of a tall rampike at the river's edge. I had never had a freshly-killed, wild adult Bald Eagle to sketch. I stalked the great bird and brought it down. Its weight—about twelve pounds (five kilograms)—surprised and alarmed me. It was a big female; so, as with most birds of prey, it was

73

larger and heavier than the male. In addition to its weight, when lifted by its feet, its immense wings flopped open making it extremely difficult to get past the intertwined mass of Devil's Club that edged the bear trails. (The bird's wing span was seven-feet-one-inch.) Having no string, I had to use my mosquito head-net. I pulled the net over the eagle's head and eased the wide end down until it covered the back, chest, and "wrist" joints of those troublesome wings. Then I drew the strings tight and tied them securely. My eagle was now trussed like a fowl ready for the oven, yet the fine mesh allowed air circulation and did not unduly ruffle the feathers. I was quite pleased with my ingenuity.

It was not long before I was to regret this action bitterly. The "little critters" crowd decided that it was time for lunch. I assumed that they were the ordinary blackflies. No. These were red—a tawny orange-red, and slightly larger. The eagle was in my left hand, the gun was in my right. My hat, which kept being swept off by the Devil's Club, was in my coat pocket under nine or ten birds. (The Devil's Club, with an appropriate scientific name, *Echinopanax horridum,* (horrid spiny herb) has broad, maple-like leaves, often two feet across. Sharp thorns on both upper and lower surfaces effectively conceal the multiple, equally spiny stalks that may be ten feet long. Touch one part of this shrub and a wavering spring-like wand swats you across the face or arms. Step carefully to one side of a bush, and your foot touches another stem, recumbent and curved and waiting to act as a trigger for other top-heavy canes that embrace you around the back of the neck or grip you around the knees and dump you headlong into the whole needle-covered mass.) The Red Blackflies swarmed over my exposed parts. They came at me like diminutive kamikaze; nothing I could do deterred them. I could do precious little: I had no insect repellent and both hands were occupied. They stormed me behind the ears, charged into my eyes and mouth, and seemed particularly pleased with my brow at the hairline, as well as my hands and wrists. No flesh was sacred.

By now, I was half running, half stumbling. Every few yards I put down one of my burdens and took frenzied revenge. In a panic I wiped them off my neck and ears. My hands were smeared with blood and thick wads of mashed carcasses. It was really a useless gesture: it gave only a moment's respite during which I made no onward progress. As soon as I picked up my eagle or my gun, they were on me again in undiminished numbers. I considered abandoning my eagle, but quickly dismissed the idea. To kill such a magnificent creature and jettison it because of some flies was unthinkable. I thought of hiding the gun and so freeing a hand to swat with. I could hardly see by now, however, and feared that I'd never find it again. With eyelids nearly swollen shut, I plunged on. I had only one desire: to reach camp and dive into the tent.

The ordeal was to last another full hour. I was on the point of abandoning both gun and eagle when I saw the fish weir that stretched across the river just near our camp. There was one last, wallowing, interminable effort, then finally the stumbling out of the woods. I remember very little of the last few hundred yards. My legs were rubbery, and I was sobbing. As I weaved into the camp area I was just about blind, but what I could see was a tremendous relief. It was Doug Deeks striding toward me. He pulled the gun out of my nerveless hand. When I tried to put the eagle down my fingers wouldn't unfold: Doug had to pry them off. Both hands were swollen into great loathsome-looking balloons. Doug steered me into the tent; I collapsed on my sleeping bag. He then ran to the river to get a pailful of cold water; he plunged my hands into it and soaked a towel, which he wrapped around my head. The relief was indescribable. I sat up to try to remove my boots, but the laces slid through my bulbous fingers. Doug had to untie them and pull them off. My eyes were now swollen to mere slits; my ears, always prominent, stuck out like a chimpanzee's; my lips were so inflamed that when I tried to explain what had happened, I couldn't enunciate. Doug helped me off with my shirt and pants, and I crawled into my sleeping bag. Completely exhausted, I fell asleep immediately.

A high fever accompanied by delerium soon broke my sleep. Doug had the billycan on the fire, and he forced me to drink large quantities of hot liquids. Unknown to me, he had plastered me with antiseptic lotion wherever I had been exposed to the "little critters". Although I spent a miserable night, I was able to get up in the morning, and open my eyes. The swellings were down some, but my hands, arms, and armpits ached, and my ears looked like over-ripe tomatoes. With some difficulty, I was able to sketch the eagle. Although it is still unfinished, I was able to capture the subtleties of the various shades of yellows of its eyes, beak, and powerful feet. So, by afternoon I was feeling quite normal—after twenty-four hours of panic and pain.

My curiosity increased as my discomfort decreased. What exactly was the species of my assailants? On a hunch I entered the tent and began a search of the canvas along the ridgepole and around the mosquito bar that covered the entrance. As I expected, I found at least a dozen of these red raiders frantically trying to escape because of their dread of closed places. With understandable enthusiasm I popped them into a phial of alcohol and eventually brought them back to Toronto. My revenge was sweetened when the Museum's curator of entomology identified them as the Red Blackfly, new to the R.O.M.'s insect collection.

The Big Brown
of the Malaspina

My most intimate experience with a Big Brown Bear left me saddened and a little sorry to be a human being. At dawn on an early July day, I left our Black glacier camp armed with a .410 pistol, intending to collect some small birds. I walked southwest toward the massive Malaspina glacier. It had rained steadily all night, and was now one of those grey, overcast mornings typical of the northwest coast. On my right rose the mountains wrapped in a blanket of misty cloud, on my left, the ice-choked waters of Disenchantment Bay, grey, with visibility obscured by an ice fog hanging a few feet above the surface. As the air was damp and chilly, I wore a heavy woollen mackinaw, sealskin mitts—and a mosquito head-net. As it wasn't a day for dawdling, I strode briskly along using mostly an age-old bear trail that was worn deeply into the soil near the beach.

The bird population was interesting, though not abundant. Willow Ptarmigan cackled noisily as they ran through the bent, stunted vegetation. There were four or five Parasitic Jaegers in the completely sooty-brown "dark phase" that is virtually unknown in the eastern Arctic. Flocks of Surf Scoters rode the undulating swells between the ice packs like floating black corks tied together by invisible lines. Goldencrowned Sparrows sang their plaintive three-syllabled call that on this dreary morning seemed to suggest a falsely defiant *I don't care.* Glaucouswinged Gulls beat lazily back and forth over the floes, their cries harmonizing with the weather and the loneliness of this place. A few Pelagic Cormorants huddled on a rock, their necks and bodies hunched down and their feathers fluffed out. They didn't mind swimming in the icy water, but they seemed disconsolate in the cool, clammy air.

I crossed the boulder-strewn, barren terminal moraine of Graliano glacier, "the Growler", thereby reaching much higher ground. From here I could see the rounded, tree-covered dome of Amphitheatre Knob jutting out of the low-hanging, misty cloud. I promised myself that, on a clearer day, I would climb up to it—and beyond, to investigate the enticingly named Floral Hills and Blossom "Island". It was an exhilarating experience to be in uninhabited wilderness with the nearest humans, my companions in camp excepted, perhaps forty miles (sixty-five kilometres) away, with the twelve-mile (twenty-kilometre) Yakutat Bay in between. Even the grey, foggy day added to the enjoyment. I climbed up a long esker (a ridge of gravelly moraine) that stuck out from the dead face of "the Growler". From its crest I could look out on the Malaspina, the largest Alaskan glacier. It covers fifteen hundred square miles (3385 km.^{2}), has a front of sixty miles (ninety-six kilometres) on the ocean, and runs more than thirty miles (forty-eight kilometres) from the St. Elias range, which feeds it. At only one point, near Icy Cape, does the ice reach down to the sea. The rest of its front is dead. It presented a strange sight: miles upon miles of grey, loosely-piled moraines, scooped and channelled by streams that change their beds annually. Patches of Sitka Spruce and alders, and extensive gardens of blazing pink Fireweed, dotted the region. On the landward side of the terminal moraines, and sloping gently up to the mountains, was the crystal vastness of the Malaspina, an immense sheet of shimmering ice. Above and beyond towered the masses of naked rock of the St.

Elias Alps, chiselled and sculpted, their upward reaches capped in perpetual snow. Looking toward the sea, the sparkling water was flecked with aquamarine drift-ice. To a son of the Prairies, the strangeness of this place was extramundane.

I pressed on to Esker Creek, turbulent and swollen by heavy rain that not only contributed its own water but hastened melting on the Seward glacier to the northwest. (The meltwater from this glacier was the source of Kwik, Kame, and Osau creeks that, with Esker Creek, now roared across the moraine of the Malaspina.) Although swollen, the excess water widened Esker Creek rather than greatly increasing its depth. It was therefore wadeable; so, I pulled up my hip-waders, fastened their harness to my belt, and started across. I had been aware of a rumbling sound, but it was not until I was out near the middle of the creek that I realized what was causing it. Orange to grapefruit-sized boulders were being trundled along the creek-bottom by the force of the current. My feet, each carefully placed and balanced on the rocky bottom at each step, dislodged several water-rounded boulders that darted downstream, rumbling and clattering. To lose one's balance and fall into that rushing water might have been disastrous for it was mostly ice water. When I reached the shore, I was shivering and my legs were slightly numb from the chill that had penetrated rubber boots, trousers, and heavy socks. I was now beyond the mouth of Disenchantment Bay and on the black-sand beach of the northwest shore of ice-free Yakutat Bay.

I wandered aimlessly along in a euphoric state known only to a naturalist, anticipating nothing in particular, not straining to see —yet somehow aware of everything about me, of the total environment. I was jarred to the alert by a small wisp of steam rising from a dark mound on the gravelly sand. Fresh "bearberry mash". Keeping a sharp lookout, I went over to it. To this enormous heap, and from it, led the biggest bear-pugs that I had ever seen. Even as I looked at one of them, a few grains of matted sand crumpled and rolled into the depression made by the heel. From these signs and from what I knew of the casual ramblings of bears, this fellow couldn't be far away; he was probably quite close. Just in front of me was a huge boulder, a chunk of the St. Elias Alps that had been trundled to this spot by glacial ice when the Malaspina had been active. I hurried toward it: I didn't want to face this giant with a .410 pistol! The boulder was at least twelve feet high, and equally wide and long—the size of a small garage. I crawled to the top so that I could better decide in which way to retreat. I slithered across the top on my belly—but not far. I don't think that I have ever stopped all motion, even breathing, as quickly, before or since. Not one hundred feet away was the bear, an enormous Big Brown Bear. His luxuriant fur was a rich, golden-brown, darker on the legs, shoulders, ears, and around the eyes. He looked like an oversized brown-and-gold Giant Panda.

His keen ears must have detected some sound as I clambered up the boulder, for he was alert and testing the air with his nose. His big, dished face was pointed directly at me, probably zeroed in by both his huge ears that acted as parabolic reflectors and his violently snuffing nose, rather than by his little, dimly-seeing, piggy eyes. He would have no fear as I was probably the first human that he had ever seen in this uninhabited, seldom-visited Malaspina.

He stood there for an eternity; then, with slow deliberation, shuffled toward my boulder. I thought of sliding backward, dropping off the rock, and retreating in all haste along the beach. (The nearest climbable trees were well over a hundred yards away.) But I hesitated; then it was too late. His waddling was deceptively quick; in a few seconds he was so close that I could see only his head and back over the edge. Then he lowered his head, and I could hear snuffing resembling that of a misfiring vacuum cleaner. He was moving around my boulder; he would soon pick up my scent. I tried to slide around silently so that I could keep him in sight, but the buttons on my mackinaw made a slight scraping sound. *Ursus* heard it. He rose up on his ridiculously short hind legs. (I was glad that they were short for even then he towered up a good seven feet.) But he couldn't see up on top of the boulder. His upper lip curled back exposing vast, bright pink gums and long blunt, yellow canine teeth. I lay as flat as a hound's ear, and he dropped back on all fours. I had often read of people who, in certain circumstances, feared that their heartbeats could be heard. I was now one of them. I could feel and hear mine. They sounded like the mating hoots of a Blue Grouse rooster.

The Big Brown Bear continued his course round my boulder. In a moment he would reach my footprints. I thought of letting out with the biggest bellow that I could summon. I was afraid, however, that the best that I could muster would be a mouse-like squeak. Fire my pistol? No. Save its single shot as a last resort, perhaps to blind him if he came up the boulder, which I knew he could do as readily as I had. I lay still and waited. It wasn't hard to do as I didn't have the courage to do anything else. He veered away some twenty feet from the rock, but continued on a line to my scent—and he found it. He stood for a moment, sniffing. Then the hairs on his big shoulder hump rose like those on an angry dog. He bared his great fangs, slavered, uttered a grunt that was half vocal, half the expulsion of the hated human stink from his nostrils, turned about and, with undisguised terror, bolted for the trees, which a moment before I had looked at longingly as my sanctuary.

It was some time before I moved off my boulder. I sat up and lit my pipe. I won't say that I wasn't relieved, but surging over any other emotion was a feeling of chagrin that I belonged to a species that had, through a brief and inglorious history, alienated and imparted abject fear into the instinct of one of the world's most magnificent creatures. Finally, I climbed down, feeling weary and provoked, and trudged back to camp. I didn't mention my encounter to my bear-hunting companions as I planned to go back in the hope of seeing more of the Big Brown Bear. I felt a proprietory interest in him: he was my bear, and I wanted him alive and free.

I saw him again two days later. I had enough respect for him that, in addition to the .410 pistol, I had a Winchester 30.06 slung over my shoulder. It was my third visit to the area, and I figured that if he were still there he might be familiar with my scent and would not panic so readily. Today, he was eating wild strawberries. I have never tasted wild fruit as delicious as the strawberries that grow on the cool plateaus and glacial moraines of Alaska. I felt a fellow-feeling as I picked a few and ate them as I watched him. He was about a hundred and fifty yards away. I could see the great hump of his shoulders and the shimmering highlights of his shining coat. I was sure that it was the same bear because he was big and his colour pattern quite unusual. He was thoroughly enjoying his fruit salad; only occasionally did he raise his head and test the air.

Suddenly he caught my scent, turned his head, and looked at me, sitting in plain view on a rock. I whipped the rifle off my shoulder and almost reflexively cocked the hammer. I wasn't scared enough to

80

run or to do anything as foolish as to fire at him, but I could hear that Blue Grouse hooting in my chest again. My Big Brown Bear, however, just turned about and slowly walked away, abandoning his beloved strawberries.

It was nearly a week later that, more or less by accident, I encountered him again. It was a fine day and I was taking my long-promised trip up the margin of the Malaspina. I had climbed over Amphitheatre Knob and the Floral Hills, and had reached the edges of Blossom "Island". The last two areas supposedly harboured an almost tropical vegetation, including varieties of trees and plants that were not to be found anywhere else in the Yakutat Bay region. Although my scepticism was confirmed, they were rather remarkable places. They didn't appear to have been recently scoured by glacial ice, but were, in effect, old nunataks (peaks of rock rising above the surrounding glacial ice). The growth of trees, shrubs, ferns, and mosses certainly was lush, but might easily have been tiny pieces of the coastal rain forest transplanted from the Situk River lowlands. The trees were mostly Sitka Spruce and the shrubs were Salmonberry, Devil's Club, alders,and willows. In more open grassy areas were heathers, Deer Cabbage, and dwarf rhododendrons. The birds and mammals were the same as those in nearby areas. Red Squirrels scolded from the spruces; Steller's Jays, Fox Sparrows, Ravens, Hermit and Greycheeked thrushes, Robins, and Pine Grosbeaks enlivened the forest. The only stranger was the Blackcapped Chickadee which, I found, replaced, on the timbered parts of the Malaspina, the common Chestnut-backed Chickadee. I collected a satisfactory bag of birds including a fine specimen of the Parasitic Jaeger in the dark phase, which is totally sooty brown with a black cap. The most exciting animal that I saw was a beautiful Silver Fox. I also had a few mammals in my collection, the result of my running a trapline near the Black glacier. So, with a good deal of work to do before dark, I started back to camp in mid-afternoon.

The easiest route was the gradually sloping moraine bordering Esker Creek. Its mouth was where the big Brown Bear appeared to live. I was carrying only a double-barrelled shotgun and the morning's collection as I walked along, engrossed in my own thoughts. Suddenly there he was—not fifty yards away. Once again the giant was berrying in a patch of Salmonberry bushes. When he saw me, he stood upright and peered with his inadequate little eyes. It was his nose, however, that told him the whole story. He dropped to his four feet with a "Big Brown snort". It was a terrifying voluminous sound—only a few decibels below the puff of an old-time coal-burning locomotive. Then he turned and fled, blundering off toward the sheltering forest.

I never went back.

I Missed
the Third Boat

It was at the height of the spawning run of Sockeye and Humpback salmon. The upper reaches of the Situk River stank with dead, rotting fish. The waters were almost glutinous with milt, roe, and slime as thousands of expiring fish mated frantically in their extremity. Both sexes, scintillating silvery creatures a week ago, were now a dark dirty red, their fins frayed and their gill covers exuding revolting fungus growths. The males had huge humps on their backs. Their jaws were distorted into evil-looking snouts, curved apart beyond all possibility of occlusion. The gums were receded exposing a bristling array of wolf-like teeth that they would never again use, for neither sex would ever eat again: just spawn and die; there would be no survivors. To quote Bill Berry (sometime employee of the United States Bureau of Fisheries), "Pacific Salmon are born orphans and die childless." Darting about in the shallows, between and under the sluggish salmon, were scores of Dolly Varden Trout, eagerly gulping the newly-laid eggs. On the sandbars and perched in nearby trees were Bald Eagles and Ospreys satiated with salmon. Once we had twenty-three eagles in view at one time. It was an orgy.

Attracted by the odour—stronger than that of London's Billingsgate Fish Market—a large number of bears emerged from the

82

mountains to feast in the riffles. The bear is essentially a slothful beast. In the spring, he feeds on tender grasses, glacier lilies, and Deer Cabbage, as well as the roots, stems, and leaves of other herbs. This diet is varied with an occasional mouse, marmot, and a tasty mess of ants or beetles. When berries ripen, he is the best berrier in the business, gorging himself on wild strawberries, huckleberries, and salmonberries. But the gourmand comes out in him when the salmon run. Jack Fletcher suggested that I accompany him on another trip up to the headwaters of the Situk in an attempt to collect one of these gourmands. Doug Deeks had bagged a fine Grizzly over on the Malaspina, and its skin and skull were packed and ready for shipment to the Museum; specimens of other bears had eluded us.

"Forget the goddamn dicky birds for once, and just take the 30.06," entreated Jack. "Between us we ought to get a Big Brownie or a Blue." ("Blue" Bear is another name for the Glacier Bear, a rare colour phase of the Black Bear. It is a sort of Maltese grey-blue, pepper-and-salt colour, with a tan muzzle. It is restricted to the region of the St. Elias Alps.) With some reluctance, I consented: there were as yet unobtained birds that I needed to round out my collection. In addition, I had vivid memories of my experience with the Red Blackflies of the Situk.

On the way upriver, each of us chose what we considered likely spots for ambush. I selected a bend of the river into which projected an extensive gravel bar, pocked and pitted with platter-sized bear tracks. The shallows were choked with spawning salmon. I checked the wind direction: I'd have to be pretty unwashed to be sniffed over the reek of rotting fish. I crawled under a dome of spruce branches that concealed me, but that gave me command of the entire bar. Jack took the canoe and worked downriver to his hideout about a mile away.

It was one of the few times that I've waited in ambush or stalked an animal in which I experienced no excitement of the hunt. I wasn't really concerned whether a bear came or not. I didn't want to shoot one, nor did I want the work of preparing it for the Museum. Besides, it was pleasant sitting there with nothing to do but watch the fish and the eagles, and listen to the evening sounds. The bear-hunters were, however, paying for the expedition; so, it would be unfortunate if they went home nearly empty-handed.

83

The light gradually dimmed. In a four-hour span, all I saw were one young Grizzly, who entertained me by charging about the riffles grabbing salmon between his jaws, and a couple of rather puny Black Bears. A Great Blue Heron stabbed and mutilated a salmon carcass washed up on the gravel. It was almost dark when I pricked up my ears, alerted by the chuckling cry of a Screech Owl, a bird not known to occur nearly so far north. It was answered by another, possibly two. In a few moments he appeared, silhouetted against the still bright shine of the sky. I could see his prominent ear-tufts: it was definitely a Screech Owl.

Instinctively the rifle was at my shoulder, the hammer cocked. But this was no bird gun! It was a 30.06 with an impact of 3500 foot pounds and loaded with soft-nosed bullets intended for bear. The owl was no more than a hundred feet away; even so, it was a small target in the dusk. If I fired, bear-hunting was over for the night. If I missed, it would be embarrassing; if I hit, would there be anything left of a seven-inch owl? What does a museum-collector do? I fired. The shoulders of Mt. Tebenkoff echoed to the impulsive explosion of the 30.06, bounced it back against the mountains ringing Russell Fiord, re-echoed it, and poured it down over the forested flatlands. In mountain country, one wonders if the sound of a shot will ever cease. The owl flew twenty feet from his perch, faster than his own wings had ever carried him, and landed in the river. I waded out, kicking aside spawning salmon, and retrieved him. He had a gaping hole through the chest and back, but very few feathers were missing. His soaked feathers made him look like a badly worn, Tlingit hair-seal moccasin.

Half an hour later, as I was sitting on the gravel bar trying, in the light of a lantern, to remove the skin from the pulverized carcass, I heard the soft sound of a paddle. Jack steered the canoe up and grounded it on the bar.

"What happened?" he yelled while alighting.

"I got a Screech Owl."

"A *what*?"

"A Screech Owl."

"You bloody fool! You've missed the third boat!" This was an allusion to the Alaskan maxim that he who misses three boats to the outside is "round the bend" and will *never* leave. I explained as calmly as I could:

"Look, Jack, many people have collected bears—Grizzlys, Big Browns, Blacks, Blues—around Yakutat, but *nobody* ever got one of these before."

"I'll be damned; I still can't believe it—that you'd shoot that damned thing when there are bears around. It's the last time I'll ever have anything to do with a cheechako naturalist!"

"Jack," I said patiently, "this could well turn out to be the prize of our expedition. I wish I could get some more. I'm coming back out here with a shotgun tomorrow evening. I know that there are one or two more right here."

"Not with any bloody help from me you won't," he growled, and sat down in silence on the sandbar as I finished preparing my specimen. (Filled, hemstitched, and painstakingly shaped, it eventually ended up as quite an acceptable scientific specimen.) Through the night, we sat together near my sandbar, but not a bruin showed in the moonlight. At the first paling of the sky and dimming of the stars, a light mist rose from the river.

"May as well drift down slowly and hope that we can come up on one quietly," Jack said grumpily. Subdued, I silently agreed. We launched the canoe, letting the sluggish current carry it downstream, steering only enough to keep us off exposed bars and in deeper water near the banks. We had travelled only a few hundred yards and were silently gliding along under overhanging spruce branches when we startled a whole fleet of Common Mergansers—two ducks and their pooled broods numbering in all about twenty. They went spattering off ahead of us, to settle down near the shore a hundred yards ahead. This was disastrous—for bear-hunting: the wild splashing of still flightless young ducks warned everything of our approach. We tried to get past them by crossing the narrow river and dragging the canoe over a gravel bar into deep water near the opposite bank. In so doing we disturbed another brood of a dozen, which charged off downriver, running on the surface and flapping their inadequate wings and making a hell of a racket. At this, the first twenty panicked and raced down to join them. Now we had more than thirty mergansers heralding our approach. Nothing we could do would make them turn back. Soon another family joined them. The situation was ludicrous. In an hour's time we had nearly a hundred loudly pattering, splashing, squawking mergansers retreating before us.

I started to laugh. Although at first Jack glowered and dug his paddle in farther, he too saw the humour of the situation. As we tied up the canoe, I said, "Sorry, Jack; all that work for nothing."

"Oh, not quite," he replied, with a touch of sarcasm. "After all, *you* got an owl!" I knew that his good humour was restored.

The little Situk River Screech Owl was taken 250 miles (400 kilometres) to the northwest of the then known range of the species. To my knowledge it remains unique. It was certainly the most important take of that Yakutat expedition—a fact that Jack generously admitted later.

FIVE

The Mexico Expedition

Aztec Thrush

Bandidos and the Soroché:
My First Taste of the Tropics

In 1946, my wife Audrey and I went on a field trip to Mexico. We travelled by bus to Linares and spent a few weeks observing and collecting in the Mexican desert in the region between the Pablillo and Comacho rivers. From there we went on to Mexico City, and spent two weeks exploring one of the world's most fascinating cities and the nearby archaelogical sites. We then moved on to Cuernavaca and thence to the tiny village of Tepoztlan (not to be confused with Tepotzotlan) in the state of Morelos. We did a little collecting there, but I came down with a cold and the *soroché,* or mountain sickness, a debilitation caused by high altitude. This, combined with a situation in which we found ourselves in danger both from *Bandidos* and the Mexican army, curtailed our activities.

We caught the ancient *Rio* bus in Cuernavaca and headed for the village of Tepoztlan. We had paid forty-five centavos (about four cents) each for the fare. (At least transportation costs were not going to bankrupt us.) The name of the bus line (second class) gave us pause. It was "Auto-Transportes Ometochtli, s.c.l." Ometochtli, "two rabbits", was the Nahuatl god of *pulque* who presided over the collective orgies and debauchery of ancient Tepoztlan. Actually, the trip was infinitely more enjoyable than many for which we had paid much more.

No one on the bus, not even the driver, spoke English. All spoke Mexican and all spoke it without pause. It mattered not that José was near the front of the bus and his amigo Manuel at the rear: they carried on a conversation just the same, only louder. Maria shouted the gossip to Consuela, five rows back. No one even considered changing seats. The talk, the gossip, the jokes were for everyone anyway.

There were chickens and small pigs, a turkey and some ducks, all hobbled under the long seat at the back. They added their *clucks* and *oinks* and *quacks* to the din on the bus of Babel.

There were sacks and bundles of melons, sugar, salt, rice, beans, noodles, and dried codfish heaped everywhere. Everybody had a load. The baggage rack on the roof was full. A box had been tied onto a spare tire at the back. The overflow had to be carried in the interior, most of it piled at the rear or under the seats. The driver was hemmed in with bundles. Only the aisle was clear.

We had just started off when a big bag burst and scattered its contents of mammee apples on the floor. The road was steeply winding and undulating, and as we tore downhill the mammees, shaped like big avocado pears, careened erratically down the aisle to the front of the bus, only to reverse and trundle like drunken sailors to the rear as we climbed the next incline. Nobody bothered about them. Time enough to collect them when the owner reached her destination.

There was plenty of entertainment inside the bus and plenty more outside. We were travelling through the great mountain plateau of central Mexico, the scene dominated by the snow-capped volcanoes of Popocatepetl and Ixtaccihuatl, both over 18,000 feet. There were rows and fields of giant magueys, the big Mexican agave, or century plant. Its fibre, known as istle, is used for cordage, nets, baskets—an important home industry for the Tepoztecans. Its fermented juice becomes pulque. It is claimed that pulque was "invented" in Tepoztlan (probably by the god-devil Ometochtli!). Distilled, the maguey juice produces tequila.

There were adobe huts, small villages, and even a few *jacals*. These are the homes of the poorest peasants, constructed of close-set wooden stakes or cornstalks plastered with mud, thatched roofs, and mud floors.

For me, also, there were Caracaras and Vermilion Flycatchers, Zonetailed Hawks, and a bird that I had long wanted to see—the Grey Silky Flycatcher. It is closely related to that strange, crested, black bird of the southwestern desert of the United States and adjacent Mexico, the Phainopepla, or Black Silky Flycatcher. They

90

are not related to the tyrant flycatchers nor to the Old World flycatchers; they are rather closer to the waxwings. They have the same neat, well-groomed plumage and erect best-behaviour posture. They look like well scrubbed children going to Sunday school, making other birds look like street urchins. They are more slender and long-tailed than waxwings, and this high-altitude Mexican representative was coloured in soft grey-blue. (I collected one at Tepoztlan later, and marvelled at the soft beauty of its colouring: pale grey, almost whitish crown and crest, the flanks and undertail-coverts bright yellow and golden, the wings black, and tail flashing black and white—a truly aristocratically handsome bird in both form and colour.

The bus trip was over too quickly. While we were anxious to see the country around Tepoztlan, the ride had been most enjoyable—at times, hilarious.

Tepoztlan is one of the more ancient of Mexican villages, having an estimated two thousand years of continuous occupation, and lies about seventy miles south of Mexico City. It is located on a slope with the northern part about six hundred feet higher than the south. All north-south roads are paved with cobblestones and are alternately sloped and terraced—the ancient Aztec method of dealing with a grade. At first, we thought this was exceptionally quaint and pictur-esque. Later, we were cursing all Aztec road engineers: their product was not meant for wheels. It wasn't even very good for burros.

All around the village are beautiful high buttes rising one thousand feet above the village, nearly fifteen hundred in some places. These rugged, craggy bluffs form a natural fortress, and many times in its tumultuous past Tepoztlan's villagers took refuge in them. Again, lovely legend, lovely scenery, and lovely collecting grounds; again, however, we were soon cursing them as the refuge of *bandidos* who were to play a large part in curtailing our activities.

We had made arrangements to stay at the Y.M.C.A. camp *Camohmile*, some four miles from the main plaza of Tepoztlan. The bus passengers all had their own bundles. I was unable to find anyone to help with ours, and there was only one way to get to *Camohmile*: walk. We had two suitcases and my gun box. The latter was heavy for it contained, in addition to the double-barrelled gun, the ammuni-tion and my taxidermy tools. Audrey carried one suitcase, I the other,

91

and I slung the gun box up on my shoulder. Fortunately, it was not hot, and the threatening thunderstorm held off until we reached the camp. But to say that we were enervated is to put it mildly.

We were assigned to a small shack that had room in it for a bunk on each side and very little else. There was a rough bench with a porcelain bowl and water pitcher. Other amenities included horse blankets and an outhouse.

On the first night we discovered the fleas, or rather they discovered us. It has been claimed that fleas are repelled by a horse blanket. We repudiate this. It is probably true that dog fleas (the ones that attack humans) don't care for horses. But these Mexican fleas had never heard the theory. They hopped about on the blankets and bit us with gusto. If the yarn is true, we can only conclude that these blankets had never seen a horse, but then how does one account for their barnyard smell? Or, are burros not horses to a flea?

As we went to breakfast the next morning, we heard gunshots up in the forested hills. We inquired about them and were informed the hills were full of *bandidos* (draft evaders, who were now living off the land by raiding, stealing, and pillaging from the local people). The shots might have been fired by the *bandidos* or by an army patrol hunting them down. It was very disturbing. We recalled the train trip from Monterey to Mexico City during which armed soldiers—a whole platoon of them—had ridden on top of the railway cars with rifles at the ready. Going into the hills alone and carrying a gun could make me fair game for either side, and I suspected there would be a lot of shooting first and identification afterward.

I did make a few trips up to the pine forest on the mountains and down to the relatively humid oak-fir-pine of the valley. On several occasions I had to forego some of the most inviting portions of the forest when I heard shots emanating from them.

One day I walked right into an army patrol. They were a little taken aback to find a *Norteamericano* with bird shot instead of the brigand they expected. Their embarrassment was compounded when I offered my collecting permit for their inspection. None of them could read, but they could recognize my photograph and the great seal of Mexico on the imposingly bulky document. When I told them that I was a Canadian and showed them my specimens—a Canyon wren, a Yelloweyed Junco, a Blue Mockingbird, and a Rufous-capped Brush-Finch—they gave up and let me go.

Then I caught a cold. A heavy cold in the head and chest. Climbing up the rugged crags and down the steep hillsides with the shortness of breath provoked by altitude was bad enough. Now, with nasals plugged and head ringing, sneezing and coughing, I began to know the *soroché,* the mountain sickness that plagues the lowlander. I had been in higher country many times before, but never with a bad cold that in itself was reducing my oxygen intake and absorption. Every part of one's metabolism is slowed down including, worst of all, digestion and peristalsis. You become sluggish. It was disappointing to feel this way when I had a job I desperately wanted to do. There were fabulous birds in this country. Strange warblers like the Painted and Slatethroated Redstarts, the Chestnutchested Warbler, and—the finest one of the family—the beautiful, silvery eared Red Warbler. There were Russet and Orangebilled Nightingale-Thrushes, Brownbacked Solitaires, and Yellow Grosbeaks, a half dozen Mexican species of hummingbirds including the Green Violet-ear, the Beautiful Hummer, the Bumblebee Hummer, and the Sparklingtailed Hummer. One day, I scared up what I took to be a Stygian Owl, one much like a big, dark Longeared Owl. There were several wrens, and, in the lower country, there were Longtailed Wood Partridges and Rufescent Tinamou. I could hear them and see them, but I was gradually losing the energy and desire to pursue, stalk, and collect them.

I knew it was finished the day I saw the Aztec Thrush. I had climbed up the craggy mountain, avoiding the easier going along a trail that led to other hills and forested slopes because of gunfire in that direction. I was dizzy and listless and sat on the edge of a ledge of rock in a quiet, cool forest of oak. I was debating going back to the camp when I saw the Aztec Thrush. It is a big thrush, heavy as a robin, and beautifully patterned in brown and buff and white. No other thrush remotely resembles its colouration. It was one of the birds I really wanted. Now if I could climb forty feet I would be in range. I slipped off the gun's safety catch and started to rise. I didn't even get my knees straight before I sat down again. I looked at the thrush through the binoculars. It was gorgeous. I had to have it. I

93

summoned all my energy, lifted myself a foot off the rock and dropped back onto it. The cold and the *soroché* had me. I looked longingly at the thrush and made another effort. It was no use.

At length he flew off and disappeared. That at least was a relief. The teasing was over. After a half-hour rest, I made my way slowly and dejectedly down to the flat lands, down to the cabin. Audrey was there.

"Did you know," she asked as I lay down on my pallet, "that the director's son was kidnapped from this place last year and held for ransom? And that some of the staff were in on it? There was almost a rupture of diplomatic relations between the United States and Mexico until they released him."

"Are those who did it still here?"

"Still here," she replied, "and I think you should give up going into the hills, especially carrying a gun. Either the army or the bandits might take a shot at you. Even if they do talk first—well, if you're as successful at communicating with the *soldados* or the *bandidos* as you were with that goatherder out near the Pablillo, I'll never see you again!"

"I think you're right. I will pack it up and take it easy. I feel miserable and just haven't the energy to go tearing up these crags anyway. All those little *soldados* and *bandidos* are the last straw."

Something out of my Irish ancestry reminded me;

> *Up the airy mountain,*
> *Down the rushy glen,*
> *We daren't go a-hunting*
> *For fear of little men.*

It's the only stanza of the poem by William Allingham that I know. Someday I must look up the rest of that poem. I'm interested to know if he mentioned the *soroché*.

94

SIX

The Trinidad Expedition

Bushmaster

Beware, Bushmaster!

The expedition to Trinidad in the spring of 1957 had as its main objective the collecting of the largest of the highly venomous pit vipers, the Bushmaster. We wanted to reproduce a scene showing this reptile in its natural setting as a feature exhibit in our Gallery of World Reptiles. This meant, of course, that we had to collect, preserve or make moulds of the major vegetational elements that make up the snake's habitat.

Trinidad is geographically part of the West Indies, but biologically distinctly South American. It is a relatively small island, roughly fifty miles long and thirty miles wide. It has two promontories that reach out from its northwest and southwest corners to within seven miles of the continental mass of South America. It is separated from Venezuela by an "inland sea", the Gulf of Paria. This proximity to the continent makes it easy to understand its botanical and faunal affinities to South America rather than to the West Indies.

Topographically, the island can be divided into five belts formed by three ranges of hills, running east and west, and their intervening lowlands. We worked mostly in the hills paralleling the north coast and known as the Northern Range. Its highest peaks are El Cerro del Aripo, 3,085 feet, El Tucuché, 3,072 feet, and Morne Bleu, 2,761 feet. Nearly all of the valleys of the Northern Range are transverse and the principal ones open to the south. The slopes are precipitous and, as the area is one of heavy rainfall, it is clothed with dense evergreen rain forest. This is the home of the Bushmaster, which, unlike the more numerous and equally deadly Fer-de-lance, shuns the low country and lives mainly in the high forest.

97

The glare of sunlight was dazzling. We had just emerged from the inky blackness of the deep cave inhabited by the bizarre Guacharos, or Oilbirds. It was a relief to be out in the open air again, high on the shoulder of Mount Aripo with the fresh, aromatic breeze of the Trade Winds slowly and gently supplanting the mouldering odour of decay and filth in our nostrils.

Here there was the fragrance of Pink and Yellow Pouis, of *Cordia*, and of Wild Sage. Underfoot were the dry, dead leaves and the good, firm earth. Big healthy green plants, ferns, arums, and heliconias embowered us. Birds sang cheerfully in the sunshine.

A few minutes before, we had been in total darkness, broken only by the frail beams of our headlamps. Bats, mostly freetails, but some the fearsome *Desmodus rufus,* the Vampire, had been whirling about our heads. The rocks of the cavern floor had been slippery with dung, the air heavy with the fetid reek of fungus, decay, and dankness augmented by the effluvium from immense mounds of bat and Guacharo droppings. The only vegetation had been man-high etiolated palms, living in the darkness on the nourishment from their own kernels and doomed to die when this ran out. They grew in the cave because palm nuts are the food of the Guacharos. At night, these strange birds go out to feed on the nuts. The following day, deep in the cave and with their digestible portions assimilated by the birds, the nuts are expelled with other wastes to fall on the cavern floor and take hopeless root. Of sounds there were only the whispering wings and chittering of the bats, the howls and growls and chaffering of the Guacharos and the occasional trickle of water seepage.

It had been worth the effort: the long hike up the side of the mountain, through the forest, to the cave; the strenuous and dangerous climbs within it; the half mile of crawling, slithering, and hanging on by toes and fingertips to see the extraordinary Guacharos, but it was deliverance to be out in the open again. We were tired and dirty, and the evil smell of the cave clung to our clothes.

We found a forest path that bordered a tiny, clear, bubbling stream, and wandered along it. We stopped to listen to the fine melodic song of the Black and Grey Thrush. We watched the strange performance of the Black and White Manakin, the *Casse-noisette,* the "nutcracker" to the Trinidadian. The dance, engaged in by two or more males, and always close to the ground, consists of the birds

98

leaping back and forth between two branches, each invariably landing in such a manner that he faces the spot he has just come from. As he lands he snaps his wings, producing a sharp crack resembling the breaking of a hard-shelled nut or the explosion of a small firecracker. On this occasion, two males were in a frenzy of leaping activity. The moment one landed the other "took off". The result was a tarantella to the snapping of castanets. There came a little troop of White-flanked Antbirds, flitting restlessly about the tangled masses of twisted lianas. Dark little birds, the males entirely black below, they frequently flashed a semaphore of brilliant white when they lifted their wings to expose their snowy flanks. We discovered a White-throated Leafscraper, a small, earthy brown-coloured bird resembling in its actions a little thrush. It wasn't scraping leaves; so, I added it to my special list of "silly-ass" bird names. (I've never seen a Nuthatch hatching a nut, a Bananaquit quitting a banana, a Plantaineater dining on one, a Woodhewer chopping wood, and certainly not a Leaf-love being amorous with the foliage!)

We were watching a Yellowcrested Woodpecker that shouted lustily as he went about his carpentry, his high shaggy crest blowing sideways in the wind, when it happened. It happened as it so often does, when you least expect it. I had found my first live, free Bushmaster.

We had come from Toronto to Trinidad to collect the material for a diorama of the Bushmaster in the rain forest of the Northern Range. All this had been accomplished long since. We had a fine plaster mould of a big Bushmaster, which we would reproduce in latex back at the Museum. We had two fine specimens for the research collection, and we had all of the accessory plant material we needed. All this was now on the high seas in the hold of a northbound ship. My companions had already flown off to Toronto, and I was putting in time until Audrey's arrival for a holiday.

The two specimens of the longest venomous snake of the New World had been brought to us, dead, by cocoa workers. We had, for over a month, searched the floor of the high forest on El Tucuché, El Cerro del Aripo, the Heights of Guanapo, the Arima-Blanchisseuse road, and Morne Bleu without success. But with the help of cocoa cutters, the job had been done, and the excitement and anticipation were over. I had ceased to look for Bushmasters—and so I found one.

I think I knew that I had found my Bushmaster before I saw him; I heard him first. It could, I suppose, just as easily have turned out to be a *Cribo* or a *Tigre* (large nonvenomous snakes), but sometimes a naturalist has a kind of sixth sense and, on this occasion, almost instinctively I knew I had come upon a Bushmaster. For one thing the climbing snakes were eliminated, for the distinctive rusting sound of a snake vibrating his tail in the dead leaves is peculiar to those that live on the ground among them, and there were not too many kinds of ground snakes in the forest.

I had never heard a Bushmaster before, but I had heard plenty of rattlesnakes, Fox Snakes, King Snakes, and Rat Snakes. The sound has a characteristic rhythm to it, be it a rattler waving his rattles in the air or a Rat Snake beating the tip of his tail among noisy, dry, dead leaves. To those who know the sound, it is as distinctive as that of a reclining dog wagging his tail on a wooden floor. This Bushmaster, rattling the dead leaves of the Aripo forest, produced a noise that could have come from a Fox Snake doing the same thing at Fish Point on Pelee Island in Lake Erie.

He was in a slight clearing, not far from the stream, and partially sheltered by some arums, already beginning to loop himself into a defensive coil. He had, I suppose, been stimulated to buzz by the vibrations set up by our footsteps as he could not have seen us until we rounded into the clearing. Now his forked tongue was flicking rapidly in and out, smelling us. The tongue itself cannot smell, of course, but its delicate tips carry minute particles to highly developed sensory cells in the anterior portion of the roof of the mouth. These are located in two tiny pits that are known as "Jacobson's organ". They are not developed in man, other mammals, or birds.

His "Jacobson" had identified us, and once again I was assailed by the realization of man's fearful accomplishment—that of terrorizing everything. It seemed unlikely that he had ever encountered humans before, yet his intuition, the immediate apprehension of his mind, without reasoning, told him to flee. It was only by adroit foot work and the aid of a stick that I was able to steer him out into the clearing and force him again into his defensive spiral. He was of a delicate clay colour suffused with pinkish orange, and with bold, irregular jet-black lozenges evenly spaced along his length. His underparts were white with a porcellaneous glaze. His big blunt head, rounder and less triangular than those of the rattlers or Fer-de-lances, was equipped with outsized venom glands, and his mouth, I knew, concealed inch-long fangs. I had been warned by many Trinidadians that a Bushmaster is aggressive. He won't flee—"He come after you, man!"

I said to Walter, my guide, "It seems he has only one objective, to get away from us. What about this bit about Bushmasters chasing after people? This chap is behaving like any other snake; in fact rattlers are more inclined to stand their ground. Have you ever been pursued by one? Do you know of anyone who has?"

He grinned sheepishly, "No. *Mapipire zanana,* he's really a mild snake. He won't come after you. He bites when he's stepped on or cornered, when he's afraid he can't escape." *Mapipire zanana,* "the pineapple poisonous snake": his Trinidadian name stems from his rugose, highly-keeled scales that resemble the rough skin of the pineapple.

He lay there making no effort to strike, even when my stick moved close. Every so often he made a half-hearted attempt to escape. But mostly he just lay there and buzzed his tail in the leaves. It seemed strange behaviour for a creature with no external ears and one who couldn't hear his own sound. Did he know he was making a noise by detecting the transmitted vibrations from his tail's contact with the leaves?

I didn't do much but look at him and steer him back when he tried to bolt. I suppose I should have tried to find out more about his behaviour, but I really couldn't find it in my conscience to taunt or tantalize him into action. I had that familiar feeling of a slight depression, a "let-down" sensation that comes upon me when I see fear in grand and puissant animals.

I had one great consolation. Thanks to the cocoa workers, I had no need to collect this Bushmaster. I knew that the two we had in pickle had been doomed the minute the men with cutlasses had found them. Every Bushmaster encountered by coffee or cocoa crews, lumbermen or whatever, is slashed into a dozen pieces and left to the ants and other little jungle undertakers. The cutlass wielders had not mutilated the ones they brought us. They knew enough about the weak neck-vertebrae of the vipers to dispatch them with a neck-breaking blow with the blunt edge of the knife.

I didn't keep our Bushmaster out in the clearing long. The

afternoon sun was fiery hot. Few reptiles can withstand long exposure to direct, hot sunlight. Even desert snakes will expire on five to ten minutes exposure. The Bushmaster was showing unmistakeable signs of discomfort. He began making more determined efforts to escape and finally we let him go. He didn't go in haste. I suppose he was already debilitated by the exposure, but I forced on myself the conviction that his unhurried departure could be attributed to his dignity.

Walter seemed a bit dumbfounded; he glanced at me, at the heavy machete hanging from my belt, and at the *mapipire*. Undoubtedly it was the first Bushmaster he had seen or heard of that was not summarily dispatched. It was, perhaps, the most pleasurable part of the whole experience to watch *Lachesis muta* crawl safely into the shade of the big patch of sheltering arums and disappear.

Lachesis was one of the three fates of classical mythology, the disposer of lots, the life span of human beings. Appropriate. *Muta* means, of course, mute. But then what snake isn't, save for its' hissing? Mine at least was making quite a racket with his tail.

Flame Birds
of the Caroni

Just south of Port-of-Spain, on the west coast of Trinidad, lies the Caroni swamp. With a coastal front of more than ten miles on the gulf of Paria and extending inland up to six miles, it is one of the most attractive areas of the island to a naturalist. It is composed of areas of open water, herbaceous swamp, and freshwater swamp-forest dotted with palm stands. Along the coast is an extensive mangrove swamp, on the landward side of which, where the water is somewhat saline, is an almost pure crop of leather fern growing to eight feet in height and forming an almost completely closed canopy overhead. This is perhaps one of the most splendid fern growths in the world. It is natural that such an area with an abundance of water and great diversity of vegetational habitats should be attractive to many kinds of animals. So it was that we took time out from our work in the northern range to spend a day in the Caroni.

We arranged to have a boat left at the end of the canal that penetrates deeply into the swamp, and early one day drove down the Caroni road through the low, flat country to the south of the Northern Range. We were treated to the sight of scores of migrant Forktailed Flycatchers, a bird resembling an Eastern Kingbird, but possessing a foot-long scissors-like tail. They breed in Venezuela and other South and Central American countries, but large flocks pour into Trinidad in the non-breeding season. There were Maizebirds, like small meadowlarks with bright mandarin red instead of golden yellow breasts, and flocks of Boattailed Grackles. Blueblack Grassquits were common in the sugar-cane and rice fields, leaping vertically one and a half to two feet, delivering a brief flight song during these aerial unfurlings and dropping like stones to the same perch. When ten or twelve of these tiny black finches go through their performance in one small field, it is a most amusing sight. Almost continuously, and often three or four at a time, they pop up out of the grass or cane and drop back. It was as if someone had dropped a dozen black India rubber balls on a hard, level surface. More reserved Grey Seedfinches edged foot over foot to the tops of cane, delivered their melodic song and slid down out of sight. Because of its pleasing voice, this is a popular cage-bird, known in Trinidad as the *Picoplat* (Silverbill). Its song in a cage never sounded so full, sweet, and rich as in the cane fields, but then I am a hopeless romantic about such things. To me, enjoyment depends largely on sympathetic association. The song of a wild, free bird imparts much that is joyous and stimulating. That of a caged one has its undertones of melancholy, even though the bird may be unaware of them.

Glossy Cowbirds and Rice Grackles perched on fence wires or walked about in short grass looking and acting very much like the familiar Brownheaded Cowbirds and Bronzed Grackles of our countryside. Every paddy-field and wet savannah had one or more Streaked Herons. These, too, resembled a North American species,

103

the Green Heron. Their behaviour was similar: standing motionless until some small prey, frog, fish or aquatic insect, approached closely enough for a darting thrust of the dagger-like bill. A harsh *chowk* was the extent of their vocalization.

The most entertaining of all were the Smoothbilled Anis. Several times we stopped to watch their grotesque antics. Their contortive acrobatics were accompanied by wheezing, whispering sibilations, unbird-like and impossible of interpretation.

When we reached the canal, seven of us managed to cram ourselves into the boat. Unfortunately the water level was low and the canal banks high, margined with shrubs and tall grass. For a while we didn't see much but the ditch banks. The embankment, however, didn't lack interest. There were frequent slimy mud-bars and shrubby, muddy, sloping sidewalls on which were several species of elegantly coloured and patterned crabs. On the stems of shrubs reposed numerous large pond-snails. Once a big Green Iguana dropped from a high branch into the water with a resounding splash and swam ashore, strongly and swiftly. All four limbs were applied closely to the body; so, it was propelled only by the powerful, laterally-compressed tail. When he reached the opposite bank, he scrambled quickly into the undergrowth. Again, a large slender-winged hawk appeared only a few yards away, sailing low over the thick grass. When it saw the boatload of people, it swerved abruptly upward, its long thin shanks kicking and wings beating violently as it took evasive action. Its Marsh Hawk-like form and black topside proclaimed it a Longwinged Harrier.

There were stretches where the channel cut through large acreages of open water fringed and dotted with waterlilies and Water Hyacinth. Here we observed Purple Gallinules, Moorhens, a Caribbean Coot, and numbers of Wattled Jaçanas. The latter were strange fowl: rather slim birds, about nine inches long, rail-like in head and body, they were strikingly coloured with black head, neck, and breast, and the rest of the body deep rich chestnut. The wings were bright chartreuse, each flight feather tipped with dark brown. Their beaks were bright yellow with a frontal lobe and two chicken-like wattles hanging from the gape scarlet. The bend of the Jaçana's wing is equipped with a sharp, thorn-like yellow spur. The most remarkable feature of the Jaçana are its legs and feet, however. The legs are long and the slender toes extraordinarily so. These strange birds travel about on the open blanket of floating aquatic plants. Their long toes so distribute their weight that they can run easily over floating leaves that would not sustain the weight of a more conventional bird. In the vernacular they are "lily-trotters", a most appropriate name. Frequently they raise and spread their meretricious wings over their backs as if proud of their garishness.

As we penetrated deeper into the swamp, the waterway became more ill-defined. Alternately we travelled across broad expanses of drowned land and through narrow channels in the swamp-forest. Travelling by boat under the closed canopy of a swamp is an eerie experience. Much of the forest floor is inundated, and the canopy, formed of sub-dominant trees, is much lower than in the tropical rain forest. The trees are covered with deep moss and draped with an abundance of air-plants. The development of flaring, plank-like buttresses at the bases of the trees is pronounced, especially those of the Bloodwood trees. The Bloodwood is so named because of the rich, arterial blood-red of the sap. When the trunk is wounded by the stroke of a cutlass, the thick viscid liquid pours forth. I once got some of this sap on my hand and its resemblance to blood was almost frightening. It even dried to a flaky red-brown as does coagulated gore.

In the swamp-forest we encountered the tiny Pygmy Kingfisher. Only four inches from crown to tail-tip, it is glossy green above and orange-chestnut below. I regretted that I had not the opportunity to watch it longer because I wondered what aquatic food the little mite captured in that brown, murky water. It had a choice of fish fry, small tadpoles, and insect larvae.

On one extent of stinking black mud there was a colony of fiddler crabs. Each male had one gigantic reddish-brown claw, shaped and coloured like a violin and held as by a virtuoso. The huge claw, as great in bulk and nearly twice as long as the body, was waved and brandished in what I suppose the little crustaceans felt was a threatening gesture. It was really more as if they were beckoning, and this behaviour has given them the alternate name of "calling crabs". If we moved quickly, they disappeared into burrows of which there was a labyrinthine abundance in the mud. When we sat quietly for a while, they emerged again with tiny euphonious sounds, not vocal, but resulting from suction of water and air in the ooze as the crabs climbed to the surface. The males' resemblance to violinists was heightened when they were feeding because the small claw picked up the food and seemed to move across the rigidly held "fiddle" on its way to the crab's mouth as if the performer were drawing the bow across the strings.

We emerged from the swamp into an area of drowned land, a lake with numerous twisted, gnarled, and weathered tree trunks protruding from the water. The lake was margined with a semi-floating mass of Water Hyacinth, Water Tobacco, and lily pads. One big tree that had died, literally from drowning, some years before served as a perch for a dozen Black Vultures and a Wood Stork. On another sat a Plumbeous Kite and yet another had two Whitefaced Tree Ducks. On a long mud bar, bordered by dense shrubbery, were herons —dozens of them: Little Blues, Snowy and Great White Egrets, Tricoloured Herons, Yellowcrowned Night Herons, and two tiny Variegated Bitterns. There were, however, two other species that took my attention because of the unconventional nature of their beaks. The first was a Boatbilled Heron. He sat in a dark, shady nook, on a tree limb five or six feet above the water. His neck was drawn down on his shoulders and he looked at first like a Black-crowned Night Heron. But the beak was grotesquely broad and flattened dorso-ventrally like the mouth of a huge Bullfrog. Then I saw the Roseate Spoonbills. There were four of them wading in shallow water near the mud bar, birds the size of geese and of the most exquisite shade of shell pink with a splash of carmine red on the shoulders. These, I thought, could be rated among the world's most beautiful birds were it not for the greenish, naked, vulture-like head terminating in a grotesque beak. Nearly seven inches long, it ends not in a spoon but in a great, rounded spatula. There was no question as to its efficiency though. As they waded sedately along, their bills were swung, partially open, laterally to and fro and with considerable elegance sifting and filtering out aquatic insects and small arthropods from the watery mud. The spoonbills had another incongruity: the short tail was straw-coloured, not at all in colour harmony with the gorgeous pink of the rest of the plumage. This bird, it seemed, was poorly planned from an artistic standpoint, and badly needed the services of a designer and colour consultant.

106

By now the sun's rays were tinged with the warmer light of early evening and the spoonbills were assuming a more ruddy orange glow. Smaller birds, having been rather inactive during the heat of the day, were taking advantage of the remaining cooler hours of daylight. An Equinocial Yellowthroat broke into its distinctive and monotonous song of about a dozen "tweets" rapidly repeated from a patch of shrubby bushes. Flocks of Yellowheaded Marsh Birds, looking like miniature Yellowheaded Blackbirds, took to flight into low trees bordering the water. Two species of black and white flycatchers were present and conspicuous. The Whiteshouldered Water Tyrant, resembling in its pattern a diminutive magpie, perched on limbs overhanging the water, wagging its tail and darting out over the surface to snap up emerging insects. The other species—the Whiteheaded Water Tyrant—was all black save for a pure white head. Its behaviour was a little more sedate. These two little birds are well known to the Trinidadian, who has his own inimitable names for them: the former is the "washerwoman", the latter the "widow". Would that zoologists of more recent years had had such facility with appropriate names; perhaps then we wouldn't have such horrendous appellations as the "Eastern Ochrefronted Hylophilus", a small vireo known in Trinidad simply as the "wood-bird".

To the west of us, on higher ground, was a stand of Cocorite Palms. This palm is extremely resistent to fire damage, and often after a burn or exhausting cultivation the Cocorites will spring up in the manner of fireweed. It frequently results in a deflected climax of pure Cocorite Palm, however. It is a most attractive plant. The stem is relatively short, but the many feathery leaves, of upright growth, are ten to twelve feet long. The trees grow in closed ranks so that a stand is dense and lush. We were watching a tiny Bat Falcon tormenting a big Black Crab Hawk over the Cocorite stand when Jake Kenny shouted, "Scarlet Ibises".

We forgot everything else to focus our attention on the scimitar-shaped flock of big birds approaching from the southwest. They came with the speed and directness of teal, with a rush and roar of surprisingly rapid yet full, powerful wing strokes. Their colour, hit by the now deeply slanting rays of the sun, was magnificent. How does one describe it? Scarlet, vermilion, cinnabar, flame, fluorescent—in the orange-red sunlight against a backdrop of darkest green foliage, their brilliance almost hurt the eyes. They flew low in the manner of Golden Plovers or Knots, swerving and banking in harmony; sweeping upward over a clump of bushes and down again nearly to the water's surface without hesitation and as one. Suddenly they checked, dropped their undercarriages, and braked. Almost as one bird, they alighted in a low spreading tree, a tree with its feet in water. More flocks were coming, some composed of only five or six, others thirty or more. Some were flying a hundred feet high, others, like the first, skimming the tree tops. Once a great almost solid square of about sixty passed close by only twenty feet above the lake. The sound of their wings was like a strong wind through a pine forest.

It seemed that the ibises' first concern on alighting and finding a roosting spot was to keep their bowels open. The semi-liquid excreta made a most distinctive *plip* as it hit the water. It wasn't exactly music, but it was a delight to listen to it. It was perhaps erratic, like a beginner picking out the letters on a typewriter or a child commencing his first piano lesson. To us it was a sound of the wild, as worthy as the song of a thrush.

There was a half hour of flighting ibises, each flock glowing redder than the last. How could the rays of the sinking sun tinge these red birds still redder? Yet it did.

The flocks were pitching into the low trees that were wading in the water of the swamp. The trees soon blossomed with great scarlet, living, avian inflorescence. In later years, in South America, in India and in Africa, as I viewed the red blooms of Kapok, Tulip trees or Nandi Flames, I was often transported back in time and space to Trinidad. Such was the marvel of the Flame Birds of the Caroni.

In the High Forest

On Mount El Tucuché in Trinidad there is an enchanted forest. It doesn't look like a corporeal forest, but rather like an Arthur Rackham illustration come to three-dimensional life. The trees, stilt-rooted or buttressed, are gnarled and stunted with long, straggling, digital limbs—clawed tentacles. Their branch-scars and knots are big and swollen like arthritic joints. The trees grow only thirty to forty feet high, and beneath them are small palms and tree ferns six to ten feet tall. Everything is festooned with a prodigal growth of mosses and long-whiskered lichens. Thick, twisty lianas twine and hide about the trunks and arms of the trees, some crooking out as if peering at you. You half expect to see white-bearded gnomes living in gigantic toadstools.

The sun is excluded by a vaporous mist so thick that it condenses on your face and clothing. The air is chilly and the light is grey-green and eerie. Everything is grey-green and eerie. This is the "Elfin Wildwood", a tiny patch of cloud forest caused by a fortuitous caprice of El Tucuché's configuration. On the western shoulder of the mountain, at about 2,000 feet, there is a concavity which looks as if some gargantuan prehistoric monster had taken a sizeable bite out of the hillside. Protected in the lee of the mountain from the northeast trade winds, warm tropical air climbs up and reaches a saturation point in moisture and is held in the depression where its water vapour dissolves into fog, dew, and misty rain. An almost perpetual cloud hangs over El Tucuché's shoulder like an epaulette concealing the charming pixie forest from all except those who climb a long steep trail.

It is a silent place save for the tranquil, melodious murmuring of the fall of tiny droplets of water on soft, wet leaves. On my first visit, I stood a long time while no animal voice broke the silence. I thought how suitable it would be if the only denizens of the magic woodland were elves, big-eyed mice, and round fluffy owls.

Then, as if conjured up by a spell, there *was* an owl. He was a big owl, a foot and a half long, and he appeared to be wearing enormous white-rimmed glasses and a long white beard. He was a Spectacled Owl; tawny buff on the breast with the rest of him blackish brown, except for a thick white line that ran over each eye and down along his beak: his "spectacles". A broad band of white covered his throat and ended in a point on his chest: his "beard". He sat on a nearly-horizontal moss-covered limb like a venerable old pundit, slowly moving his head from side to side, the better to see and appraise me. He didn't stay long, but took soundless flight. I was delighted that the first bird I saw in the Elfin Forest should be so appropriate.

On another day I saw an even more fitting bird in the enchanted woodland. He was as fay-like as the forest. I stopped still as I detected an alien movement among the fern leaves. It was not that there was no other movement: every leaf, every twig, every long strand of lichen danced a slow and graceful *valse triste* as droplets of water fell upon them. This movement was deliberate and had a degree of purpose to it. Its architect soon emerged from under the ferns and onto a patch of bare mud.

It had the body-size of an American Robin or European Blackbird, but it had been equipped with the most absurdly short tail, about an inch and a half long, which it carried at the perpendicular. It walked with an air of affected delicacy, the stubby upright tail jerking forward at each mincing step taken by the long spindly legs. It was not brightly coloured: earthy brown above and slate grey below. Its face was black with a conspicuous white ring about the eye. Rather, it was its extraordinary configuration for a song bird and its quaint deportment that lent it an individuality that commanded attention.

I couldn't put a name to it immediately, but I knew it was one of that large neo-tropical group known as Antbirds. There was, at that date, no field guide to the birds of Trinidad; I had, however, prepared my own keys to the identification of the terrestrial vertebrates of the island, and this somewhat soiled and soggy notebook was in my pocket. I had sketched in most of the Antbirds and it was not difficult

110

to decide that I had before me a Blackfaced Antthrush, known to the Trinidadian as *bois-coq*. Even as I returned the "field guide" to my pocket, *bois-coq* stretched himself up to his full height, ruffled the hackles on his neck, pointed his beak nearly straight up, and uttered a loud, clear whistle followed by three more on a descending scale. The little cock could crow! And he looked like a little rooster as he did so. Having delivered himself of this exhausting effort, he collapsed down upon himself into a fuzzy ball. Even his "knees" sagged.

On other days I encountered many animals in the Elfin Forest, but none seemed so spookishly suited to its magical mood as the big wise owl and the crowing *bois-coq*.

No climb up El Tucuché was without its adventure and its reward. The trail skirts the foot of Maracas Falls that cascades down 340 feet of sheer precipitous rock and throws off great clouds of spray. The near vertical walls on either side, bathed constantly in spume, support an exuberant growth of mosses, ferns, bromeliads, and philodendrons. I never passed it without spending a few minutes scrambling and slithering over the boulders at its base, smoothed and slippery from centuries of exposure to the tiny airborne droplets that drifted from the cataract. I was always sure of seeing a pair of Green Kingfishers and a number of Short-tailed or other Swifts. Once a Blackthroated Mango, a hummingbird nearly five inches long, probed at the flowers of a milkweed. It was a scintillating bronze-green above, black below, with the sides of its chest gleaming iridescent blue. Its big fan tail changed from chestnut to magenta to purple and bronze depending on the angle at which it received and reflected the light. Eventually, it perched on the branch of a small Cecropia tree. Several times its long tongue slid out beyond the end of its inch-long bill as if it were licking its lips after its repast of nectar.

Along the margins of the trickling streams below the cataract, small attractive Trinidad Arrow Poison Frogs were abundant. The skin of many frogs contains mucous glands that emit poisonous secretions if the animal is roughly handled. In some South American genera, the discharge is highly toxic, and it was to one of these groups that the little Trinidadian "Borgias" belonged. Indians of tropical America used a concoction of this poison on arrowheads when hunting monkeys and large birds. The victims were almost instantly paralyzed and soon died. I captured a number of these frogs that, when gently handled, do not exude their venom. They are remarkable in other ways. The new laid eggs are attached to the father's back were they soon hatch into tadpoles. For several weeks, "papa" becomes a hopping nursery. The tadpoles cling to his back and he carries them about, frequently dunking them in water. When they reach an advanced stage of development, they swim free during one of these baths and enter upon a life of independence. "Papa" resumes *his* life of independence until he next meets an attractive female. Some of the males I examined showed evidence of having been nursemaids as the skin of their backs was macerated and pockmarked.

On one soggy stretch of trail lived giant earthworms —"gentlemen of the road", Serrano, our guide, called them. They reach a length of over three feet and are as thick as a garden hose. Usually we didn't see them, we just heard them. Almost every footfall caused a big worm, stretched out in the ooze beneath the surface, to retract its great length with a sucking noise like the final rush of bath water gurgling down the drain.

It has been my wont on all my field trips, arctic or tropical, winter or summer, rainy or dry season, to spend at least one night awake and out-of-doors. Noctivagant solitude in the high forest of El Tucuché is a fulfilling experience. The animals of the darkness are astir, frog voices boom, pipe, and drumroll, and orthopterous insects skirl and whine, but the din has a lilting cadence to which one quickly becomes acclimatized. In fact it is somewhat soporific. It is when something to silence them occurs—perhaps the ground shudder caused by the fall of a heavy fruit—that the hiatus in sound rushes in on you with the urgency of a thunderclap. All your senses seem to "sit bolt upright".

A flashlight beam will pick up the eyeshine of many otherwise invisible creatures—the glowing red orbs of an Agouti or the bright, emerald-green mirrors of spiders. Shone on the soggy, dead leaves at your feet, the light reveals myriads of small creatures going about their sunless course of existence, each in its tiny way contributing to the endurance of the parquetry of the forest. Slanted upward, the beam attracts moths and other airborne insects, each suddenly glaringly visible. Big meandering beetles fly laboriously into the shaft of radiance, and blunder back out into the surrounding darkness. In turn, bats, drawn by the fluttering moths, sweep back and forth, each sweep expunging abruptly a dancing point of light that had been a moth.

Once, in the dark, I found myself being nipped with greater frequency than usual. The torch revealed that I had been sitting close to the path of a work gang of Leafcutter, or Parasol, Ants busily engaged in denuding a nearby tree. After removing myself to a more comfortable distance, I watched the conveyor belt of activity. Hordes of them, empty-jawed, streamed past comparable hordes hurrying the opposite way each carrying a neatly-scissored portion of leaf fifty times its own size. Their scurrying shadows thrown on a ditchbank by the torchlight and magnified a hundredfold was something out of a bizarre horror movie. With the lamp, I traced the lines to a big Pois Doux tree and finally lost them eighty feet up in the leafy crown. The ants were engaged in collecting the leaves that would be carried to a chambered nest a dozen feet below the surface. There the leaves would be chewed to tiny bits and prepared as compost for their underground gardens of fungus upon which they subsist.

The aroma of the jungle is more pungent at night: musty, aromatic, mouldy, spicy, fetid, and incensed—the amalgam of rotting vegetation, of fragrant flowers, of the sea breeze, and of stagnant frog-ponds, all synthesized into one great redolent brew. But the most powerful and lasting impression is of the night itself, warm, deep, and profoundly mysterious. No night in temperate regions, no matter how dark or hot, has the nature and complexion of the nocturnal hours of the tropical forest. But it is not only that one learns much about the forest and its dwellers; more important perhaps is that one acquires a feeling of calmness in it. The soft, voluptuous blackness inspires serenity.

I saw yet another face of the rain forest on what started out as a bright sunny day. Ario Gatti, my assistant, and I entered the forest armed with folding pruning saws and cutlasses with the objective of collecting a number of lianas for use in our exhibit. The forests of Central and South America are richer in big woody creepers and vines than those of Asia or Africa. There are lianas a foot in diameter, lianas over five hundred feet long—greater than the length of any tree; there are round lianas, spirally twisted ones, some fluted, some crenelated, some winged, some with raised nodes resembling nightmarishly extended, huge string-bean pods.

I had left Ario with a twisty liana that he was to cut into four-foot lengths, label, and tie into a bundle for eventual fumigation and shipment home. I walked on deeper into the forest. I am easily distracted, especially in a plant and animal-rich rain-forest. I was surrounded by things that cried out for investigation. Strange bird-songs kept luring me deeper into the jungle. There was the steely ringing *bonck* of the Anvil Bird, the *Campanero,* or "bell-ringer". Its resounding forceful cry, perhaps the most characteristic sound of the day-time forest of Trinidad, has been, with validity, compared to the clang of a blacksmith's hammer on the anvil. Sometimes one would presage the sonorous bell-note with a series of lesser utterances: *tonk, a-tonk, a-tonk, a-tonk—Bonck!* I heard one deliver fifteen *tonks* before the final crashing clang. He did so from the crown of a Pink Poui, a tree so tall that it was identifiable only by the circular carpet of fallen blossoms that littered the forest floor beneath it. A Trinidad Squirrel chattered at me. He was so like the familiar Canadian Red Squirrel that I just had to approach and renew old friendship. A big patch of Shamebush, the "sensitive plant" of florists, had to be touched so that it folded up its compound leaves and virtually disappeared—then I waited and watched as it slowly and surreptitiously unfolded itself. There was a Blunt-headed Tree Snake, thin as a darning needle yet a yard long, extending its tenuous body two feet out from its anchorage, then recoiling at the touch of a fingertip, vibrating like a violin string. Not without reason is it called by the Trinidadian *Mapipere a Corde Violan,* the fiddle-string poisonous snake. A rear-fang that kills its prey of small frogs and insects with its venom, it just can't be induced to bite a human or any animal too big for its tiny gullet. Huge, opalescent blue *Morpho* butterflies flew with the speed of birds, usually high over my head, but sometimes low over the water of the mountain streams.

I was a long way from the road and the trail when the storm broke. There is nothing so total, so unqualified as a tropical storm. The rainfall is so absolute that one almost drowns. In half a minute, one abandons any thought of shelter. It is pointless to seek it, one can't get any wetter. The deluge is teeming down through the forest canopy, cascading off the foliage and pouring down, not in raindrops, but in drenching streams as from a thousand faucets. Then, as suddenly as it started, the storm is over. It still rains as every leaf of the hundreds of billions in the forest drips. First there is the drip of water from the leaf surfaces, then, as each tree, each shrub soaks up ground water, soaks it up to the point where it absorbs too much, the marvellous adaptation of some tropical trees is revealed. A little valve at the tip of each "drip-tip" leaf opens up and starts to drip water, ridding the system of excess. Long after a storm, with clear skies above and in brilliant sunshine, the forest rains.

With a bundle of sodden lianas on my shoulder, I started back. I soon realized that I was lost. I had been certain that I was retracing my steps, but nothing was familiar. I had never been here before, everything was strange. I took stock as best I could and plodded on.

The contour of the forest floor was steep, in some places about one in one. Lianas not only hung between the trees at head height and caused detours but crept along the ground, cunningly concealed and artfully designed "jungle trippers". Many shrubs and vines have some skilfully planned formula for inhibiting human progress. Some have almost animated, sinewy tendrils, some thorns or fishhook spines, some are glutinous and sticky, and some have whip-like branches. All clutch and grasp and restrain one's progress. Some are aggressive about it, but most have a kind of fawning, ingratiating cajolery, a sort of "wait a bit, stay here with me" tactic. It is almost indecent. Mats of rotting leaves on the slippery mud imitate scatter rugs on a freshly-waxed floor. Big patches of terrestrial arums and dumbcanes, *Dieffenbachia,* restrict one's view of the ground, discon-certing in Bushmaster and Fer-de-lance country. My eyes smarted with salty perspiration, and there were frequent attacks by sand flies. Worst of all, I started to think of tall, cool Planter's Punches back in Jake Kenny's comfortable living-room.

Was that the same big stand of Roseau Palms, armed with circlets of three-inch, vicious, black, brittle, needle-sharp spines that had been passed on the way in? It had to be, yet everything else was strange. The Roseaus hadn't been hedged in with foliage like this. A minute later there was no doubt. There on the ground was the purple cartridge casing, ejected when I had collected *Plica,* the Spiny Tree Lizard, for use in our exhibit. I knew where I was and it would now be easy to get out to the road and the car. Nonetheless, I was amazed at the completely changed aspect of the forest. Every branch, every liana and shrub was bowed down by its weight of water, external and

115

internal. I began to enjoy the experience, for after the storm it was a new forest, bearing little resemblance to the one that went before. Where I had walked upright with ease, I now had to duck under dripping branches: yet another fascinating facet of the wondrous rain-forest.

A Frog Called Paradox

My work in the Northern Range was concluded, the collected material packed and awaiting shipment to the Museum. Now, to enjoy myself: this of course meant exploring more of the island and making the acquaintance of more of the animals that lived on it. It was with a grand relaxed feeling that Jake Kenny, my host, and I travelled up the O'Meara road to the Churchill-Roosevelt Highway and turned east toward the Nariva Swamp on the Atlantic coast. We were entertained on the way by Maizebirds, Forktailed Flycatchers, Greybreasted Saltators, Lesser Seedfinches (Chickichongs), Glossy Grassquits, Tropical Mockingbirds, Rice Grackles, Smoothbilled Anis, Scalybreasted Ground Doves, and many other species. We turned onto the Eastern Main road two miles west of Valencia, proceeded on to Upper Manzanilla, then down the Plum Mitan road until we were due west of the swamp. We drove as far as possible along a short side road, one that would be impassable in the rainy season, with some misgivings for the sky to the north was blanketed with slaty-black clouds that rose into flat-topped thunderheads periodically illuminated by lightning. Ten minutes of tropical rain and this road would not be negotiable by car. We felt that the storm would likely play itself out over the Northern Range; so, we parked the car and went on foot into the swamp. The Nariva Swamp is somewhat more extensive than the Caroni, and, in places, more inclined to be brackish. Its vegetational character proved to be quite different from that of the Caroni. The transition from swamp-forest to herbaceous swamp dotted with stands of Cabbage Palms was abrupt. The vegetation of the latter consists to a large extent of Mota Grass that reaches a height of from eight to ten feet and superficially resembles Papyrus. There is also plenty of Bamboo Grass and Cascadura Grass. Morning Glories grow in profusion and confusion. Jake, intent on amphibians, was irresistably drawn toward a patch of shallow, open water whereas I walked along a dike toward a "hammock" of Cabbage Palms.

Three or four Blacknecked Stilts rose up, uttering their yelping *pip pip* calls. Stilts are among the most fragile-looking of birds. Slender of body with long needle-like beaks, they have thin pink legs, ten inches long and little thicker than a matchstick. They are extremely active, however, running about ploughing the water and probing the mud with their fine bills in search of food, and I have yet to see one with a broken leg! An abrupt, raucous series of *kak, kak, kak* notes informed me that a Clapper Rail was nearby and conscious of my presence. I could see his "chicken-tracks" in the mud along the edge of the dike.

I soon entered the stand of palms and almost immediately startled a Squirrel Cuckoo that ran rapidly, perhaps more like a big lizard than a squirrel, along the rib of a palm frond and glided off in effortless and noiseless flight toward an area of swamp jungle a hundred yards distant. This cuckoo is a most handsome species: chestnut above and pinkish below, it has a red eye and pale apple-green beak. Its total length is about seventeen inches of which ten are tail. It started to call from the jungle, its voice being a two-syllable squawking *chuk-kurr*. I wanted to see more of this bird and pursued it across marshy ground to the edge of the jungle. This proved to be difficult to penetrate as its margins were a hopeless tangle of thorn-bushes and vines, and I hadn't a *machette*. Even after I had wormed and bulled my way through the "edge", I found the interior to be equally difficult. The rather short trees were as heavily burdened with airplants and lianas as those of the rain-forest in the hills. The evil Roseau Palm with its circlets of long, needle-sharp black spines around the trunk formed a larger part of the composition of this

"forest" than I had ever seen in the Northern Range. As I was sup-
posed to be enjoying myself, I didn't penetrate very far, but instead found a looping liana the girth of a man's arm and with the loop
at just the right height to sit on. It was like idling in a child's swing.

I started sucking the back of my hand to make the squeaking noise
that often attracts inquisitive birds, and was quickly rewarded by the
appearance of an Antvireo. A moment later a Whiteflanked Antbird
appeared and was soon joined by a Whitethroated Leafscraper. A
second and third antbird and then a Goldenheaded Manakin
materialized. This was much better than fighting through lianas.
The sudden appearance of so many birds and the high percentage of
formicivorous species suggested that army ants were on the move not
too far away. I examined the surrounding area warily, but saw
nothing of the voracious horde. Still, I kept them in mind because I
wasn't anxious to try to flee through that brushy, spiky tangle while
being attacked by them, as their bites are sharply painful.

The squeaking had been so successful that I decided to try an
imitation of the call of the Pygmy Owl, a half spoken, half whistled
kook, like blowing into the neck of an empty bottle. I had used this
call with great success in Alaska to decoy chickadees, jays, juncoes,
and other small birds. They come to annoy the "owl" and will remain
to search for him almost as long as one cares to continue kook-ing.
Once I attracted a Pygmy Owl with this call. The fierce little gnome
was obviously spoiling for a brawl with one of his own kind, but as a
number of small passerines, or perching birds, had arrived before
him, he literally flew into an ambush as they all went at him in
Liliputian fury and put him to rout.

When I used it now in the Nariva Swamp, however, all my
audience disappeared except the Antvireo. Perhaps my Pygmy Owl
imitation had an Alaskan rather than a Trinidadian accent! I felt quite
crestfallen, but continued to whistle. It brought no results until at
last there was a loud stage-whisper of wings followed by a thumping
crash into a Hurricane Plant, the big, round, perforated leaves of
which wandered all about the trunk of a tree directly in front of me.
Several wide black feathers rose slowly from behind a leaf and a second
or two later, around the margin of the same leaf, protruded a
five-inch thick, black beak followed by a bright blue face. It was a
twenty-inch "Tia Poco" (in the colloquial: a little old woman)—to

the ornithologist, a Sulphur-and-White-breasted Toucan. Soon it hopped with great dexterity onto a more or less horizontal liana, looked at me out of one watery, pale blue eye, which was surrounded by equally blue and heavily wrinkled bare skin, and announced with intense satisfaction, *pee-o*. It turned its head 180 degrees so that the other watery, pale blue eye could examine me.

The view must have looked the same because, with diagnosis confirmed, it reiterated *pee-o*. Now the tail rose with great deliberation until it stood up like a wren's. This explained the appearance of the black feathers above the leaf of the Hurricane Plant, which had been the first that I had seen of this marvellous bird. It was now leaning forward so that its head and beak were the lowest parts of it, a demonstration of the great power of its climbing feet. Both eyes now seemed to be focused on me, the bird's expression one of senile incomprehension. But it seemed that to monocular or binocular vision I looked equally droll—*pee-o*! I made a mental note to look up the word in a Spanish dictionary on my return. (I found *pio* can mean "pious", "piebald", or the "puling of chickens"—I wonder which *Tia Poco* meant?) I was so engrossed in watching this fantastic clown that I forgot to repeat the Pygmy Owl call that had brought it to me. And so it seemed satisfied that no owl was present, declared *pee-o* once more, and then, with loud flapping wingbeats, flew off. Imagine my surprise when it was joined by two (or more) of its kind that had been perched only a little farther away and that I had failed to see! It seemed incredible that crow-sized birds, black with blue faces, yellow-orange chests, red rumps, and bright cobalt-blue feet could so merge themselves with the almost uninterrupted green of the forest. They flew noisily for twenty feet or so with deep heavy wingbeats, then suddenly, as if they had changed the camber of their wings, moved through the air gracefully and silently.

The light was beginning to fade and the interior of the swamp-forest was becoming gloomy. I made my way back to the dike. I wanted to witness the evening flight of parrots to their roosts which Jake had told me about; so, I stationed myself close to the stand of Cabbage Palms. Before chasing the Cuckoo, I had noted that the ground and low shrubs under the palms were liberally spattered with bird droppings and concluded that this clump of trees was a parrot roost.

I had just settled down to watch for parrots when I became aware of a swishing sound, as though the ditchwater east of the dike was being disturbed. I thought it might be a fish and walked to the edge to investigate. There was very little light, for the shadow of the dike, lengthened by the westering sun, extended ten to twelve feet over the shallow water. But I could see, hard against the bank, a long sinuous blackish form gliding almost on top of the water. It appeared to be as thick as a man's leg. Anaconda!

The Anacondas of Trinidad were considered by some authorities to be distinct from those of Amazonia, and indeed, had been named as a separate species. I plunged in, attempting to straddle the snake—it was a collector's reflex action, the kind of thing that prompts an antique lover at an auction to bid on a piece that he can't afford—but the section of its body that I aimed for "zigged" when it should have "zagged", and I missed it, though I was able to get my hands on it. The water was a bit deeper than I had estimated, and the soft mud on the bottom a good deal more so. My hands could not encompass the snake's body, and it became thoroughly alarmed and thrashed about wildly to escape. I was drenched with a spray of muddy water. It was in my eyes and mouth and nose. I floundered, stumbled, and nearly went down; then I lost my tenuous hold on its hard, smooth body, slippery because of its wetness. Its side brushed against my waist as I made another lunge for it, this time at its tail, which now appeared above the surface. I touched it but couldn't get a grip. In seconds the big snake submerged, and in the blackness of the water disappeared from sight. Once I saw bubbles as it exhaled under water, but I realized that, wallowing through the mud, I could not reach the spot in time. I also realized that even if I could catch up to it I could not possibly handle it alone. I estimated its length (from what I had seen of it and from its girth, which I judged to be about twenty inches) at better than nine feet. It was by no means a large Anaconda; there are authentic records of up to twenty-five feet, but nonetheless it was a formidable reptile. As I clambered back up on the dike, I actually felt relieved that the snake had tried only to escape and had done this so easily, for I had begun to think of the thirteen-foot Anaconda that we had had alive at the Museum a few months before. I thought of the many long, curved teeth in its jaws, teeth that break off readily and remain in a wound. Though not venomous, the bite of an Anaconda or a large Boa can be painful and dangerous.

I was breathing hard, more from excitement than exertion. I sat down to recover my composure and to scrape off the evil-smelling mud that clung to my shoes, socks, and trousers. I was thus engaged when the comparative quiet of the evening was shattered by an uproar of staccato squawks that sounded like a dozen ancient and long-ungreased wagon wheels being forcibly revolved. I looked up in time to see a flock of stout, rapidly-flying parrots disappear into the Cabbage Palms. The discordant cries that were ejected from the palms suggested that all parrot notes are polyhedral and that their expulsion is not accomplished without great but not untold agony. My binoculars were lying in the grass a few yards away where I had dropped them before making my ill-advised and unsuccessful assault on the Anaconda. I had just picked them up when a second and a third flight of parrots raced in from some feeding grounds to the west. A flock of parrots with a purpose—such as these had in hurrying to their roost—is a dramatic sight. Each bird tapering from the big, blunt head to the slender tail gives the suggestion of powerful and deliberate action. The long wings are driven rapidly through a deep arc. Perhaps it is the straight-backed, horizontal carriage of the body, like the shaft of an arrow, that gives them their forceful, unwavering appearance. Through the binoculars I could see that the new arrivals were of the bulk of pigeons, and mainly bright green with light yellow cheeks. They were Amazon Parrots, a species ranging all across northern South America. More flocks arrived, some travelling high and fast and making for other roosts deeper in the swamp, and some pitching into the Cabbage Palms nearby, twisting, turning, and squalling as they sought out unoccupied, or occupied, perches. Before the light failed, I saw two other kinds of parrots. There were several flocks of small black-backed Sevencoloured Parrots and one of long, slender Small Redbellied Macaws. The latter are only half the length of the big macaws familiar to zoo and park visitors, but in all respects are true macaws. They are green and peacock blue with the breast pinkish and the belly rich blood-red. The undersides of their flight feathers change from brown to yellow depending on the angle of light refraction, as in shot silk.

121

I watched the parrots until darkness made further observation impossible, but I could see Jake out on the wet mud-flats leaping about with acrobatic vigour. I knew that he had found something of interest; so, I decided to join him. On the way I lifted my "head-lamp" torch from the car and started across the mud. Jake had found a spot inhabited by one of the world's most remarkable amphibians, the Paradox Frog. It is a "paradox" because of the singularly dispro-portionate size of the tadpole and the adult frog. The former is the giant among tadpoles, reaching a length of ten inches and is two to three times the bulk of the three-and-a-half-inch mature animal. Fortunately, the adults don't have to look after these children. In fact, like all tadpoles, they are well able to fend for themselves; these monsters are carnivorous and gulp down the smaller tadpoles of other species or their own! The adults are strictly aquatic; their heavy, flabby bodies seem almost without bones, and they have been known to suffocate from their inability to perform respiration when removed from water into the lighter medium of air—almost as much a travesty for an amphibian as is Burmeister's Tree Frog, which, if placed in water without a raft to cling to, will drown!

Capturing Paradox Frogs proved to be a most difficult and exas-perating task. They spraddled low in the murky water with just the eyes and snout or half of the head above the surface. Even a stealthy approach was invariably detected and the frogs would submerge instantly. Finally, we struck on the solution by approaching them from the front and blinding them in the beam of the torch. This permitted one quick lunge at them. More often than not, though, we grasped only a handful of mud or, if we clutched a frog, had it squirt out of our grip and disappear into the dark water; it was like trying to pick up a handful of slippery jelly. After many tries, however, we managed to capture a few specimens, which were placed in wet cotton bags for transport back to Jake's lab. (Later, we had a chance to observe them in a tub of water. There was nothing very remarkable about their appearance save for their soft fatness. They varied from greenish through olive to blackish with some yellow on the throat and chest. Otherwise they looked just like most other frogs. But, as I watched them, I became aware of the very mobile thumb, which was used to grasp floating leaves and twigs for firm anchorage, and also the "outsized" hind feet with their wide flexible webs—truly efficient paddles. Here indeed was a true "skin-diver".)

Darkness enveloped us with the blunt abruptness of the tropics and, regretfully, we called it a day. It was only when we reached Sangre Grande on the way back that we realized that we hadn't eaten since breakfast. I doubt if we'd have thought of it even then had it not been for the racks of multicoloured fruits and vegetables displayed on the main street. As we stopped the car, we heard the sweet, sad song of a tinamou far away while nearby a Granular Toad uttered his short modulated trill. We purchased two hands of "figs" as the tiny, fragrant, tree-ripened lady finger bananas and apple bananas are called in Trinidad. We consumed all the sweet, luscious fruits before we arrived at Maracas—and paid for it with an excessive "looseness" the next day.

Studies of the Anvil bird, Trinidad

SEVEN

The Ecuador and Galápagos Expedition

Darwin's finches, the Galápagos Islands

To the "Infernal Paradise"

Galápagos! The very name is enough to excite a naturalist. It conjures up visions of strange reptiles and birds, species found nowhere else in the world except on this tiny volcanic archipelago that straddles the equator in the Pacific Ocean six hundred miles west of Ecuador. *Las Islas Encantadas* they were christened by Spanish buccaneers in awe of the perverse and seemingly self-willed currents that sweep through the channels and bights, and invest the islands with an apparent magic ability to repel sailing ships seeking a landfall or, conversely, to draw them, siren-like, toward shore against their wishes. These capricious ocean streams may be understood by modern navigators and no longer incite superstitious wonder, but the Galápagos are still, to the naturalist, the Enchanted Isles. They have been called the cradle of modern biology because it was on these islands that Charles Darwin found the clue to the processes by which new forms of life appear on earth. The narrative of Darwin's Galápagos-inspired ratiocinations cannot be recounted here. It is sufficient to say that one of the most eventful experiences that can befall a naturalist is to visit this bizarre group of islands and retrace Darwin's footsteps.

My opportunity presented itself in 1965. I was asked to join a party from the Canadian Broadcasting Corporation. On the 6th of April, we assembled at Toronto International Airport. My associates were John Livingston, director of C.B.C. science service, James Murray, producer; Rolph Blakstad, cameraman; William Banting; and George McAfee handling the difficult assignment of looking after the party's supplies, finances, itineraries. Our first stop was New York, where we were joined by Dr. Roger Tory Peterson, artist,

127

lecturer, photographer, and ornithologist who was to help interpret Charles Darwin and his theory of evolution for television audiences. Later we were joined by Dr. W. W. H. Gunn of Toronto, an expert in the recording of animal voices.

It was mid-afternoon when we reached Quito, Ecuador. The approach to the landing field was breath-taking even though most of the surrounding mountains were obscured in shadowy cloud. On a clear day it must be magnificient. In any weather, the plane has to sideslip around Mount Pichincha, through the passes, bank around mountain shoulders and then drop swiftly to the tarmac.

It was a day threatening rain, and the temperature by contrast to that of Cali in Colombia, our prior stop, seemed almost freezing. We were not too warm in sweaters and jackets as we travelled to the Hotel Quito. All of us were charmed by the city, a quaint mixture of Spanish baroque and Moorish geometry and honeycomb. Businessmen in grey worsted hurried along the street past Indians squatting in the arcades, motionless in their dark blue or grey woollen ponchos, brown trilbies, and splayed bare feet. Where but in Quito could one see the narrow row of smooth paving stones inset along the middle of the cobblestone street for those who walk barefooted? Nine and a half thousand feet above sea level, it is a city of good hotels, excellent restaurants, ancient monasteries, fenestrated walls, and rococo cathedrals. Remote and difficult of access until linked with Guayaquil by rail, it has preserved its character as an ancient, mountain city ringed by snow-clad volcanoes. There are more than twenty noble volcanic summits surrounding the Quito valley: some perfect cones, some truncated, some with jagged sunken crests, some with smooth, ice-covered gleaming domes such as the magnificent but dreaded Cotopaxi (19,347).

When I awoke the next morning, I found hazy sunlight coming through the wide picture window of my room on the second floor. The window overlooked the extensive and well-kept garden; it overlooked the old city in the valley far below; and it looked up to the towering mountains to the south and east and west. A flash of white in the garden attracted my attention and resolved itself into a biggish grey-brown bird whose tail was long and brilliantly white save for two dark brown central feathers. It was the size of and behaved like a mockingbird, but proved to be a Mountain Ground Tyrant, a

128

flycatcher confined to the high Andes and singularly distinctive in behaviour from other members of its family. It stayed close to the ground, hopping about on the drystone walls and on the grass, and reminded me of an Oldworld Rock Thrush. I didn't get a chance to watch it long for probing at the flowers of a huge fuchsia was a very large glittering green hummingbird with two long black streamer tail-feathers, a Blacktailed Trainbearer, one of the most elegant birds I have ever seen. It must have been ten inches long with the tail making up more than half of this. Then a flock of eight or ten small finches arrived with erratic bounding flight and pitched into a small bush directly beneath my window. They went to work with almost febrile industry to dissect the small seed pods on the shrub. These finches were brilliantly olive and chrome yellow with black heads and gaily banded black and yellow wings. That they were goldfinches was evident, and a quick reference to my notes showed them to be Southern Siskins. In the flower beds, I saw Andean Sparrows and blackbacked Vermilion Flycatchers. The air seemed filled with Brownbellied Swallows. If I needed something to get the sleep out of my eyes, the view from the window provided it. I was shaved and dressed and down to breakfast in record time. I wanted a few minutes at least in that garden! Unfortunately I didn't get it, at least not that day, as there were too many things to be done and our plane left for Guayaquil later in the morning.

Guayaquil was a sharp contrast to Quito. After a short but interesting flight over the western cordilleras of the Andes, we landed 9,500 feet lower than our take-off point in the steaming seaport metropolis of Equador. Of sights and sounds there were enough, but of smells there was completeness. The first impressions blatantly assailed the nostrils rather than the eyes and ears. The smell of tropical heat, of human bodies, of fruit (fresh and not-so-fresh), of wet wool, of burros, of diesel fumes, of rancid cooking fat, of hibiscus, flamboyants, and bougainvillea, of coffee and cacao, of cogent perfume, and of smells too indelicate to mention. It is strange how quickly the nose adjusts. (I doubt if the short-order cook ever smells the onions he is frying.) In half an hour all the odours mingled, merged, and harmonized into an amalgam, the hot strong smell of a tropical seaport awakening nostalgic recollections of other strange and far away places. Then gradually they dwindled and evanesced.

We had planned to sail from Guayaquil for the Galápagos on the monthly supply ship, the *Cristobal Carrier*. We found the sailing date had been set back to near the end of April, and it was now only the 8th! Three weeks in Guayaquil with the Galápagos beckoning was unthinkable. A solution was found the next day. A military aircraft was chartered from Transportes Aeronaves Militarios Ecuadoriana (known as T.A.M.E. or "Tommy"). They could fly us over on April 10th.

In the evening, we wandered about the fascinating market streets of the city, buying panama hats. It is in the region just north of Guayaquil that the *toquilla* fibre is produced. This permits the manufacture of the finest straw hats, those known as Montecristis and Jipijapas being the finest grades.

The following morning, we made our way to Guayaquil airport in a fleet of four taxis, each with at least one member of our party and a stack of luggage. The T.A.M.E. plane was waiting. There was some difficulty fitting all our equipment into the luggage compartment, especially several huge wooden crates that had been enthusiastically nailed up by the C.B.C.'s shipping department. Try as they might, the loading crew couldn't fit them in. At last it was decided that the crates would have to be opened and the contents distributed, some in the luggage compartment and some in the passengers' seats. This was duly accomplished, but not without great effort and expenditure of some round Spanish expletives uttered with fine theatrical emphasis. The luck of the draw placed a gigantic carton, from which the top had been removed, on the floor directly in front of the loading door. It was filled to the brim with rolls of snowy white toilet tissue! Enough, it seemed, to do twenty men for a year. What with our Entero-vioform and Kaopectate, I thought we were well-equipped to cope with Montezuma's Revenge! It became doubly amusing when we discovered that, without our prior knowledge, we were to be hosts to a number of free-loading, high-brass officers of the Ecuadorian Army and their wives. The high-spirited chatter of the ladies trailed off into embarrassed silence as they entered the plane. It was evident that some high-born Latin ladies do not yet admit to the existence of certain things.

The flight across the sea to the Galápagos was, we learned later, exceptional in that it was uneventful and the pilot found his target without much difficulty. He flew low over the islands in a great circle for, we suspected, the benefit of the army brass. This, at any rate, was to our advantage as it gave us a fine introductory view of the islands, of their rugged cliffs, their vast lava flows, their forests of cactus, and of the mist-shrouded, luxurient higher slopes of the craters.

The plane touched down on Baltra Island landing strip, a relic of the war in the Pacific. The strip itself was in excellent condition —but that was all. There was not a soul in sight, and only one building; no vegetation on the bare lava save for a few patches of scrubby bushes and discouraged-looking cacti. We disembarked and started to unload our supplies and equipment—thirty-four boxes, some as big as bathtubs, plus personal dunnage bags and suitcases. It made an imposing pile of matériel in the shadow of the aircraft's wing. It was in fact the third largest object within our range of vision, exceeded only by the four-engined aircraft and the shack that served as the air terminal, radio house, and beacon tower. The sun beat down with fierce intensity, and the only shade was under the plane's wing. John Livingston said fervently, "We made the right decision to bring everything we need for survival from safety pins and chocolate bars to antibiotics."

A car came and took away the air crew and the army officers and their wives. We waited an hour, vaguely uneasy and wondering if there might have been some foul-up in the arrangements that had been made with the Charles Darwin Research Station to meet us. There was no sign of life on the island unless one included the woebegone cacti in that category. I guess that is why several of us exclaimed as the butterfly fluttered across the tarmac. I dashed after it, knocked it down with my hat, and we examined it. We decided it was a Queen, a butterfly common in the Gulf States, New Mexico, and Arizona. Satisfied, we let it fly off. Little did we know then that this first living animal that we encountered on the Galápagos had never before been recorded on the islands. Later, I captured and preserved several at Tagus Cave on Isabela Island (Albemarle). (It should be noted that the islands have English names as well as Spanish names.) Then John and Roger Peterson and I took a short walk to look at one of the big cacti. It stood about nine feet in height, the first of its dinner-plate green pads being four or five feet from the ground and supported by a reddish-brown flaky-barked bole about

131

ten inches in diameter. At the time it seemed quite impressive, but before another twenty-four hours had passed, we were to see tree-cacti that dwarfed it. Resting in the shade on one of the bristling pads were two Striped Sphinx Moths. These insects I knew well, having observed them all the way from Canada to Florida. As we walked back toward the plane and the shade, we saw our first Galápagos vertebrate—a Magnificent Frigate bird that sailed lazily and effortlessly in the blue sky over the coast a few hundred yards away. This was too much. I had seen three kinds of animals on the Galápagos and all of them were old friends from Florida!

Another hour used itself up with maddening waiting. We were alone with fifty pieces of baggage, a locked-up aircraft, and no means of communicating the fact of our existence. I heard a feeble bird song that seemed to emanate from a low shrub far down and at the edge of the air-strip. For something to do, John and I walked down and, in the fading light, got a glimpse of one of Darwin's finches. We were excitedly debating its precise identity when we heard the coughing and chugging of a truck. We hurried back leaving our bird unidentified and arrived just as the truck with backfires and puffs of smoke came bowling up to the aircraft. As it pulled to a halt, a tall lean young man with a shock of blond hair and bare feet leaped out and said,

"I say, I'm Richard Foster from the station. Frightfully sorry to keep you waiting here, but I had a bit of trouble with the vehicle. The *Beagle* is anchored at the dock waiting to take you to Academy Bay. Welcome to the Galápagos!" We were to develop a great affection for this personable, talented, and resourceful young man who was then serving as first mate on the *Beagle II*. This ship, skippered by the almost legendary Carl Angermeyer, was a fifty-five-foot Looe lugger, which I prefer to call a square-rigged brigantine. It was the ship on which the staff of the UNESCO-sponsored Charles Darwin Research Foundation for the Galápagos had commuted between the various islands in their capacities as researchers and wardens.

Within minutes, the first load had been stowed in the truck and it roared off. It would take three trips to transport all our junk and our persons. I volunteered to remain for the last load. As the second truckload disappeared I was left entirely alone with a pile of baggage and an airplane. The sun was touching the waterline of the western horizon and darkness was creeping quickly over the landscape. In a matter of minutes, the sun drowned itself in the Pacific and intense darkness prevailed. It was a weird and fitting nightfall on the Galápagos; there was not a sound, no hum of mosquitoes, no cry of night fowl, not even the ghostly whisper of a moth's wing or the murmuring of the wind. An age-old total, silent darkness on one of earth's newest yet most primeval fragments of land. It was congruent to be in solitary isolation on such an occasion, for, above all, the Galápagos are islands of mood. For all their primitive harshness, they have a serenity and tranquility of agelessness that is unique. I wondered, no, I knew how Charles Darwin felt 130 years before, when he first made landfall on these islands. I felt that it was this strange unearthly capacity of theirs to transport a person in time and space into the past or into the future that put Darwin in the frame of mind to conceive his momentous theories. Virtually all the world's remote island groups are the refugia of now unique forms of animals and plants, and, in varying degrees, exemplify the principles that revealed themselves to Darwin on Galápagos. Was it the mental "atmosphere" that acted as the catalyst?

Reverie doesn't last long. It shouldn't. When prolonged it has a habit of becoming maudlin. Mine was broken by the sound of a tremendous backfire and the sudden glare of headlights on the runway. The truck rolled up and Richard bounced out, as fresh and buoyant as, I was to discover, he always was. The last boxes were heaved into the truck and we rattled away, heading for the dock and the *Beagle.* The activity was revitalizing. I was eager to see and experience the real Galápagos, and each burst of action brought it closer. In a few minutes, the truck stopped on the dock. The night was so black that to this day I don't know what the dock was like or how big it was. But I could see the lights of the *Beagle* and her dim outline on the water. Vaguely I could make out her good lines and tall masts. Our torches flashed and revealed the vertical ladder on the dockside down to the longboat far below. The boxes were somehow lowered into this longboat and, finally, in the dark, I made my way down. Richard was already aboard; the outboard kicked over, and soon we were clambering up the ship's ladder onto the *Beagle,* which was rocking gently with the tide, and rocking violently with laughter, for Carl Angermeyer was there.

133

The evening passed quickly. There were yarns and questions, plans and even a bit of music from Carl and his accordion. We would spend the night at anchor and proceed to the station at Academy Bay on Santa Cruz Island (Indefatigable) at daybreak. That night we slept on deck. The day had been a full one, not only of physical effort but also packed with excitement and emotion. I was an old hand at expeditions, but somehow this one had rekindled all my youthful enthusiasm and anticipation. It was a long time before I went to sleep. Even in the darkness there was the great constellation of the Southern Cross to enthuse over. Finally, the hypnotic effect of the quietly lapping water and the rhythmic swaying of the ship lulled me to sleep (the ship seemed to be stationary; it was the celestial equator that was rocking from lee to starboard and back again sending the stars scudding back and forth across the yardarm).

I awoke as the first pale streaks of dawn enlivened the sky. A line of Brown Pelicans flapped majestically by through the gloom. I arose and looked about. A Spotted Sandpiper skimmed along the lava boulders by the shore, skimmed past a Great Blue Heron standing motionless on a rock. What was this? Galápagos? It might as well have been one of the Florida Keys.

Then suddenly *it* was there. Swimming jauntily along near the shore, with little more than its head out of the water, bill pointed up at a saucy angle, and barely twenty miles south of the equator, was a *penguin*! A wild, living Galápagos Penguin. *This* wasn't Florida.

A quick wash and breakfast and it was up anchor. The twin diesels were running smoothly and *Beagle II* put out to sea. Carl had promised that we should have a worthy introduction to the Galápagos. A place in which he took as much pride as if he had made it himself, boulder by boulder, was tiny Plaza Island. He proposed to put us ashore there, where he said we would see a great variety of animal life with very little effort. It was mid-morning when the longboat drew alongside a low black lava spit on which basked a dozen Sea Lions. They were quite unconcerned by our approach, lazily lifting sleepy heads with blinking eyes, then disregarding us and going back to blissful dozing as if we were not at all their affair. We were forced to step over two or three of them in order to make our way up the lava shore. They were all females or young animals. We had just got nicely ashore when the "lobo" bull appeared. He was

134

highly exercised at our intrusion into his harem. Our numbers must have been disconcerting to him for he confined his actions to loud howling and racing up and down with great commotion from one end of his harem to the other, but he didn't leave the water. We left him to his bellowing and climbed a gentle slope to a most entrancing plateau. The lava rock and scattered lava blocks and boulders were covered by a most harmoniously coloured growth of lichens; pale greys and yellows predominated, but there were others of gold and verdigris, of rust and ochre and cerulean hue. The sky was crossed and recrossed by hordes of gliding and soaring birds. There were Bluefooted and Masked Boobies, Magnificent Frigate-birds, Brown Pelicans, Redbilled Tropicbirds, and the endemic Forktailed Gulls. As I walked along, big, clumsy golden-orange Land Iguanas, crenellated like mythical dragons, lumbered out of my path for two or three yards, then stopped and looked me over with amiable indifference, the lids drooping over their beautiful soft orange-brown eyes. Unhurried movements enabled me to approach these heavy-bodied monsters (a large one may be well over four feet long) to within a few feet. Plaza boasts one of the few remaining colonies of this fascinating reptile numbering somewhere between fifty and a hundred. They feed almost exclusively on the fruit and pads of the prickly pear cacti.

The ground beneath my feet was honeycombed with the nesting burrows of Audubon's Shearwaters, an enormous raft of which floated on the water just offshore. We soon crossed the island to the opposite coast, which was precipitous, with innumerable ledges and crags on which were nesting Forktailed Gulls and Bluefooted Boobies. The Forktail is, I think, the most attractive of all gulls. Its form is more graceful and its head relatively smaller and finer than in most species. The wings are long and elegantly patterned in three triangular shapes of pearl grey, black, and snowy white. The feet are pink, and there is a distinct rosy flush on the otherwise white underparts. The anterior third of the black beak is yellowish. The head is black with a white spot at the base of the bill. But its most striking feature is the enormous, radiant, dark brown eye surrounded by a wide naked eyelid of the most intense vermilion. The great size of the eye is probably a by-product of its night-feeding habit. It is perhaps the only consistently night-feeding gull in the world. Its voice is decidedly ungull-like, being a curious, rapidly repeated clicking sound, given with the beak held wide open and the tongue vibrating, the latter probably activated by rather than producing the sound. It also had a mournful gull-like wailing note that we sometimes heard far out at sea; the clicking sound, however, is delivered frequently at night as the birds approach their nest (each of which has a single egg or chick). It seems likely that the clicking call has sonar-like implications, the bouncing echoes from the sheer cliff-faces aiding in orientation.

The white spot at the base of the bill also has nocturnal significance. Gulls swallow the food that they gather to bring to their young, and are stimulated to regurgitate it when the chick pecks at the parent's bill. In most gulls of diurnal habit, there is a black or red spot on the bill which serves as a trigger target for the chick to peck at. Red and black are virtually invisible in darkness and would be useless to a nocturnal gull. But the white trigger target of the Forktail is prominent at night. Why the Forktailed Gull became nocturnal is conjectural. Some have put forward the theory that it is to avoid the piratical attacks of freebooting Frigate-birds, which acquire much of their food by aerial attacks that force other species to drop or disgorge their hard-earned provisions. I think it is more likely that their favoured prey—squids and other crustaceans—is photophobic and rises to the surface only after dark.

I was able to work my way down the cliff to within a few feet of an almost fully grown but still flightless chick. It was a very pretty little bird with a clove-brown mantle, each feather of which was edged with white. The white head was decorated with a pale brown crescent covering the occiput and the ear coverts. The eyes were big and brown like those of its parents. The chick's head and parts of its body still bore straggly wisps of pale down, which imparted a very juvenile and ingratiating appearance. The nest on which it sat was most untidy and reeked of guano in which I could see what I took to be the pens (the internal, horny shell), the indigestible portions of squids. Soon the adults returned and alighted on the nest ledge—one stood within arm's length of me—and though they kept a wary eye on me they showed no great alarm. Finally the near one waddled over and stood so close to me that once again I had to put on my reading glasses. As I was studying the gorgeous colouring of its eyelid, it looked me squarely in the face, opened its bill and nearly burst my eardrums with a staccato burst of shrill clicks. I could look right down its throat. As it called it spread its long pointed wings and held them open. It was a salutary warning that I was trespassing on private property—a warning that should be respected. It pleased me to acknowledge it and I withdrew, partly because they had already performed for me more than adequately, partly because there were other things to see, but mostly because I didn't want another ear-shattering blast.

A sparrow-sized bird drew attention to his location in a giant cactus with a pleasant song that sounded to me as though he were reiterating *Beagle, Beagle.* It was a Medium Ground Finch, the first of the celebrated Darwin's finches that I could really observe and identify. His black beak was stout, resembling that of a Purple Finch or a Brown-headed Cowbird. It was obviously a seed-eater and seemed a most ordinary sort of bird, giving no hint of the astounding behaviour that I was soon to see in other members of his group. A few minutes later I saw and heard another, this one somewhat smaller, with a sharp-pointed, goldfinch-like bill and singing an undistinguished junco-style *zib-zib-zib-zib-zib.* This was the Small Ground Finch. Song, size, and bill-shape were the only characteristics by which it could be distinguished from the larger bird. I had, in the brief time available to me before leaving on the trip, boned up on the Darwin's finches from such literature as I could readily lay my hands on. There were no really good illustrations. Now I had grave doubts about my ability to identify some of the more obscure species, which we were certain to encounter later. The next bird that appeared on Plaza Island, however, could have been named by the veriest tyro birdwatcher: a Yellow Warbler. Aside from being a somewhat brighter yellow and wearing a coppery red skullcap, it was precisely like the familiar bird that, at this date, was streaming in multitudes through Mexico on its spring migration to occupy, within the next six weeks, virtually all the timbered regions of the United States and Canada. This one, happily singing its well-known song, had been hatched on the Galápagos and would never leave Plaza. Already some of the singular anomalies of the Galápagos were presenting themselves. First, two kinds of land birds found nowhere else in the world, then one that occurs from Alaska and Hudson Bay to Peru.

As always, time, the enemy, caught up with me, and it was

imperative that we leave if we were to make Academy Bay in daylight. While Richard Foster kept the bull Sea Lion occupied, we climbed once again through and over his harem into the longboat and headed out to the *Beagle*. Our first trip ashore on the Galápagos had served to convince us that what we had heard of the indifference of the animals to the presence of humans was in no way an exaggeration.

The sea was calm and Carl ran close to the shore. The coastline of Santa Cruz Island was indeed awesome. It was alternately fearsomely exciting and calmly beautiful. There were sheer, two-hundred-foot cliffs, vast areas of tortured black lava rock, tumbled and twisted in nightmarish abandon, quiet-water coves of deepest and purest blue, and stretches of roaring, crashing surf. If this was Galápagos on a placid sunny day, what was it like in a storm? The vegetation observable from the deck consisted mainly of gigantic arborescent, or tree-like, prickly pear cacti; tall columnar, candelabra cacti (looking like gaunt, underfed Saguaros), and bare, white-barked, crooked shrubs that appeared leafless and lifeless. I'm sure that in the minds of most of us were the words of Captain Robert Fitzroy, commander of the original *Beagle,* which brought Darwin to the islands in 1835: "A fit shore for pandemonium!"

I realized that if we were going to land on some of the more remote and incommodious stretches of coast, which of course would be necessary if we were to visit certain bird colonies, we were in for a watery baptism, if not total immersion. I didn't dwell on this as there was a wealth of marine life to divert my attention. There were Right Whales, Pacific Bottlenosed Dolphins, Galápagos and Madeiran Storm Petrels, Redfooted Boobies, and Flying Fishes as well as the now familiar Pelicans, Frigates, Tropicbirds, and Masked and Blue-footed Boobies.

At 3:00 p.m., we entered the fiord-like approaches to Academy Bay and in a few minutes dropped anchor. Almost immediately a most outlandish boat approached at terrific speed, then cut its engine and was manoeuvered gracefully alongside the *Beagle*. Carl told me that it was a *panga,* a frail-looking craft with, apparently, a displacement of nil. It skimmed over the surface like a dead leaf. Its sole occupant was a lean, tanned, youngish man puffing a pipe and sporting a jaunty soft brown fedora. He came lightly up the ship's

138

ladder and Carl introduced us to Roger Perry, Director of the Research Station.

At last we had arrived at our destination, the research station from which for two months we would explore the "Infernal Paradise".

A Most Singular Group of Finches

I am sitting on a chair-sized boulder in a forest of arborescent cacti on Santa Cruz Island when something lands with a soft thump on my head, something alive. It lands lightly, but there is the unmistakeable sensation of small, sharp claws scrabbling around on my scalp and in a moment a tuft of my hair is being pulled. Apparently the hair is too firmly rooted because a female Cactus Ground Finch flutters from my head and perches on my right shin, which is crossed horizontally over my left knee. There is a fleeting moment of inquiry as she looks directly up at my eyes, then a big-footed sidewise sidling down to the exposed top of a white woollen sock. Acacia thorns and cactus spines have torn and snagged the wool, and loops and ends of ravelled knitting protrude. A loose, frayed end is grasped in her long powerful bill, her neck is humped, and she tugs, holding and bracing with big, almost intelligent feet. It is a hard struggle, but she perseveres, and finally a two-inch strand of yarn comes loose. She flies about forty feet into the pads of a tall prickly pear cactus and disappears into a neat globular nest, the entrance to which is a golf ball-sized hole on its "equator". To a Darwin's finch, for such it is, I am no more than a fortuitous source of nest-lining material.

The incident didn't surprise me, for when it happened I had spent over a month on the Galápagos Islands and had long since ceased to be

139

amazed by the remarkable behaviour of Darwin's finches. I had learned to expect almost anything of them except, perhaps, that they should behave like prosaic birds.

Of the thirteen distinct species inhabiting the archipelago, *Geospiza scandens,* the Cactus Ground Finch, was my favourite. Its middle name, "ground", is somewhat of a misnomer, for it spends most of its time up in the cacti: Galápagos cacti, both the Prickly Pear, *Opuntia Echios,* and the Candelabra, *Cereus thousarii,* which are tree-sized, often reaching thirty feet in height.

Scandens, "the climber", is the cheeky one, the clown, the acrobat. Feeding largely on the nectar of cactus flowers and the pulp of cactus fruits, its big powerful feet enable it to perform gymnastic feats, hanging upsidedown like a chickadee does, and climbing like a woodpecker or a nuthatch does, vertically obverse or reverse. Of all the remarkable Darwin's finches, the Cactus Ground shows the greatest indifference to humans. Man is merely a perambulatory part of this finch's environment, something to be investigated; his ears and fingernails are to be nibbled, tested for edibility; his clothing is to be examined for the presence of food or the stuff of nest building. My washing, hung on a line to dry in the equatorial sun—towels, blankets, socks, undershirts—undefended for a whole morning because of my absence, was a sorry sight at noon. Wisps and strands and loops of wool and thread projected at erratic angles.

Once, I gave Roger Peterson a haircut, and as quickly as the silvery locks fell on the gravel between his feet, a hen *scandens* gathered them by the beakful and carried them to her nest. How appropriate that a Darwin's finch was lining her nest with hair of the high priest of birdwatching!

Six, including *scandens,* of Darwin's finches belong in the genus *Geospiza,* the so-called ground finches. They range from goldfinch size to bluebird size. All have short, stumpy tails and are coloured essentially alike: charcoal black in the males and striped sepia brown and whitish in the females and juveniles—modest attire indeed for one of the world's most extraordinary groups of birds. At first, they are difficult to distinguish but, with familiarity, one learns that they have different feeding habits (and hence differently-shaped bills), different songs, and, if I may be excused an anthropomorphism, different temperaments.

140

As might be expected the largest is also the mildest. *Geospiza magnirostris,* "great beak", the Large Ground Finch has a huge turgid bill that makes that of an Evening Grosbeak or Hawfinch seem puny in comparison. It is, of course, a seed-cracker. It is not aggressive, but it will brook no undue act of crowding or gluttony on the part of other species or members of its own. All the *Geospizas* are inordinately fond of rice, and daily this grain was spread in front of our dormitory doors to attract them. In less than a week, numbers of finches would converge as soon as we emerged from our rooms, and were hopping about our feet with an expectant air before the first rice grains hit the ground. A shower of rice was the signal for a Donnybrook, and it was on these occasions that the dignity of the dominant *magnirostris* manifested itself. No uncouth brawling, no pecking or squalling; if another finch intruded on *his* patch of rice it was sent sprawling by a deliberate sidelong half-kick, half-shove of one big *magnirostris* foot.

The beak of *magnirostris* on Santa Cruz Island is large, but that of the population on San Salvador Island verges on the ridiculous. It is so huge that, face-on, nothing of the head except the beak is visible, save for two beady eyes projecting slightly beyond its margins.

The most common of all the Darwin's finches is *Geospiza fortis,* "the strong", the Medium Ground Finch. Like *scandens,* it has the quarrelsome disposition and toughness of a House Sparrow. I wonder what would happen if the latter ever reached the Galápagos? I suspect that the "squidger", the House Sparrow, would meet his match. *Fortis* and *scandens* possess all its slum-urchin virility plus a superior physique. Their feet are disproportionately large and strong, though anything but awkward. Unlike those of the sparrow, they can be used independently. One dexterous foot will reach out and the toes will grasp and hold an insect or fruit in a powerful grip, reminiscent of a grackle or jay, while the beak tears it apart. They are ample winged and swift flyers. Both are loud and incessant singers. (Was it because we had Charles Darwin and his ship the *Beagle* so much in mind that *scandens* seemed to sing *Charley-D, Charley-D,* and *fortis, Beagle, Beagle?*)

The strength of the Darwin's finches is amazing; consider *Geospiza conirostris,* "cone beak", the Large Cactus Ground Finch, which dwells on Espanola Island (Hood). This is the stone-mover, the bulldozer. Sometimes it furrows through loose fine gravel, using its

141

beak as a plough to stir up scorpions, centipedes, and other delectables. Sometimes it flips stones sideways like a turnstone overturning pieces three or four times its own weight.

Remarkable? But wait—these are Darwin's finches, and with these there is always more to come. *Conirostris* has been observed to move stones thirteen to fifteen times its own weight by the expedient of bracing the top of its head against a larger rock, placing both feet against the stone slated for dislodgement and kicking! Comparisons are odious, but a man of a hundred and fifty pounds would have to tumble a stone weighing over a ton to equal this performance!

Every adventure on Galápagos seems somehow to feature a Darwin's finch. It is as if they must have centre stage, the starring role. I was on the shore of Santa Cruz Island one day, traversing the smooth, wave-polished coastal boulders. The sea was an intense turquoise with gouts of white surf breaking over raven-coloured reefs. The horizon was lost in heat shimmer . . . the next landfall in that direction? The Marquesas. How far? Three and a half thousand miles. Scarlet Rock Crabs scuttled about over the black lava rocks. One evil monster was daintily picking the flesh from a still-twitching, belly-up young member of his own family. His claws ended in little spoons rather than points. Fascinating horror to watch the cannibal slowly, deliberately, and without malice or emotion, spooning up his colleague.

Big, gentle, but hideous-looking Marine Iguanas were all facing one way like an audience at a play, drinking in the sun's warmth. Some were still wet. They had returned to shore from a feeding expedition to the algae and seaweed-covered rocks beneath the cold Humboldt Current that washes the Galápagos Islands. They allowed close approach. But one spat at me. He didn't really spit, he snorted-sneezed, ejected air from his nostrils and with it came a watery jet. The salt-extracting gland in his head runs the saline solution down his nostrils for ejection—a marvellous adaption of many marine creatures for ridding themselves of excessive, lethal salts. I was amused to find that if I spat at Iguanas, they spat back.

The longer I watched them the less ugly they appeared. Finally, I convinced myself that they were rather handsome animals. The dark eyes are soft and lustrous. Their bearing and expression is one of pride and good breeding. Most of them were shedding, and flaps and tatters of translucent epidermis, yellowed as with age, clung like old rags. The shabby genteel!

Then from out of nowhere, another Darwin's finch; this one was a *Geospiza fuliginosa*, "one prone to sootiness", the Small Ground Finch. He is indeed sooty black, but in size and shape of beak resembles a perky Savannah Sparrow. Without hesitation he jumped on the back of an elderly Iguana. He hopped jauntily along a few inches of the body of the four-foot dragon, then suddenly stooped and picked off a tick. This was crushed and eaten with obvious relish. Then another and another as he edged up toward the lizard's head. Only when he pulled one off the Iguana's eyelid did the lizard react. It blinked its eye. At last, having deticked his host, the finch tore off a small loose fragment of dead skin from the reptile's side and flew off with it. What for? Nest lining perhaps. I did, however, have a fellow feeling for the old sea monster. Each of us had had the treatment from the Darwin's finches. Each had been used for the finches' selfish purposes and had been abandoned like an old shoe.

Could this tick-eating habit have led to the more revolting behaviour of *Geospiza difficilis*, "the difficult", the Sharp-beaked Ground Finch? It has developed the habit of probing at the "elbow" and "forearm" of the wings of Masked Boobies until they ooze blood, which the little feathered vampire then proceeds to drink. Could it have acquired this "taste" for gore from eating blood-filled ticks?

The *Geospizas* are astonishing birds, but they seem commonplace beside those known as the Woodpecker Finch, *Cactospiza pallida*, "the pale". I met this bird one hot day on Santa Cruz Island. I had travelled on foot into the cactus forest, about a mile inland from the coast. In places the walking was easy, with broad plateaus of weathered lava as flat as a billiard table and cracked into great level building blocks dotted with cacti and shrubs. *Palo Santos* trees, gaunt, white, lichen-encrusted, skeleton-like, predominated.

Then an area where it looked as though all hell had broken loose. The lava was split, twisted, and contorted into fantastic shapes of curled and jagged form; here, sharp pinnacles, three feet tall; there, great masses of ropey lava "frozen" into solidity as it flowed. The whole was spattered with lichens, as was the lava on Plaza Island. Low lying areas are filled with pools of rain water from the severe thunderstorms of the preceding few days, an infrequent phenomenon in the

143

dry Galápagos. Yet, on the water's surface, whirligigs, or water beetles, dart and gyrate; there are also numerous tadpole shrimps clinging to the submerged vegetation or swimming lazily about. How long, as eggs, have they lain visable but imprisoned in the parched earth before being released by the rains?

Then I heard a bird-song new to my experience. I struggled over the rough lava that was strewn with big shattered-faced boulders of the same material. A wide growth of *Discaria,* like an enormous, bright green mass of crucifixion thorns, its tiny green leaves so few and so small as to be readily overlooked, caused me a long, difficult detour. Just such a spot must have prompted Darwin to compare the islands to "the cultivated portions of hell". Eventually I came close to the singer and located him in a big prickly pear. He is not an impressive-looking bird. Tanager-sized, drab olive-brown above, off-white below with faint watered streaks on the breast; but I felt a surge of excitement and anticipation as I realized he was the fabulous Woodpecker Finch, the "tool-user". He didn't disappoint me. He scrambled over a cactus pad and, with his beak, wrenched loose a two-inch long cactus spine. He flew, carrying the spine in his bill, to a spindly *Croton* tree and proceeded to climb up its skinny branches, examining them with myopic intensity. His actions reminded me of a West Indian Bananaquit. Suddenly, he stopped and inserted the point of the spine into a small hole in the bark. With a forward and sideway movement of the head, he slid the spine through the inner edges of his beak until he gripped it near its tip. There was a slight wrenching motion and the spine was withdrawn with a small, fat, wriggling, white grub impaled upon it. The base of the spine was lowered into contact with the tree limb and secured there by a strong-clawed grasping foot. The beak, thus freed, daintily removes the grub. I thought how well he would deal with an olive in a martini! As he flew off to the next tree, a little sliver whirled gently down onto my outstretched palm—his toothpick! I carefully folded a piece of paper about it and put it into my pocket. It is the very one now held in the beak of the mounted Woodpecker Finch in the Galápagos diorama that I afterward created for the Royal Ontario Museum. Let no one say, "the Woodpecker Finch doesn't use that kind of pick."

The next day I found his mate and her nest, a globular structure similar to those of the other Darwin's finches. I returned to the area many times to watch them perform, and I never failed to be impressed by their behaviour. It should be emphasized that no other non-human uses a tool with such consistent regularity—not even the great man-like apes. It was the one act by a Darwin's finch from which I could not escape a feeling of incredulity.

Other methods of extracting wood-boring insects are used by the Woodpecker Finch. It will pick away soft wood in the manner of a woodpecker (hence its English name), and I have observed it enlarging holes in soft wood by picking and prizing with open beak and using only the upper mandible. It also uses this method to flake away lichens and loose bark in its search for insects, rather like using one blade of an open pair of scissors.

But in some ways, perhaps, the most remarkable of all is the Warbler Finch, *Certhidea olivacea,* which by way of some evolutionary process has become in effect a warbler. Europeans would say that it looks and behaves like a Willow Warbler; Americans would say that it appears to be closely related to a Tennessee or Nashville Warbler. Yet, it is neither *Sylviidae* The Old World Warblers, nor *Parulidae* The New World Warblers, but a true finch. The beak has become long and attenuated; just such a beak as required by the Old and New World Warblers for their diet of small caterpillars and other insects. Is it really possible that before the fortuitous advent of the Yellow Warbler on Galápagos some finches (seed eaters) developed the equipment to live as warblers, to fill an unoccupied niche—there were no such birds on Galápagos— and to evolve in actuality to the equivalent of warblers? It was the only one of the Darwin's finches that I felt was in danger. There were too many Yellow Warblers, a more recent immigrant and a species adapted through many more generations to the niche that nature chose for the Galápagos Warbler Finch.

The four remaining species are, to the best of our knowledge, less spectacular; but don't count on it, however, because they are after all Darwin's finches and any one of them can be expected suddenly to unveil startling behaviour. Three of them are known as the "vaulted beaks", *Camarhynchus,* in reference to the shape of their bills, which rather resemble those of parrots. All are mainly insect eaters and seldom descend to the ground. The largest, *Camarhynchus psittacula,* "little parrot", the Large Insectivorous Tree Finch, indeed has a parrot-like appearance, and climbs about somewhat like one. The smallest, *C.parvulus*, "the small", the Small Insectivorous Tree Finch, reminded me of a vireo in its actions, but it displays individuality by not infrequently clinging or even hanging by *one* middle toe when hunting insects.

The last and, to me, the one most finch-like in form and deportment—its gentleness suggesting a bullfinch or Pine Grosbeak—is *Platyspiza crassirostris*, "coarse billed flat finch". As befits its quiet nature, it is thought to be a strict vegetarian; thus, it is called the Vegetarian Tree Finch. Only once did I see one of these birds riled, and that was when Bill Gunn, using a tape recorder, played back the finch's own song within a few yards of its nest, and on which its mate brooded. The apparent intrusion of another singing male of its own species on its territory soon had the finch beside itself with excitement. In a human, its behaviour would have been called righteous indignation. The bird hopped about the recorder, even on top of it, singing vigorously and working itself up into a veritable frenzy. The finch relaxed only when the recorder was turned off.

It has been suggested that the Darwin's finches and other Galápagos animals owe their "fearlessness" to a lack of natural enemies. Yet, they do have instinctive fears. They are not disturbed by slow deliberate motion, but sudden or rapid movements do alarm them. The swiftly moving shadow of a pelican or frigate bird, the waving of my butterfly net or the approach of a mockingbird, *Nesomimus,* was sufficient to alert them and on occasion send them into panic. Their fear of the mockingbirds, at first surprising to me, was soon explained, for these are aggressive, semi-predatory birds, sometimes behaving like jays, grackles or shrikes. On one occasion, as I watched a flock of Darwin's finches feeding on rice before the door, there came the *frou-frou* of soft wing-beats, and a Blackeared Mockingbird swooped into the flock, struck a juvenile Small Ground Finch with its beak, and I believe its wings and feet, and knocked it senseless amid a puff of dislodged finch feathers. I'm sure it would have killed it had I not reflexively intervened. I had been encouraging the finches to come to the area in order that the cinematographers could photograph them. Afterward, I regretted that I had interfered.

146

I should have watched to see what would happen. The little finch revived after a few moments of grogginess; then it amazed me by commencing to eat rice while held firmly in my hand. Once again a Darwin's finch had "stolen the show".

There were other predatory creatures on the islands: the Galápagos Hawk, now rare, was once abundant and, though its normal diet appears to be Lava Lizards, Galápagos Snakes, young Marine Iguanas, and Painted Grasshoppers, it is certainly not averse to a plump young Darwin's finch. Then there are the wild dogs, cats, and rats that, for over a century, have roamed the islands in their hundreds. The appearance of any one of these has as frightening an effect on the finches as it would have on a Song Sparrow or a Yellowhammer.

The finches become terrified if trapped indoors, even in a full-windowed and sun-splashed room. On several occasions I saw them knock themselves out in their desperate efforts to escape. Yet seconds later, the same birds, liberated outdoors, will return to perch unconcernedly on one's hand to feed on rice. These fears have obvious causes, tangible and comprehensible; even their claustrophobia. They also suffer from the vague, strange fears known as "dreads", familiar to those who have studied colonies of gulls or terns or watched feeding flocks of migrant shorebirds. Without apparent reason, a feeding group of Darwin's finches would "freeze", go silent, and in unison start into the air.

Scattering in every direction, they alight some yards away, peer about in an alerted manner, and then return to the food supply as if nothing had happened.

What is most remarkable about this is that "dreads" are not individual, but examples of "herd obedience", as if there existed a community of thought. Yet, Darwin's finches are not normally gregarious and come together in flocks only under such artificial conditions as those created by our bonuses of rice.

Are there in this "most singular group of finches" the instincts of now vanished progenitors that were, like many finches, gregarious on their migrations?

The Black Island

The *Beagle II* had just dropped anchor when John Livingston pointed down on the brigantine's starboard: "There," he stage-whispered, "a Flightless Cormorant." My first glance was enough to tell me that here indeed was a bird that had no need for the power of flight, that is, until the scene changed and— *enter* Man.

We were looking almost directly down on the bird as it swam, completely submerged, alongside the *Beagle*. We could see the shining air-bubbles still clinging to its feathers. It was propelling itself along solely by the paddling of its outsized webbed feet, the tiny useless wings pressed close upon its back. It swam as well as a fish—actually it must swim better than most fish for it pursues and catches them for a living. It angled away from the *Beagle* and surfaced, floating low in the water like a surfaced submarine. Its head on the end of a long but thick snaky neck was held with the beak raised slightly above the horizontal.

To see this bird and the Galápagos Penguin were the two main reasons for our coming to Fernandina Island (Narborough). We were now anchored off Point Espinosa, one of the few places where a landing is possible on the "Black Island".

The landward view was one of wild, forlorn desolation. The mountain sides were almost entirely covered with black, twisted slag, the result of repeated flows of lava from the main volcano and other numerous craters that pockmark the slopes. The blackened mass was relieved only by a few struggling patches of scrubby brush. The level ground, save for one stretch of sandy beach bordered on one side by mangroves, was lava.

148

"It's a moonscape," I said to John. "It looks like a big cinder out of the earth's furnace."

The longboat had been brought alongside, and we climbed down the ship's ladder and boarded. The landing on the sandy beach was easy, but we were hardly prepared for what happened to the long, low slag-heaps of lava bordering it. The whole area rose about two inches and walked two or three feet farther away! Although there *was* lava underneath, what we had been looking at was an expansive, densely-packed assemblage of lava-coloured Marine Iguanas. I couldn't even hazard a guess as to their number.

The living shoreline didn't walk far. It settled down and forgot about us as we walked up the sand beach within twenty feet of it. Curiosity-impelled sea lions had converged on us from both sides and floundered up to inspect us. They looked at us as if they expected us to perform some unusual antics for their entertainment. I felt boorishly rude as I turned my back on them and hurried off toward the lava boulders near the water's edge, for on those boulders stood a half dozen Flightless Cormorants. Sea lions I had seen before and could see on almost any of the islands of the Galápagos, but only on Fernandina or Isabela would I have the opportunity of meeting the unique cormorants.

They were sitting at the water's edge and about two feet above it. Needlessly, I approached slowly and cautiously so as not to frighten them off. I was walking through a densely-packed swarm of Iguanas that opened up a narrow path for me and closed in behind. I was in the centre of a moving lacuna in a sea of iguanas. The cormorants showed no disposition to take to the water or indulge in any evasive action whatsoever. One had its quaint little wings extended, spread out to dry in characteristic cormorant fashion.

I stopped about ten feet from the birds and squatted down on my haunches to watch them. Drops of water were slowly forming at the end of each long, hooked beak. Each drop gradually grew, became a full and pendant tear-drop, and then fell like the drip from a leaky tap. "Faulty plumbing", I mused. That it was certainly not. It was a very efficient, life-saving procedure. Their salt extracting apparatus was at work, ridding them of the excess salts acquired in their strictly marine feeding. I moved closer. Five feet, three feet, two. Finally I had to don my reading glasses, the better to see the details of the sea-blue-green irises, each with a hair-thin circle of silvery-white surrounding the pupil.

(Galápagos is the only place I have ever kept a list of the birds and reptiles that I approached closely enough to require the use of my reading glasses, which improve my vision at distances of from twelve to twenty-four inches. My list, without trying too hard, for I had other things to do, reached nineteen. I had been on the Galápagos only a short time when I dropped my binoculars on a concrete floor knocking the prisms out of alignment. When one of my companions commiserated, I could cheerfully say, "It's all right, I've still got my reading glasses.")

I noticed that one of the cormorants had a band on its leg. It would be amusing, I thought, to see if I could read the number and report it to Roger Perry at the Darwin Research Station. (A cormorant has a much flattened so-called "tarsus". Actually it's the metatarsus. The metal band, or ring, used by bird banders is placed on the "foot" rather than the leg. A bird walks on its toes and the first bend we see is its ankle not its knee.) The band, fitting snugly, was a very flat ellipse about the "leg". It was simple to read the first half of the inscription and number, but to determine the last portion I had to crane my neck around in front of the bird with my nose almost between its feet. As I completed jotting down the number, I was wondering if that strong hooked beak would suddenly take a chunk out of my right ear. I withdrew slowly and glanced up at the bird's head. Unbelievable as it may seem, its eyes were closed and its head rolled back on its neck. Totally unconcerned by my almost contactual proximity, the cormorant was dozing in the sun. (I wonder how many bird-banding returns have been made without capturing or even laying a finger on the bird?) Less than a minute after I straightened up and was squatting beside it to study its form, it lifted one foot, the one with the band on it, tucked it up into the belly feathers, swayed a moment while it achieved balance on the other foot, laid its head across its back with the beak under its back feathers, and went to sleep!

The degenerate wings of the Galápagos cormorant are a striking example of genetic loss of function. For ages flight was unnecessary. It had no serious enemies. Even today, the most dangerous threat to the continued existence of the several hundred birds left does not involve its flightlessness. It's the lobster industry. The deep-diving cormorants are frequently caught by and drowned in lobster traps.

Soon one of the birds felt the pangs of hunger. It waddled awkwardly to the very edge of the rocks and jumped off into the sea, landing a belly-whopper with a resounding watery splat. Another followed. The sounds of the splashes awakened my erstwhile friend who, tripping over his own widely webbed feet (all four toes are connected by webs so that it has three webs instead of two as do ducks and geese), and with his abbreviated wings flapping to keep balance, rushed up to the edge and leaped off into the water.

The photographic crew was busily engaged with another group of cormorants; so, I set off to explore on my own in the opposite direction. I soon found what I was looking for—penguins.

There were two of them standing on the wave-polished lava at the water's edge, their shiny white breasts conspicuous against black lava or deep blue water. Once again I approached gingerly, and once again without cause. When I was some twenty feet away, they began to walk toward me, their flipper-like wings waving. We all stopped when my feet were no more than thirty inches from theirs. I leaned forward at the waist to look at them and soon realized that they did not possess binocular vision. First one side of the head was presented so that the right eye could examine me, then with a speed that made the movement almost imperceptible the head swung a full 180°, and the left now glared its disapproval. This was repeated at intervals of a few seconds during the time I stood there. I realized that, even while they had been approaching, their heads had been swinging in this singular fashion. I was puzzled. I extended one arm as far to the side as I could, then brought my hand, fingertips foremost, as nearly in a direct line with the point of a penguin beak as possible. Almost instantly the head swung at a right angle presenting to the hand its profile and one baleful eye. If they haven't good forward vision, how on earth do they ever pursue and capture a skinny target like an anchovy? I had to conclude that they have binocular vision only when looking down; that the chin and throat are narrower than the crown of the head so that only in looking up must they turn sideways and look out of one eye. I believe the fact that they often swim with the eyes submerged and looking down, and that while on land the beak is tilted strongly upward as if they were looking under it, helps to substantiate this theory.

Those familiar with the curious ocular qualities of a bittern will appreciate the point.

I kept my hand a good ten inches from the penguin's beak with its razor-sharp cutting edges. Years before I had the assignment of painting a scenic backdrop for an exhibit of live Blackfooted Penguins, close South African relatives of the ones I now watched, for the Children's Zoo at the Canadian National Exhibition. The penguins were in the enclosure as I worked, and I was having a difficult time because each time I painted a penguin on the backdrop, the living ones would toddle over and stand beside it. One of the keepers tried to shoo them away, but they wouldn't budge. Finally, he reached down and snatched one of them up. The inch-and-a-half-long, pencil-thick slice taken off the side of his hand by the infuriated penguin was removed as neatly as if by a pair of surgical scissors.

As I was watching the first pair, two more appeared in the water. They swam toward the shore and, when close to the rocks, lifted their heads so that the beaks were raised about 45°, and literally leaped out of the water. One landed upright on his feet, the other on his belly. The latter clung frantically with his flipper wings and pulled himself upright. They were obviously in a great hurry to join their compatriots in examining something new. They progressed by a series of waddles and hops balancing every move with outstretched and wavering flippers, like a small boy walking a fence. One leaped almost straight up, landing on his feet, in negotiating a fifteen-inch boulder. When they reached us, they examined me in the same manner as the first pair, but one of the newcomers was a bit too brash. He walked over with the rocking motion natural to fat, short-legged people and tried to bite my foot. I was wearing only light sneakers, so I danced back a step or two. Then one of them started chattering his beak and another let go with a bray like a donkey. I decided I'd had about enough of them, especially when I noted the approach of two more. I am a somewhat reserved person and resented this self-assertive, impertinent approach to friendship. I felt it was obtrusive, flippant, and premature; so I chased them all toward the sea. When they reached the edge of the boulders, they either jumped in feet first with flippers flailing or simply leaned forward and fell in full length. I decided that they were rather absurd and could never be numbered among my favourite birds.

Now the eerie black landscape and weird, twisted shapes of the lava behind me beckoned. I walked along the beach in order to bypass the dense growth of mangroves that grew along its edges. Aside from numerous mangrove crabs, there was no sign of life. I began to think that the only creatures that made use of this slag heap of ashes were those creatures that came ashore and found it a convenient resting place. I was meditating on this when I heard a curious sort of chirping whine. It came from deep in the mangroves and was unlike any sound I had heard before. It was impossible to climb through or over the thick-set compact mass of mangrove, but it seemed possible to penetrate by crawling under the curving stilt roots. It was wet but fairly firm sandy-mud underneath. I was about fifty feet in when I heard the bleating sound again. It was right in front of me and I saw it almost immediately: a tiny pup sea lion. The little chap was not much more than a foot long and looked like a big russet-coloured slug. I had no chance to observe him further for there came a hollow, snorting cough. His mother was coming at me through the mangroves. That she was angry was evident to both eye and ear. Her mouth, armed with sharp teeth, was open and she never ceased bellowing.

Now getting in under the mangrove roots head-first had been difficult; backing out was well-nigh impossible, except that I was being urged on by an infuriated sea lion matron. Fortunately I was carrying a butterfly net, and I used the handle to poke her in the chest and make her keep her distance. I considered letting out a fierce, aggressive bellow. That might have stopped her big husband, the "lobo", but I was old enough and experienced enough to know that that kind of behaviour never works with a female of any species. I just kept poking her in the chest, scrabbling backward on elbows and knees, and talking to her. At last I emerged to where I could stand up and quickly get out into the open. She didn't follow me, chiefly because, at that moment, the cub bleated again, setting off an instinct more powerful than the pursuit of an enemy—the need to return to her offspring. It was then that I realized that I had backed out of that awful mangrove tangle faster than I had crawled in.

153

I finally reached the vast field of black lava. At its edges, it had not been bad walking. In fact it had "treads". It was pahoehoe, smooth, billowy, or ropy lava that had congealed "frozen" as it flowed. Visualize the folds of whipped cream or chocolate pudding pushing away from the blades of your electric beater as the cream stiffens. Abruptly the lava became rough; at best riven with cracks, voids, and crevasses lumped with shapeless and unshapely masses; at worst, a field of stalagmites, contorted and perverted, in such closed ranks that there was no foot-room between them, and so tall that there was no leg-length above them. There were places that I stopped and looked at totally impassable stretches of visible horizon. Others may have stood where I had; no one had set foot a dozen yards ahead.

In places, there were fumaroles, some bucket-sized, others much larger. Their cones looked like black plasticene pots fashioned by inept four-year-olds—melted, sagging, and drooping like candle wax exposed to the sun; they were, however, hard and rang like iron when tapped. Some were big and lusty and evil-looking: witches' cauldrons in a nightmare. Everything was black. On the lava near the shore, there had been small cacti, shaped like phallic images: orange, tan, and greenish orange; here there was nothing, nothing but blackness. For something to do, I tried to analyze the kinds of black: this patch is ebon, that jet. The lighter points of stalagmites were charcoal or even sooty. The shiny parts polished by wind and weather were like a raven's wing. The shadows in the crevasses were dark black, a suitable home for black cacodemons.

My aimless musing was startlingly shattered by a rapid, scurrying movement of something black across the lava. A living creature. It was a lava lizard, about eight inches long, and he was *black*. He joined a female who was as black as her mate, and smaller; when they remained motionless, they were invisible. Their relatives on Santa Cruz, San Salvador, Plaza, and Isabela islands had been gaily coloured, the males in various shades of cerulean, powder blue, and green, speckled with black, and showing brilliant red underparts when displaying. The females were usually greyish brown with brilliant scarlet about the chin and mouth—I accused them of using too much lipstick. On this black island, even the lizards were black. Closer inspection revealed that there *was* a tiny bit of sepia on the male's chest and on the female's lips, but essentially they were black.

154

On my approach, they scuttled away, leaping across a deep chasm nearly two feet wide in the process. The male cleared it with ease, the female fell a little short, but landed clinging to the vertical face of the far wall a few inches from the top, and instantly scrambled up and hurried after her mate. None of the lava lizards I had seen on the other islands had shown this propensity for jumping. Were black colour and leaping ability by-products of living on this chinked and fissured black island?

By skirting the more inhospitable areas, I had penetrated a quarter of a mile inland. Then I gave up; the surface was becoming more and more treacherous for walking, and it was obvious that there was little to be seen. I returned to shore. Two gulls stood on the black rocks. They were facing each other and going through a kind of ritual. The beaks were pointed to the zenith in a strange, stiff manner—"hams", overacting. As they returned to horizontal, one bird uttered a short, conversational *tut*. It appeared to trigger the main performance that consisted of looking straight at each other, opening their brilliant red mouths as wide as possible, and letting go with derisive and uncouth laughter: *eh-ha haha haha*. There was no doubt that they were Laughing Gulls, their form and their behaviour were those of Laughing Gulls, but they were *black*, charcoal grey-black like the lava they sat on. They were Lava Gulls.

Then, a stealthy dark bird walked in slow motion near a tide pool. The big orange-red crabs moved a little to one side. The mahogany-red and blackish young ones scuttled sideways down the boulders to creep into crevices or cling to vertical rock faces out of reach from above or below. The bird paid them no attention. He stalked slowly and deliberately to a low rock, its surface only a few inches above the pool. He looked, in form and action, exactly like a Striated or a Green Heron, but he was almost uniformly coastal lava-coloured. It was as if he had been anodized in a tank with electrodes and lava. That's all he was—a Green Heron that by some unexplained evolutionary process had assumed the colour of his surroundings even as the Laughing Gulls had become Lava Gulls. According to the taxonomists' *Systema,* however, my little bird was a Galápagos Heron with the distinctive scientific name of *Butorides sundevallii.* He stood motionless, with superhuman intensity of concentration upon the water below him; suddenly, he darted forward and down. His toes never left the rock

155

they were clinging to, but for a second, he was upsidedown. His wings gave a flick as he righted himself, and his neck a slight convulsion as he swallowed. I missed seeing what he caught, perhaps a mudskipper or some unfortunate marine invertebrate that had been trapped by the ebb tide in the pool. His legs and feet were of a darker colour than those of his continental counterparts and seemed heavily blotched with lava black. He walked with his head drawn down on his shoulders, like a man snuggling his ears into his coat collar on a cold winter's day. His strides were comically long, his incongruously big toes carefully folded together as he lifted them and which he equally solicitously unfolded and spread as he put them down. At the edge of a boulder, he launched into the air. His flight was initially awkward, but after he had gathered in his neck and dangling legs, he looked better, even if there was a jerky wing action suggesting a slightly arthritic condition.

I passed the mangrove tangle, wondering what the fond mother sea lion and her pup were doing; discretion told me not to try to find out. A black Medium Ground Finch sang *beegie-burgie* from the mangrove. I was relieved when I heard and saw a Yellow Warbler, not black but brilliant sunshine yellow marked with venetian red. I wondered how long his offspring and theirs would live on black Fernandina before they too turned black.

The longboat was waiting; Jorgé and Richard were waving. Time to go aboard the *Beagle* for a supper of clawless lobster. Trudging down the beach, I reflected on the blackness. Iguanas, Lava Lizards, finches, gulls, herons—all black. If white man lived on this black island for a sufficient number of generations, would he too become black? Shades of Darwin.

This Devil's Island

To see *Beagle II* under full canvas was a thrilling sight. To be aboard her with sails filled by a freshening wind was intoxicating. The flap of canvas and the creaking of her timbers as she scudded along made one appreciate the drama and romance of the days of sail.

This particular day was sunny and breezy with big white cumulus clouds billowing up on the southern horizon.

"It's a Jacques sky," commented Roger Peterson. This in reference to the surging clouds painted by Francis Lee Jacques, who, of all nature artists, perhaps captured more of the atmosphere of sea and sky and rock than any other.

There was plenty of excitement. A school of enormous Hammerhead Sharks, five or six of them, had circled and convoyed the ship for a nautical mile. Two of them must have exceeded fifteen feet in length. We climbed the rigging to look almost directly down on them, marvelling at the extraordinary conformation of their heads clearly outlined in the almost transparent sea. Carl Angermeyer informed us that their flesh was so extremely bitter it was inedible. As I had no desire to catch and eat one, I added this tidbit to my store of useless knowledge.

Later, we were startled by an explosive report off our starboard side, and soon we were being treated to a fantastic display of leaping Manta Rays (Greater Devilfish). There were about twenty of them; all, so far as we could determine, young, for none seemed more than twelve feet in the spread of its pectoral fins. They were full of exuberance, of the sheer joy of living. Each would surface, tread water as it were, with fully spread "wing-fins" gripping the surface of the ocean. Cephalic, or head, fins, projecting forward like a pair of horn-like appendages on either side of the mouth, were waving and vibrating. Then, with a superb effort, the pectorals would slap the surface of the sea and the big fish would soar into the air. Up, up each went, ten, twelve and more feet, "wings" beating rhythmically, "flying" perhaps five yards, then stretching and extending the great sails with a slight upward dihedral and dropping back into the sea. Invariably they hit the water surface on a level, horizontal plane and produced a report like a cannon-shot that reverberated off the walls of a distant cove. The sea at the time was only slightly ruffled by the breeze, but there was a long rolling swell, probably enough to give added impetus to the Mantas' leaps.

We watched them for a long time, until they moved their playground away from the direction in which we were proceeding. Their exultance in the "games", it seemed to me, could be equalled only among mammals. I was reminded of playful porpoises.

Carl was guiding the *Beagle* into James Bay on San Salvador Island (also known as Santiago and James). We sailed by the vast lava flow that had reached the sea. It resembled a great Cimmerian glacier. "This is the true Black Glacier," I thought, recalling the grey-brown, moraine spattered Alaskan Black glacier at the foot of which I had camped some years before. The darksome front of the lava flow, jagged, broken, and perpendicular was indeed a glacier that had been formed of malleable rock flow instead of *névé,* or compressed snow.

We anchored off James Bay and went ashore in the longboat. My first impression of San Salvador (other than that barren, horrendous lava river that we had passed) was of a more hospitable island than any of the Galápagos I had visited. There were areas of deep soil and grass, and vascular plants and *real* trees—trees big enough to house the enormous nests of Galápagos Hawks. One vast expanse was covered with magenta-flowered wild portulaca about which hovered blue-black carpenter bees and pink and white day-flying moths. I felt sure that they were the same species that is common in the salt-marshes of Florida, though these were in the dry uplands.

I wanted to see the lagoon with its flock of scarlet flamingos; so, I walked along a pleasant sandy beach upon which reposed sea lions and a half dozen fur seals. The scarcity of the latter was alarming. There had been sixty in the colony at James Bay in 1962, only three years before. I hoped that there were more off in the sea. As I reflected on the difficulty of policing these remote islands to prevent fishermen from killing the fur seals and sea lions, which they looked upon as "competitors", I was passing a rookery of honking, barking sea lions. I had just about passed it and had reached a stretch of lava rock when the "lobo", the harem-master, appeared. He was furious. He took me for an invader of his home-site, for a competing bull trespassing and wanting some of his wives. He charged along the beach after me, giving voice to a throaty roar. The thing to do when attacked by a "lobo" is to run, but only if the footing is suitable. Mine wasn't; it was rough lava rock. The second thing is to avoid falling. He is not likely to make actual physical contact while you are standing taller than he is. Another thing I had learned was to carry a stout stick when near a sea lion rookery. I had my butterfly net and when he got too close I raised one bent arm over my head so as to appear even taller and poked him in the chest with the handle of the net. That would stop him long enough for me to take three or four careful backward steps. He herded me along the lava stone bellowing like a Demogorgon; I backed up as carefully as I could while still keeping one eye on him and holding the net handle a few inches from his chest. After every few steps, or when he seemed about to charge, I would poke him in the chest. This invariably brought him up short. Soon he was a fair distance from his harem, and I think he was beginning to worry about rival "lobos" abducting his wives. He began to look back over his shoulder. I fancied I could see anxiety in his face and hear it in his voice. Finally I decided to take the offensive. I yelled, waved my arms, and whacked him across the shoulder. He capitulated, turned, and floundered off toward the water. I chased him until he plunged in, then I desisted for he swam up and down some hundred feet off shore, howling, but having given up all defence of his harem. He had surrendered them to me. It would be amusing I thought if all his wives followed me back to the *Beagle* as their new "harem-master".

I reached another stretch of white coral sand and then penetrated a jungly tangle to the lagoon that parallels the shore. The basin was surrounded by a lush growth of *acacia, bursera, maytenus, cordia, miconia,* and *croton.* There were also numbers of the deceiving Manchineel, a tree that looks like an orchard apple tree, but that possesses a caustic sap. This exudes from the leaves, and during or after a rainstorm drips to the ground. If the fluid falls on a person's skin, it can cause severe blistering. And, of course, it is one of the few trees with sufficient foliage on the Galápagos that provides shelter in a rainstorm. Its fruit, greenish and plump, resembles a crab apple. It too contains corrosive sap that burns the mucous membranes of the mouth and throat, and can and has caused human death.

On Santa Cruz Island one day, I performed the experiment of touching a torn leaf to the back of my hand (taking the precaution of doing so with a full wash basin of warm soapy water in front of me), and almost instantly felt an intense burning sensation. I quickly washed and rinsed it off in fresh running water. In spite of this, a small blister formed and five weeks later there was still a faintly discernible mark. This tree occurs also in Florida and the West Indies.

Swimming on the surface of the lagoon near its margin, under the Manchineels, were several Whitecheeked Pintails. Once again I was impressed by the similarity of situations here six hundred miles out in the Pacific with those I had encountered before, for the Whitecheeked Pintail occurs also in the West Indies. The sensation was compounded as the next birds that I saw were two American Flamingos, a species predominantly West Indian. But only *two*? The lagoon of San Salvador normally holds a population of from fifty to a hundred flamingos.

When I rejoined my companions, we paid a visit to the salt mine, a vast ugly hole in what had been one of San Salvador's prettiest spots. It had been abandoned because it hadn't been profitable to mine the salt, load, and ship it to Guayaquil. Ten men had been left behind to clear up such work as remained and were to have been taken off to Guayaquil in a week or so. That had been five months ago. They had no radio, no contact with the outside world, no ship had called, they had run out of food, their clothing was in tatters. The only thing they had plenty of was salt! Their presence and their plight were unknown even on the neighbouring inhabited islands of the Galápagos. They had, they said, been living on Galápagos Doves, that handsome, small, endemic species. Ten doves per day per man. A hundred doves a day. For nearly four months—10,000 doves! It looked as if a feather mattress had been emptied outside their cookhouse. The tame little doves had been clubbed and snared. Among the feathers I found those of the Galápagos Hawk and recalled the camp fire near the lagoon where one had been plucked and eaten. Its picked bones and feathers were scattered about. Had they also decimated the flock of flamingos?

"Take us off this Devils' Island," the men pleaded.

There were already twelve of us aboard the *Beagle,* but we took them off and delivered them to the port captain at Academy Bay where arrangements were made to get them passage to Guayaquil.

I believe our decision was influenced as much by our concern for those threatened birds, the Galápagos Doves, the Galápagos Hawks, and the flamingos as it was out of compassion for ten starving Guayaquileños.

This is but one example of the precarious state of Galápagos animals, and the more or less unpredictable menaces to their continued existence.

The Cristobal Carrier

The *Cristobal Carrier,* a converted U.S. Navy surplus LST plies between the Ecuadorian port of Guayaquil and the Galápagos Islands. In theory, she makes the trip once a month. In fact, her sailings depend upon a great many things, the most critical being how many of her seven diesels are operable at any given time. A voyage on this extraordinary vessel was at once one of delight, suspense, and incredulity; and it was droll. To begin with, the manner in which she had been converted from a war-time troop-landing ship into a "luxury" liner was most intriguing. A superstructure had been built "abaft the binnacle", and was subdivided into the tiniest double-bunked first-class cabins ever conceived. Her owners ought to have been forced to advertise that "thin people only may

161

apply for first-class passage". Second-class passengers occupied the lower deck.

First-class passengers needed food for the four-day voyage. Second class brought their own. There was no posh dining-room on an LST. Actually there wasn't much room for anything except bodies and their accoutrements. The *Cristobal Carrier* transported the wealthy to Galápagos and back, and had to have a watering place and a refuelling place for its passengers. So, where did they build the dining salon? Directly forward of the wheelhouse! As we approached the estuary of the Guayas River, the skipper required clear visibility to exercise his navigational skill. Standing at the wheel, behind a large glass port-hole, he was forced to peer forward at reefs, shallows, and other hazards to water-travelling vehicles through the milling mob of drinkers and diners. He pounded on the glass with his fist, waved them aside, poured what was probably magnificent Spanish invective on them, unheard because he was sealed in the wheelhouse. I sat over in a corner watching his choleric, apoplectic face as he yelled, gestured, and screamed at entirely unconcerned and slightly inebriated people who stood directly in his line of vision. No sound penetrated the salon except for the frantic hammering of his fists on the glass.

The *Cristobal Carrier* had a delightfully comfortable afterdeck. Here we could relax in lounge chairs, watch the sea, the birds, the whales, and Manta Rays in peace. In peace? Not entirely. The fumes from the seven diesels poured up and enveloped us and sent us choking and coughing to the rail.

But it was not all that bad a voyage. A naturalist finds compensations. Firstly, he is seeing things that transport him into a different world. Secondly, he has put up with hardships before; there has always been something worse, and wherever he goes he has rewards. There was for me in this case, the fabulous birds that live on the ocean: Wedge-tailed and Sooty Shearwaters, Bulwer's, Leach's and Black Storm Petrels, Madieran and Galápagos Storm Petrels. There had also been a Laysan Albatross, a Pinkfooted Shearwater, and a Sabine's Gull. There had even been an old friend of the twenties: a Franklin's Gull (exciting to see him here in the South Pacific; known to me previously only on the prairie sloughs of Manitoba).

On June 3, 1965, a Sperm Whale (the biggest carnivore on earth—now very rare) rose close to our leeward side, surfacing,

162

breaching. And two Pilot Whales leaping in tandem in sheer exuberance, twelve feet above the ocean surface, thrilled us from the
afterdeck.

But there had been ludicrous incidents. The voyage fluctuated,
staggered, and reeled away from the ecstatic to the ridiculous. We
sailed into Wreck Bay on San Cristobal Island, a huge bay, a
marvellous anchorage, following up an Ecuadorian destroyer that had
one of our party on board. He had picked up a "bug" somewhere
along the line and had gone into a semicoma, fortunately just as the
Ecuadorian destroyer, with a *medico* aboard, had put into Academy
Bay. The *medico* had said, "This man must not be out of my care until
I get him into hospital in Guayaquil."

The destroyer had reached Wreck Bay several hours before us and
was now riding at anchor. It was after mid-day and there wasn't a
cloud in the sky. Save for a few fishing boats near the shore and the
destroyer, the big harbour was devoid of craft. The *Carrier* thundered
in, cut its engines, and dropped anchor. Then she started to swing on
her anchor chain, the ebb of the tide drifting her stern right at the
destroyer. Bells rang, an attempt was made to start the engines, but
it was too late. It was mesmerizing to watch the gap between the two
ships dwindling, to stand by the rail and watch an unavoidable
collision in the making, slowly and deliberately. The sailors on the
destroyer were gesticulating, waving us off, as if by willing it and
shouting they could ward off the inevitable. Then the crash. The
heavy *Carrier* sent the smaller ship careening off, having struck her
amidship and scraping along her length. No real damage was done;
only a few yards of paint had been removed. For our part, we thought
it a somewhat unduly exuberant manner of greeting our colleague on
the destroyer. Only the *Cristobal Carrier* could have done it in that
ample harbour.

The first two days of the voyage had not been too bad. On the third
day things deteriorated; the smells got worse, the food got worse, the
service stayed the same—it couldn't get worse. The closer we got to
the coast, the hotter it got. Some of our passengers, including one or
two of our party, disappeared into their cabins, skipping meals and
deck strolls, reappearing only when we reached Guayaquil. The sea
wasn't rough, but there are other ways of contracting *mal-de-mer*.

Bird-watching from the salon, or the afterdeck was a time-passing

163

diversion. Most of the birds were truly pelagic ones. They are the ones that spend most of their lives on the high seas, far from the sight of land, coming ashore only to nest on the remote and inaccessible islands. There were Laysan and Blackfooted Albatrosses, their stiffly-held, long, narrow wings and heavy bodies enabling them to ride the air turbulence above the waves with effortless ease. More energetic and purposeful were the shearwaters, of which we recorded seven different species: hard, rigid wings, beating rapidly in a shallow arc, then a long, sailing glide close to the water's surface, and rising or dipping with the elevations and the depressions of the waves. There were five species of Storm Petrels, the "Mother Carey's chickens" of the mariners. These tiny birds brave the ocean storms as though under the protection of "Mother Carey", the sailor's name for the Virgin Mary.

There were other less strictly marine species: migrating Sabine's and Frankin's Gulls, Arctic Terns and Redtailed Tropic-birds. As we approached the coast of Peru and Ecuador, boobies, frigate birds, and pelicans began to appear, but it was when the *Carrier* sailed close by the nets and boats of the fishing fleet at the meeting place of the cold Humboldt and warm El Niño currents that we saw a remarkable spectacle. Around the nets and vessels were thousands of birds. Those in greatest abundance were the Guanays—big South American cormorants. The most famous of the guano birds of Peru, it has been called the most valuable wild bird in the world. They are black, glossed with oil green and steel blue, with snowy white breasts and a patch of vivid red, bare skin on the face. The last cormorants I had seen had been the Flightless Cormorants on the Galápagos. The Guanay's wings are at the other extreme. In proportion to its size, it has the longest wings of any cormorant or shag. Whereas the Galápagos bird is earth and water bound, the Guanay is a masterful flier. Long rows and strings of them, flying beak to tail, glided along close to the surface of the sea, and landed with considerable grace, for a cormorant, close to the nets.

Piqueros, or Peruvian Boobies, were present in the hundreds. They were the most active of all the fishing birds, winging rapidly over the nets and diving in a steady rain of big white arrows, sometimes singly and sometimes by the dozen, in unison.

There were scores of big Peruvian Brown Pelicans, in form and colour resembling the familiar Brown Pelican of Florida and California, but with twice the bulk. The northern birds have a wingspread of almost seven feet and weigh about eight pounds. The South American pelican is ten feet across the spread wings and weighs up to eighteen pounds. For comparison they are as large or larger than the American and Old World White Pelicans and are exceeded in size probably only by the huge Dalmatian Pelican. Most of the pelicans were floating on the surface, but a few were feeding, making shallow dives that sent up gouts of spray. Their splashes were much more boisterous than the clean jets caused by the knifing thrusts of the Piqueros. The Piqueros dived, the pelicans plunged.

Soaring majestically over all were scores of Magnificent Frigatebirds, one occasionally making his sweeping, twisting swoop at a booby that had captured an *anchoveta* and forcing it to drop or disgorge its prey, which was then retrieved by the frigate before it hit the water. What a contrast to the heavy pelicans: the frigate, with a wingspan of seven feet or more, weighs only three and a half pounds. The assembly was completed by several Great Skuas and a few gulls.

The fishing fleet itself was impressive, and so was the meeting place of warm and cold currents. Enormous masses of yellowish frothy foam marked the turbulent overlapping zone, and above it swirled a misty vapour through which we could see the hazy red setting sun. To the north, the warm El Niño water was purest deep blue; it gave way to the ship's prow like thin oil or maple syrup. To the south, the crisp Humboldt fought back with a rushing sound, and the water broke into millions of hard little beads of spray.

And so, by carrying us past this, and one of the most splendid gatherings of birds that I had ever seen, the *Cristobal Carrier* repaid us, on this last evening of the voyage, for all her earlier offences; and, unpredictable as she was, she didn't foul up a single net.

Avenida de Volcans

The morning light was still soft and subdued as the *autoferril* left Duran. It was comfortable and rode surprisingly well on the roller-coaster-like rails. For fifty miles we travelled through coastal lowlands strongly reminiscent of the flatlands of southern Thailand. Rice paddies alternated with cane and banana, cacao and coffee plantations. Great areas of swampy marsh laced with waterways made one reflect that this region, known as the Yaguachi marshes, must have been a naturalist's Eden. The *autoferril* proved to be an excellent vehicle from which to observe birds. It made enough noise as it hurried along on its iron wheels to startle into flight any birds near the tracks. Unlike a long train, however, its passengers were seated within a few feet of the wide windscreen, and flying birds could be seen forward and from the side windows before they had covered any appreciable distance.

We had excellent views of Wattled Jaçanas, Limpkins, Ibises, Herons, and two Snail Kites: the Kite, that remarkable bird that once was abundant in the marshes of Florida, a bird that has become so specialized that it feeds almost exclusively on large freshwater *Ampullaria* snails. Its beak is long, slender, and sharply curved, well adapted as a "snail-pick" to extricate the snail's body from the unbroken shell. The draining of Florida's Marshes virtually exterminated the snail, and of course with it went the Snail Kite, which only survives in the United States in pitifully small numbers in, until now, undrainable Lake Okeechobee. The two we saw were adult males, easily identified by their overall black colour with a large patch of white on the rump, by their broad wings, and by their bright

166

orange-red feet that hang loosely down as they beat, harrier style, over the marsh.

There were many small birds, but most of them were drab and defied identification. There were, however, black and white Pied Water Tyrants and Green Kingfishers, and small flycatchers like diminitive Grey Kingbirds that seemed quite unconcerned that zoologists call them Torrent Tyrannulets.

A flock of vultures quarrelled over the remains of a carcass while others sat on nearby tree-limbs, their great wings outspread to the sun. They were all Black Vultures save two handsome, creamy-white and black King Vultures. These were larger than the common blacks and their heads were blaring orange, red, and blue. At the clatter of our rail-bus, the whole flock rose and moved away with awkward, heavily flapping wings until they cleared the tops of the nearby trees; then, suddenly and almost as one, stiffened their wings and began soaring gracefully. The change from clumsy to elegant flight was dramatically swift. Riding the updraft, they rose higher and higher with barely a wing stroke. All the while the overlapping circles of their soaring flight were so symmetrical that they seemed almost to leave a tracery on the sky. Somehow it reminded me of the concentric, widening, and interlacing ripples made by raindrops on a quiet pool.

There were many things to see from the bus. Along the edges of the streams stood small thatched huts held up from the swamp on bamboo stilts, many of them with Black Vultures, the *zopillotes,* on their roofs. In the doorways or playing in the mud were children of olive-brown hue, innocent of clothing but totally unmindful of their exposure. Women trudged barefoot through the mud or sat in the shade nursing their infants. There were boats loaded with bananas, greenish-black pineapples, and *zapotes.* Eager as I was to see the high country, I wished that we could have stopped to explore some of these primitive outposts.

We passed by large plantations of coffee, shielded from the equatorial sun by strategically placed *guamote* trees, tall thin shafts with a sparse growth of narrow leaves at the top that produced a dappled shade on the coffee trees below. Occasionally, we would pass through relatively untouched rain forest. Here were tall ghostly grey trees—some with flying buttresses, others standing on stilt roots, and festooned with epiphytic plants; gay red-flowered bromeliads;

pink, white, and mauve orchids in profusion; and the whole matted with lianas that seemed to lace them all together and to the ground. One felt that a skilfully aimed stroke of a machete might destroy the intricate warp and woof of the forest and set off an unravelling that would precipitate the whole thing to the ground in a great sighing crash. Anyone who has chopped at woody South American lianas knows how far this is from reality. And yet there is some truth in it, for let one of the larger trees weaken and fall, and it carries with it or crushes innumerable other forms of life. It wrenches the other lianas free of their grasp on other trees and plunges them down in a tangled mass. It destroys the thin new growth of the understory, young trees reaching eagerly for the light above so that much of their energy is expended in vertical growth at the expense of thickness and strength. Its great limbs carry with them, like passengers in a doomed airliner, all the rich growth of airplants that adorn them, perhaps hundreds or even thousands of orchids, ferns, hair-like *Tillandsias,* climbing cacti, the nests of birds, wasps, and small arboreal mammals. The bromeliads in turn spill out the rainwater that has accumulated in the bracts of their leaves, unceremoniously dumping treefrogs, their eggs and tadpoles, insects, mosquito larvae, worms, snails, and other inhabitants of the hundreds of tiny lakes that had floated so inconspicuously a hundred feet above the ground. The splitting and crackling of the great bole may cause panic and confusion in the nests of the termites and ants. It is one of nature's disaster areas. Tropical lumbering operations kill thousands of trees, but tens of thousands of plants and animals also die unnoticed.

After passing through the town of Bucay, the *autoferril* began its dizzying ascent. In the next fifty miles we rose nearly ten thousand feet, negotiating an astonishing series of switchbacks, travelling first forward, then in reverse, up the face of an enormous sheer cliff. This span of track is called the Alausi Loop and *Nariz del Diablo* (the Devil's Nose). Far below us, with no right of way observable from the windows, the first visible patch of jungle looked like a slice of green cauliflower.

The air was rapidly becoming more chill and clouds of mist like dusty cottonwool drifted along the mountainside, sometimes enveloping the bus so that it was impossible for us to see out. We were grateful that the bus possessed flanged wheels that ran on rails. The lush green of the rain forest, the big trees, and the rank growth of lianas were left behind. Gnarled and twisted trees, shrubs and grass all clung precariously to the steep rock. There were patches of olive-green cloud forest, with fine stands of tall slender bamboos. Imperceptibly the cloud forest passed into a low forest of contorted trees— *Myricas* and *Quenuas*—nearly overwhelmed by the weight of mosses and ferns that sheathed them, and by the draperies of *Fuchsias* and *Lycopodiums* that dangled from their branches. This was the *Ceja de la montana*, the highest of the forest types of the humid western slopes of the Ecuadorian Andes. Abruptly it gives way to the Andean tundra, the cold, treeless land of rock fields, semi-bare earth, volcanic sand, and fields of *Ichu*, the peculiar bunch grass that so resembles the *tête-de-femme* of the Canadian Arctic tundra.

In a hundred miles, we had travelled from sea level to 10,800 feet, from sea to cloud, from rain forest to paramo, from 100°F. to 45°F. These cold mountain regions are given over to grazing, and scarcely anyone but the herdsmen lives there. The homes of the herdsmen were mere burrows in the earth, sheltered by a low mound of sod.

The steep climbing was over. We were up on the inter-Andean plateau, a great high valley that stretches over two hundred miles to beyond Quito, and is bordered by the towering peaks of the eastern and western cordillera of the Andes. The road, gently winding and undulating, varies in altitude from 8,500 feet at Ambato to over twelve thousand feet near Urbina; for most of its length, however, it unfolds at about ten thousand feet. It is known in Ecuador as *Avenida de Volcans,* "road of the volcanoes". But *Avenida de Volcans* can be interpreted also as "road of violent passions", and this is perhaps a more appropriate translation, for in these high valleys the destinies of Indian, Inca, and Spaniard were agonizingly consummated. It has been the stage for awesome courage and endurance, and of treachery and torture.

Pachacutec, the Inca chieftain, led his warriors into this country and the local people fled over the western cordilleras to the sanctuary of the forests. It was here that Rumiũahui, last of the Inca chiefs, and his followers made their stand and fell before the Spanish conquistadores under one of Pizzaro's captains, Belalcazar (1495-1500). It is said that Cotopaxi erupted at this time and hurled tons of ineffectual rock at the invaders. Three centuries later Simon Bolivar

(1783-1830), the liberator, crossed the Andes here with his hungry, frost-bitten army on his way to free Quito and Ecuador from Spain. The royalists were defeated at Pichincha just north of Quito.

But zoology also has its history and, today, wherever one goes in the world, one is following in the footsteps of the giants, the pioneers. On the Galápagos, it had been Darwin, Swarth, Lack, and others. Here it was Louis Fraser, George K. Cherrie, and Frank M. Chapman. The last I knew well, and one of the treasures of my library is a signed copy of his autobiography.

These men, with zoological discovery as their motive, rather than Inca gold, performed feats of daring and underwent hardship no less than their adventurous predecessors. All battled the *soroché,* the "mountain sickness" of the high altitudes. On one trip, Chapman contracted relapsing fever, probably from the bite of a tick, and was invalided out only when warned that loss of sight could be an outcome of his illness.

Just to the west, in the lower country, Cherrie was shot in the right arm by a disgruntled former camp-hand, the charge shattering the lower forearm and cutting out an inch and a half of the ulna. He killed his assailant and, on foot, covered the eighty-five miles to Santa Rosa, only to find that the weekly mail boat to Guayaquil had sailed. Hiring four paddlers, he pursued it in a canoe and caught up to it at Puerto Bolivar. Four days after the accident he arrived in Guayaquil in such a condition that he was not expected to survive the night. But Cherrie was tough; not only his life but his arm was saved.

Now directly to the east of us rose the great burning head of El Sangay, 17,500 feet above sea level. A pall of volcanic cloud hung over its symmetrical cone, a reminder of the violent eruptions of the past that more than once destroyed or caused the evacuation of the old town of Riobamba.

To both the east and west of the road loomed other great peaks. Nowhere else in the world are there two such rows of giant snow-crowned volcanoes. Twenty-three peaks over 13,500 feet flank the *Avenida de Volcans,* topped by mighty Chimborazo (20,561 feet) on the west and Cotopaxi (19,347 feet) on the east. Not one of the crests is more than twenty-five miles from the road, and many are within five. It is said that from the shoulder of Mt. Pichincha all twenty-three can be seen at once. Alas, Nature is modest about her charms and usually draws a veil of cloud over most of the Andean queens.

We soon approached a large reed-rimmed lake, the *Lago de Colta*, and ran along close to its western shore. Mountain gulls fluttered and squealed above some fishermen who were throwing out small nets from dugout style "canoes". Yellowbilled Pintails and Andean Teal swam on the tranquil water, and at one quiet bay women were washing clothes, beating the water into a froth with the shredded leaves of a century plant, the saponaceous juice of which makes an excellent soapy cleanser.

There was a welcome rest stop at Riobamba, the half-way point. It is a clean pleasant town of forty thousand people, and we were entranced by the cobblestone streets, the herdsmen in red ponchos and rope sandals, some with *chaps* of fur, and women in trilbies and the inevitable shawl, which holds bundles of fruit, vegetables or faggots, baskets or a single, large ceramic pot. I was puzzled by the technique of carrying a load in the shawl, for its ends were drawn across the upper arms and tied across the chest, effectively immobilizing all but the hands and forearms. The hands were often busily engaged in carding or spinning wool. In fact, I think that my most lasting impression of Riobamba is of hands industriously twirling the spindles and teasing out the wool. Young, firm, strong, brown hands and old grey, gnarled, wrinkled but still strong hands flashing and twirling the strands of wool as their owners trudged along the cobblestones or gossiped in the doorways.

As we descended into scrubby country on the approach to Quito, the Giant Thrush, like a huge brown robin, became quite common. We arrived in Quito just as the last light faded. The entire trip had been only from dawn to dusk, but the day had been as crowded with a variety of sights and sensations as any I had ever experienced. Yesterday's events seemed far away in time and space. The Galápagos adventure was already blurring and merging with others older and newer. It would take time, but I knew from past experience that once home it would all sort itself out.

King Vultures, Ecuador

EIGHT

An India Expedition

In 1963, I was sent to India by the Museum to do a series of biographical exhibits in diorama style. The first of these was to be a diorama of the "Roof of the World"—the Himalayas—and our base of operations was to be in Darjeeling.

I prepared to leave for India with photographer Ario Gatti late that year, and planned our arrival there to coincide with the end of the monsoon season. But for several reasons the locale and subject matter of our first exhibit were changed, and when we arrived in Calcutta our new destination was Gauhati in Assam. However, due to an impending invasion by the Chinese, we were not permitted to enter Assam. In fact, we were advised to return to Canada.

We had travelled half-way around the world and we had a ton of equipment in Calcutta: I was determined not to return to Canada empty-handed. I applied for permission to work in the Western Ghats in South India, an area strangely similar, faunally, to the hill country of Assam. This was finally although somewhat reluctantly granted, and we started the frantic task of rerouting everything and making new arrangements. Eventually, we flew to Coimbatore in western Madras, and with the invaluable aid of Mr. Giles Thurnham of Tea Estates Ltd., investigated localities in the Nilgiris, Palnis, and Anamallais. We finally settled on a region at 3,500 feet in the Anamallais (Elephant Hills), and stayed with Roger and June Hands on the Injipara estate in the Stanmore group of Tea Estates Ltd.

For six weeks we collected material that we later assembled into the Indian Monsoon forest diorama, the first of our ecological biome groups.

174

The Tree Watcher

I had to spend several chafing, impatient days in Coimbatore. I was looking foward to reaching the hills with their tea gardens, jungle *sholas,* and wild animals. I had learned, in Calcutta and Madras, however, that there were many creatures to be seen in the peaceful parts of Indian cities: a park, the river bank or the temple grounds. When my work for the day had been accomplished, I often walked to the nearest temple. In most south Indian cities these are impressive structures, but what the average visitor sees is actually the portal *gopuram,* and not the shrine itself. Some of these skyscraper pylons rise up two hundred feet and may have a dozen or more storeys. A corridor passes through the base of the *gopuram* with rooms on either side for the doorkeepers and a staircase leading up to landings of each "floor". The lower storeys have vertical sides, but those above slope inwardly, each succeeding one being smaller than the one below it. In aggregate, this forms a sort of steep-sided, flat-topped pyramid. Front, sides, and back are embellished with a crowded assemblage of brightly-coloured statues representing dieties and sacred personages from the inexhaustible resources of Hindu mythology. There are also elephants, sacred cows, demons, devils, monkeys, and goblins —mystic and weaponed figures, multiplied and repeated, in rising ranks and receding tiers up to the great horns of the roof.

During my stay in south India, I was privileged to see a number of famous temples. In the *gopuram* of the Mylapore Temple at Madras there are seven hundred figures. Others have over a thousand. I wouldn't hazard a guess at the numbers on the four huge *gopurams* of the Temple of Chidambaram, those of the eighth-century

175

Kailasanatha Temple at Canjeecaram, or those of the Great Temple of Tanjore. Perhaps the most impressive shrine was the Minaksi (the fish-eyed goddess) at Madura. It has nine *gopurams*, all well over a hundred feet high, enclosing a huge tank, or *jheel* (a sort of reservoir), called *Swarnapushpadarini*, "the Tank of the Golden Lilies".

The attraction of temple grounds was that there were usually groves of palm trees and gardens with shrubbery, which meant birds. Once, in the city of Mysore, I was taken by Sri. Subaya through the *gopurams* and into the shrine area itself. We paused a moment to inspect the *lingam* (a stylized stone phallic symbol signifying Siva), and then the shrines in the form of carts, or chariots, with carved stone wheels. I was anxious to get a look at the swallows, though, which were flying about over the big tank in the centre of the arena. They were Wiretailed and Striated Swallows. On a patch of parched grass, Pied and Common Mynas foraged. On one of the *gopurams* were a half dozen Pariah Kites.

The temples are a naturalist's observing place in the heart of Indian cities. Not only are the *gopurams* tall perches for birds, the faithful do not forget their cohabitants: food is left—a few grains of wheat or rice, some small portion of a *chapati* or a fragment of fruit—for the lesser creatures. Sacred monkeys scramble about on the steps or climb over the lower statues of the pyramid. Pariah Kites, Jungle Crows, House Crows, and Longbilled and Whitebacked Vultures perch on the summit, in the palms or strut about the grounds. Three-striped and Five-striped Palm Squirrels scurry about exploring the ledges. Gentle-appearing yet palpably belligerent Spotted Doves and Collared Turtle Doves mingle with wild and domestic Rock Doves, squabbling and quarrelling over a few cereal grains. A more inappropriate bird could hardly have been chosen as a symbol of peace than a dove. In truth they are aggressive, belligerent, and intolerant of each other. Their basic attribute is their toothsomeness. Fat, tasty, and of adequate size, they are choice prey for predatory animals. I saw many other birds and small beasts, butterflies, dragonflies, and beetles (not to mention cockroaches) in parvises of the temples. I could always be sure of a brief respite from the dust and noise and toil of the cities—only the heat followed one into these temple areas.

At last Ario and I arrived at Injipara, a tea estate at some 3,500 feet in the Anamallais, the Elephant Hills of the Western Ghats. To the north range the higher peaks, dominated by round-knobbed nine-thousand foot Anamudi, "The elephant's cranium". The upper reaches of the hills are above timberline and are clothed in long rich grass, the home of Gaur and Nilgiri Tahr.

We were given huge and comfortable rooms by Roger and June Hands in the Estate house. (Roger managed the estate and the factory.)

After we got settled in, we started to search for a suitable site for our field work, a site not far from transportation and yet in relatively untouched forest. Such a location is not easily found in densely populated India. Fortunately, on the estate there was a fine patch of jungle, called a *shola* in South India. There were tall trees with dense undergrowth of thorny shrubs and vines, and the floor of the forest was covered by ferns, Cardamom, and other plants.

The next task was to locate a suitable area within the *shola* to set up our field lab.

The natural clearing made in the forest by the fall of a giant tree provides an excellent observation area and working space, In our *shola* just such a tree had crashed at the top of a ridge. A day's work cleared away the debris and provided us with light and with clean, level ground. By roughly levelling the top of the recumbent tree trunk, we had an adequate lab-table.

We soon got used to the sounds of jungle "carpenters"—beetle larvae busily engaged in the monumental task of reducing the heart-wood of the big tree to sawdust. The odour caused by the jungle chemists took a little longer to get accustomed to. Moulds, fungi, and bacteria working on the cambium layer produced a sweetish smell of ferment, reminiscent of stale homebrew.

The surrounding forest contained the species of plants and animals that we wanted. So, for the next month we made daily trips to the forest with the necessary supplies: bags of jute, jars of formalin, gallon cans of liquid latex, bundles of plastic bags, pails of water, and an eighteen-foot ladder. All had to be carried on our backs along the crude track that we had hacked out up a steep ridge from the nearest point at which the car could be parked, a mile away.

Wherever I go on museum fieldwork, or on a holiday for that matter, I am told that the weather is "unusual". I have come to the conclusion that there is no such thing as "usual" weather. India was no exception. There was, in 1963, an abnormally prolonged south-west monsoon. During the first week at the jungle lab, our work was hampered by heavy rain. We began to understand why the cry of the Hawk-cuckoo, repeated *ad nauseum* in the rains, has given it the vernacular name of "Brain-fever bird". And the wet woods brought out the blood-sucking jungle land leeches, hordes of which travelled the forest floor like inch worms and attacked us with fine enthusiasm.

The high humidity prevented us from making moulds of tree trunks and rocks because the slow-setting moulding material would not have cured. Instead, we hunted through the dripping forest to collect the animal specimens we needed. Birds of strange form and colourful plumage abounded. There were Goldenfronted Leafbirds, as green as leaves, and betrayed only by their golden crowns and oriole-like song. Clumsy Great Pied Hornbills, as big as turkeys, flopped heavily through the tree tops, a whole flock intent on alighting on a branch with barely enough space for one, squawking raucously and tumbling and tottering in farcical manner. White-breasted Kingfishers, oddly out of place in the riverless *shola,* pounced on lizards rather than fish. Hill Mynahs, the "talking" birds of pet shops, were a nuisance; spying us, they would then warn all other creatures away with their vituperative language. There were cat-sized, wild and wary Indian Giant Squirrels, and modestly beaut-iful Grey Jungle Fowl. One day our lab site was visited by a pair of Heartspotted Woodpeckers, surely among the most whimsically incongruous birds I have ever seen. Scarcely larger than Nuthatches, they are adorned with long, flamboyant crests, very thin necks, dumpy pear-shaped bodies and very short, rounded tails. In colour, they are creamy-ochre and black, with a series of small heart-shaped spots on the sides of the breast and flanks. They climbed about like right-side-up nuthatches, and their movements were comically jerky with much bobbing and clownish, sidewise inclinations of the head. They have the seemingly inanimate jouncing jiggle of mechanical toys.

On another dark and rainy day, I collected a jet-black Racquet-tailed Drongo, which plummeted down into a dense growth of cardamom in a ravine bottom. I realized that I would never find the black bird on the dark forest floor without first clearing out the undergrowth and I set about levelling the plants and shrubs of the area with a heavy tea-pruning knife and piling them in a neat stack on a spot I had already searched. I was about to cut down a small sapling, but before doing so, I glanced up to see if, by chance, the bird had got caught in its branches. There, directly above me, not three feet from my head was a coiled Largescaled Lancehead, one of the highly venomous, green, tree-climbing pit-vipers of South India. A stroke of the knife would have brought it tumbling on top of me. Instead, it was duly photographed and added to our collection. A few moments later I found the drongo.

A bird that I particularly wanted was the Indian Lorikeet. The only place that I had seen them, however, was in the guava trees in my hostess's garden, early in the morning; I did not think hunting in her garden a guest's prerogative. Fortunately, I learned that these birds are a pest, as they destroy much of the yearly harvests. Thus, with my hostess's blessing, I planned my "garden" hunt. I ordered a 5:00 a.m. "bed-tea" and turned in early. It was still quite dark when I made my way down to the guava grove. I chose a tree that I knew the little parrots frequented, and sat down on a stone wall in optimum range for the dustshot.

Early evening and dawn are poor times for concentration. Too much is happening. I watched a shaft of sunlight pierce the leaden clouds and brighten the tawny crests of the Grass Hills; I listened to the calls of the Crow Pheasant and the Koel; and heard the distant scream of a Black Eagle. A Hoopoe called from the tennis court. A Banded Krait slithered slowly along the stone wall and disappeared into a crevice. As the light increased, the guava tree became outlined against the eastern radiance and I half-consciously marvelled at the quantity of fruit on the tree. It seemed there were scores more guavas on that tree than I had thought, but I forced myself to watch the brightening sky for flighting parrots.

Out of the corner of my eye I perceived a movement in one of the guava branches. A "guava" had sprouted a wing, which it proceeded to flutter. Another "guava" squawked. A third swung itself from a normal hanging position to perch upright above it.

Lorikeets. Dozen of them, and I had been sitting there with the shotgun on my knee for ten or fifteen minutes actually *looking* at them. They were hanging in clusters, heads down like bats; some hanging by one foot, some by both. I watched for a while and when

179

most of them were awake and climbing about, some flew off, so I took careful aim and fired. Four little round balls dropped. I picked up three Indian Lorikeets and a guava.

"What a marvellous adaptation," said Ario, when I told him about it.

"Yes," I replied, "except that these little parrots have been sleeping like that for centuries before guavas were introduced into India from tropical America."

We had almost despaired of accomplishing our work before our time ran out. The rains persisted, and the leeches kept biting. Every evening when I took to my tub, the bath water around my legs turned pink as old and new leech bites opened up. Then one morning I awoke to a cloudless sky. "Today we start on the latex moulding," I thought, and hurried through breakfast.

We needed casts of three big trees, and I decided that I wanted an Indian Ironwood, *Messua ferrea,* a Jak-fruit, *Artocarpus integra,* and a Teak, *Tectona grandis.* To bring back the real thing presented a logistics proposition beyond either our physical or fiscal resources. Also, the importation of forty feet of assorted, raw foreign lumber with all its attendant zoological and botanical tenants would have resulted I'm sure in a somewhat reluctant, if not downright truculent, attitude from Canada Customs Quarantine Service.

On earlier expeditions we had devised a method of reproducing trees and large boulders by taking rubber moulds (negative impressions) of them in the field. Upon returning to the studio in the museum, latex casts (positive impressions) are taken from the moulds. These are then wrapped around prefabricated forms of the exact size and shape of the original tree or rock, and coloured from reference sketches and colour photographs.

So, on this first sunny morning, my Tamil helper, Duroswami, and I began to "butter" the latex on a big Ironwood trunk with our hands. The rubber paste was worked into every crack and crevice of the bark from the exposed roots to a height of fifteen feet.

Just as we completed the job we heard the ill-omened resonance of thunder. The monsoon was not through with us yet! In humid weather our latex takes about three days to "mature". A heavy rain would wash it off wasting our work and, worse still, depleting our precious stock of special formula latex, unavailable in India.

180

We scrambled and floundered down the rude track to the car. The trunk held many yards of polyethylene sheeting for just such an eventuality. This we tied up in bundles as heavy as we could carry. Little ninety-pound Duroswami matched my burden and was less tuckered out when we arrived back at the tree.

Even as we reached it, the first big, heavy drops of rain fell. The sky was saturnine black to the southwest. Quickly we unfolded the long plastic streamers and Duroswami, clutching one end of a sheet, scaled the ladder like a squirrel. One end of each of a dozen streamers was securely wrapped about the tree above the latex and their free ends guyed by ropes to adjacent trees. When the task was completed, we felt that our mould was safe from all but a gale-driven rain.

While we sat under the shelter of our improvised tent, however, having a relaxing smoke and getting our breaths, I realized that our troubles were not over. A band of Nilgiri Langurs—big skinny black monkeys with ridiculous long, blonde hairdos—began to take great interest in our singular and entertaining structure. As soon as we left they would surely descend to investigate.

My concern was very nearly—but not quite—as much for the monkeys as for my mould. I could envision Langurs with hands, faces, and fur clotted with sticky latex, which is almost impossible to remove without using its specific solvent.

I decided to leave Duroswami on guard while I went to the estate to eat. Then I would return to take over watchman duty for the night. It was an unattractive prospect. I had several specimens in need of attention. The night would be cold and wet. Anyhow, I reflected, fighting off jungle leeches would keep me from falling asleep.

At the estate house I explained the situation to Roger Hands. He said that that would be unnecessary because a *chaukidar*, night watchman, could be hired for a few rupees. Indeed, a man was found who was not only willing but eager to accept the assignment. I took him back, equipped him with some food and tea and an enormous black umbrella. He spoke only Tamil, but by sketches and gestures I conveyed to him what was required.

The next morning, at daybreak, I returned to the site. I could hardly contain my mirth at the unearthly scene: dawn in the jungle, torrential rain, a ghost-like tree with its trunk encased in a glistening, smooth coat of creamy-white latex and bearing, eighteen feet above the ground, its broad translucent marquee of plastic. Beneath it sat the tiny man with dark brown skin, clad in a high-crowned, white turban, a very large white shirt, and a breachclout, and holding in his hand a huge, black, tightly-furled umbrella. He was dry, comfortable and cheerful, and the mould was intact. For three nights my "tree watcher" guarded the tree with zeal and loyalty. Once he was surrounded by Langurs and some of the big males had approached to within ten feet of him, but he had put them to flight by pointing his gigantic "brolly" at them and flipping it open.

On the third day, we made a vertical cut down one side of the cured latex and simply peeled it off in one piece, dusted it with talc, rolled it up, and tied it in a relatively small, neat cylinder. Later we did the same with a Jak-fruit tree. Moulding the Teak was another story, but eventually we were able to pack all three moulds into a tea chest for shipment home. The technique enabled us to bring back to Toronto the equivalent, for exhibit purposes, of three fifteen-foot lengths of Indian trees in a box two and a half feet square. Best of all, there was no objection from the Quarantine Service.

Sri. M. A. Badshah

There was an audience of about twenty-five people in the Club in the little town of Valparai perched up in the tea country of Anamallais, the Elephant Hills of Madras. I had been ushered into a seat in the front row. (All the back row seats were occupied by those who wanted to insure a quick and furtive exit to the bar when the lights were turned out.) I expected that, as is so often the case at "lectures", especially those to small and incapacious groups of listeners, it would be a bomb.

But when the lecturer appeared, I knew somehow that this one wouldn't be. He was a big man, well over six feet tall. He had a good face and an engaging smile. His name was Sri. M. A. Badshah, Chief Wildlife Officer for the State of Madras. I leaned back and felt better. It had been Roger Hands's suggestion that the visit to Valparai that evening might be worthwhile. I had a heavy work load that day and had begged off; the work had gone well, however, and at sunset I agreed to go. At that moment I had no idea of the benefits or the ordeals I was letting myself in for.

There was an introduction by the club president and the perfectly composed Mr. Badshah then began his talk. He had good slides of Indian Elephant, Tiger, Gaur, Nilgai, Black Buck, and Sambar. Suddenly he shifted gears. "I visited Canada a couple of years ago," he said, "and the wildlife people there took me all over and showed me their fauna. I think you might enjoy seeing a few slides of the other side of the world."

There were pictures of White-tailed Deer and Bighorn Sheep, Black Bear and Beaver. He described them well. With the next slide he said, "This is a bird that I saw and photographed in Manitoba. I can't remember its name."

It was an excellent picture of a Brown Thrasher and as I was only six feet or so from the speaker I whispered, "Brown Thrasher".

Badshah bellowed, "A gentleman here in the front row has re-minded me; it's the Brown Thrasher, a bird belonging to a family that has no representative in India."

The next slide was a Cedar Waxwing. "This one is a . . ." he hesitated and looked at me.

"Cedar Waxwing," I whispered.

A little later as he spoke of the alarming destruction of wildlife throughout the world, his slide revealed a man holding a mounted specimen of the extinct Passenger Pigeon. I had known the man for thirty-three years and saw him almost every day in the Museum. He was the ROM's assistant curator of birds!

"This," said Badshah, "is a gentleman who kindly showed me his fine collection of Passenger Pigeons in the Royal Ontario Museum in Toronto." He glanced at me and chuckled, ". . . and I can't remember *his* name."

"Jim Baillie," I whispered.

"The gentleman in the front row not only knows the birds I am showing you, but also the people!" he shouted. "I'm going to ask him to help me finish this lecture."

It wasn't difficult. The birds, after all, were those I knew well. The people were my compatriots and colleagues in Canada. By the time the evening was ended, Sri. Badshah and I were good friends.

"Why don't you come up to Mudamallai and see our animals?" he asked. "You can't leave India without seeing Gaur and Tiger and Elephants."

I promised I would try. Roger and I got back to Injipara in the wee small hours of the morning.

It was several days later when Roger said, "Look, there's no sign of the end of the monsoon here, you can't work with latex moulds in this weather, and the leeches will be insufferable in the shola. Why don't you drive up to Mysore and see the *Dasara*—the great procession with floats, elephants, camels, and bands put on by the Maharajah of Mysore? It'll be sunny and warm up there and you can stop in at Bandipur and Mudamallai on the way back."

The suggestion made sense, especially the part about avoiding jungle leeches for a few days. With Chinnaswami driving, Ario and I left the next morning. It was still raining. In order to get to the city of Mysore, we had to pass through Mudamallai and Bandipur, the adjoining wildlife sanctuaries on the Madras-Mysore border.

I asked Chinnaswami to stop at the ranger headquarters in Mudamallai. I saw the head ranger.

"I would like to make arrangements for a Rest House, or a *dak* bungalow, for two or three days, and also to arrange for a riding elephant and mahout. We'll be coming back this way in a few days."

"I'm very sorry, *Sahib,*" said the ranger with that sad, Indian negative headshake, "but all of our houses and elephants are booked solidly for two weeks. There is just no possibility of accommodating your party."

Sorely disappointed, I returned to the car.

"No soap," I said to Ario and Chinnaswami, "they just haven't got anything for us."

I was about to climb into the car when a jeep driven by a ranger came along the mainroad and turned into the ranger station.

"Hello, my friend," boomed a familiar voice, "what are *you* doing here?" It was Sri.M.A.Badshah.

"Hello," I returned, "you remember me from Valparai?"

"If you can identify all my birds and all my Canadian friends, I think I should be able to identify you!" he retorted, laughing heartily.

I explained our presence and our disappointment.

"You will remember that I invited you to come up and see our animals," he roared. "You will come back here at any time of day or night; you will come to Karkudi and stay with me in my bungalow, and you will have a good riding elephant and mahout for as long as you want them, and I will listen to no protests! *I* am in charge here."

Some of the adventures initiated by meeting Sri. Badshah in Valparai are recounted in the chapters entitled "Gaur from the Gaddi" and "Happiness is a scream in the night"; I pass over these at the moment, however, to tell of the final episode in my aquaintance with this ebullient man.

Tropical darkness had descended when I reached the Queen's Hotel in the city of Madras. It must have been after 7:00 p.m. I peeled off my limp jacket and pulled off my shoes. There was an easy chair; so I flopped into it. A few minutes rest, a wash, a bite to eat, and early to bed. It had been one of the most tiring days I could remember, not only a long, strenuous day but a hot one.

In less than five minutes there was a knock on the door. When I opened it I found myself face to face with none other than Sri.M.A. Badshah. He was smiling broadly, and his big right hand clutched a bottle of Indian whiskey. It was about one-third full.

Frankly, I was as much dismayed as pleased. Much as I liked and admired him, he was the last person I wanted to see at that moment. There would be no sleep tonight, not with this great human dynamo on my hands. But hadn't I roused him out of a sound sleep at Karkudi at 1:30 a.m. with the blast of a car horn only three weeks before? "This is a shuteye for a shuteye," I thought.

I hauled him into the room. "Come in, come in, Mr. Badshah, take the armchair. How on earth did you know I was here?"

"I knew you would be along this way sometime this week," he replied, "so, I called all the hotels that you might stay at, and asked them to let me know when one of them got a request for a reservation from you. When this one phoned me this morning, I simply called Indian Air Lines and asked for the time of arrival of the Bangalore flight. Allowed time for you to get your baggage and make the trip in, and came on over." He laughed heartily. "Let's have a drink."

"All right," I said, "I'll have room service send up some glasses and water."

The remnant of the crock soon disappeared under Sri. Badshah's masterful pouring. He looked disconsolately at the empty. Madras state has prohibition areas and the city was one of them. However, as a temporary resident of the state, I had been granted a permit for eight units (eight quarts) per month for two months. My second month still had its full quota.

"I'll get another if you will excuse me for a few minutes," I said.

I went down to the desk and was directed to the back of the small bar at which sat a few "temporary residents" and a few others who, by getting a doctor's certificate that they were alcoholics and by giving up their driving privileges, were issued a permit to consume liquor. This was not as great a hardship as it might seem because most of them had chauffeurs.

I produced my permit, a six-page, foolscap-sized chunk of cheap, heavy grey-brown wrapping paper tied together with string. It contained such illuminating statements as, "Indian-made foreign spirits means spirits manufactured and compounded in India and made in colour and flavour to resemble gin, brandy, whiskey or rum . . ." and "one unit represents one quart bottle of whiskey or other spirits, including liquor."

The domestic liquors were indeed simply appropriately diluted alcohol flavoured to loosely resemble foreign liquors. The brandy was a caramel-licorice tainted fire. Rum I think resembled explosive brown sugar and shoe polish. The gin was better, but still tasted like alcohol doctored with dime-store perfume, and made one think of Socrates. The whiskey—it had the volatility of carbon-tetrachloride. It vaporized on contact, backed up over the attic of one's mouth, hit the antrums and sinuses and poured down your nostrils. Sometimes I felt I should be looking in the mirror to see if I were breathing fire.

In a few minutes I returned to the room. I had two bottles of Indian whiskey. "One for us, and one for you," I said.

"Come," he shouted, "you must come to meet my family. Then we will go somewhere to eat and I will take you out to the Deer Park!" I supressed the groan, left a message at the desk to be called at 5:00 a.m. (my plane to Calcutta left at 6:00 a.m.) and accompanied him to his car.

There was a charming visit with his wife and family. There were several whiskies, mercifully drowned in an orange pop, and some delicious canapes. About 10:30 p.m. Badshah said, "Let us go out to eat. I will take you to a little place where I used to eat as a student."

It was a small, crowded, low-ceilinged place with about a dozen oilcloth covered tables. It had a heavy permeation of cooking and other odours that I tried not to identify. In a few minutes we had a large bowl of vegetable and chicken curry. We dipped in with the index and second finger of the right hand and scooped morsels into our mouths (the left hand is "unclean" and is reserved for such tasks as are inspired by somatic functions).

I was actually enjoying the food and the conversation until the cockroach climbed the side of the curry basin and peered over the rim. It paused and waved its antennae at me. I calculated the distance, engaged Badshah's attention, and shot out my hand waggling the fingers furiously. It scared off the cockroach, but my hand landed with a resounding *splat* in the curry. The cockroach raced across the oilcloth and down the table leg. Obviously, it was terribly surprised and insulted. Discrimination, that's what it was. As casually as possible, I wiped the curry off my hand on the grey, greasy rag provided for that purpose, which hung from a hook on the edge of the tabletop. It was hard to do without the assistance of the other hand, and when I brought it up it still had rice on it. I didn't dare consider whether I'd got the rice from the bowl or from the rag.

It was when I got the dead cockroach out of the curry bowl on one of my next scoops, that I stopped eating. I continued to take the odd scoop but managed to come up with nothing on my fingers or to deposit such as I did under the table on the floor. The heat was oppressive. There was a faint smell of some kind of pyrethrum incense in the still, stale air. I wasn't sure I could stand it much longer.

"Come on," bellowed Badshah, "we must get out to the Deer Park, it's nearly midnight."

Outside, the air had become cool. It was almost cold, but it was refreshing even if it carried a distinct tincture of human excrement.

As we walked to the car, Sri. Badshah spied a small stand behind which squatted a man wrapped in some unidentifiable form of clothing, best described as rags.

"Ho," cried Badshah, "we must have some *pann*. It's good after supper." *Pann* is a combination of the fruits of the Betel-nut Palm, *Areca catechu,* and fresh leaf of the Betel-pepper, *Piper betel.* The crushed palm fruits are placed on the leaf and smeared with lime. It is the chewing gum of the east—used by possibly eight hundred million people.

It seemed like a good idea. I'd never chewed Betel before, and I had heard that it was pleasant and stimulating. Besides, it might counteract the recurring curry. Badshah bought two and, folding the leaf around the mash, we popped them in between the lower front teeth and the lower lip and climbed into the car. Now betel stimulates a tremendous flow of saliva; so, a can was placed between us on the floor. We must have made a revolting sight driving along and expectorating a pinkish fluid into a spittoon. It was not long before I wanted to be rid of my betel, but I didn't want to appear a pantywaist; and, because there was a cool wind blowing, the car windows were closed. There was no way of furtively rolling the windows down far enough to expel the now undesirable wad. Its flavour was not unpleasant, but it was strong and strange.

The drive was longer than I had expected. Half an hour went by and still no sign of the Deer Park. I figured I could get rid of the betel once we got there without offending my host. At last I had a brain wave. "How about a drink?" I asked, and I chortled to myself when he roared, "Yes, yes my friend, the bottle's in the glove compartment." I handed it to him. He spat—but only pink saliva. The wad was shifted to his cheek; he slugged down a big shot of fire water and handed back the bottle. Hoist on my own petard, I did likewise. At least the burning rawness of a spoonful eliminated for a few moments the now pervasive taste of the betel. The betel was powerful and persistent and soon fought back. Now I had the foretaste of the betel *and* Indian whiskey added to the aftertaste of the curry, which my fancy persuaded me had a suggestion of cockroach about it.

At last we swung into the Deer Park, heavily wooded and pitch dark. I tried another ruse. "I have to relieve myself," I said, "can we stop at a convenient place?" It wasn't a lie, I had to relieve myself of the betel. He pulled up. "So do I, I'll come with you." For a moment I thought I had been frustrated again, but I dashed far into the trees, dumped the betel and, waiting for an appropriate time, returned to the car.

Now I felt better. The cool air had a bracing effect, and soon we began to see animals in the beams of the headlights. Mongooses of at least two species appeared on the road, and then we saw Blackbuck by the dozen. Before we left the park, we had seen Chital, Barking Deer, and the Indian Hare as well as Nightjars and Gerbilles on the road.

It seemed somehow insubstantial, dream-like, driving through the sanctuary deserted of cars and people, in the middle of the night. Above, the closed canopy of the forest cut out even the light of the stars. Below, just the reflection of the head-lights off tree trunks and patches of shrubbery. Then two small glowing lamps of eyeshine, quickly going out and evolving into a gorgeous spotted Chital or Blackbuck bounding across the road in the full glare of the car lights. Sometimes a dozen jack-o-lanterns would abruptly appear at once, to break up into a herd of leaping deer or antelopes.

Injipara and the tea gardens; the sad farewell to June and Roger; the long drive down the Ghat road and across the plains to Coimbatore; the drudgery of paper work at the railway station; the visit in gratitude to Mr. Koshi and the old gunsmith; the call at the Indian Airlines to pick up tickets; luncheon with the Giles Thurnhams—for me six Pintail Snipe shot the day before by Giles, and a bottle of Kingfisher beer; the dash to Coimbatore airport; afternoon tea with an Indian army officer in Banglore; the improbable seating incident which placed me beside a young Danish hygrographer who had worked in the Canadian arctic with my friend Max Dunbar; the heat and confusion of Madras airport; Badshah at the door.

Some days there is just too much! It was agonizing to try to stay awake and conversational on the trip back in to Nungambakkam, the Madras suburb where the Queen's Hotel was located. Badshah finally dropped me at the hotel at something after 4:45 a.m. I had only time to shave, pack my bags, and drop exhausted into the armchair. I had just lit a cigarette—more for something to do to keep me from falling into a dead sleep—when the phone rang.

"Good morning," said a cheerfully pleasant Indian voice. "It is time to get up. Your car is waiting at the door. It has been nice having you stay with us, *isn't it?*"

"Yes, I've enjoyed every minute of it. Thank you."

Indeed I had no complaint to make about any feature of the hostelry.

How could I? I'd spent little more than half an hour in the place.

Gaur from the Gaddi

In the undulating country, at an altitude of 3,000 to 3,800 feet, at the foot of the Nilgiri Hills lies the Mudumallai Sanctuary. The region is one of fairly heavy rainfall; hence the denseness of the forest. It is on the Madras State side of the Moyar River, which is the natural interstate boundary between Madras and Mysore. Ario and I left Mysore where we had been viewing the Dussarah festival and photographing a procession that featured bullock-drawn carts upon which were inelegantly coloured and tinselled floats, caparisoned elephants, one of them bearing the Maharajah of Mysore in a golden howdah, cavalry with pennoned lances, and many other gaudily decorated exhibits.

We had taken too much time in adjoining Bandipur Sanctuary on the Mysore side looking at wild Peafowl, Grey Jungle Fowl, Sambar, Indian Elephants, and Sloth Bears. We arrived at Karkudi and the Forest Rest House in Mudamallai about 1:30 a.m. We had been

190

assured by Sri. M.A. Badshah, however, that no matter what hour it was we would be welcome. If it were late we were to raise a clamour and he would get up. Nonetheless I had misgivings as we drove up to the dark house, surrounded by forest. It *was* an ungodly hour to come calling! As we stepped out of the car, we could hear the howling of Asian Wild Dogs off in the jungle. Nearby, a Collared Scops Owl monotonously repeated his mellow, questioning *whit?*, pausing a few seconds between each call.

Even as we considered, in whispers, what to do, our driver Chinnaswami let go with a loud blast on the car horn. This started a wild outcry from a troup of Common Langurs that must have been sleeping in a stand of bamboos not far away. It was too late to protest and besides Chinnaswami probably knew more about the protocol of early morning visiting in India than we did. Certainly his tactics brought results. The Rest House exploded with lights, the door burst open, and we were surrounded by houseboys. In moments we were escorted inside and our luggage disappeared into the deeper recesses of the house.

There were stifled yawns and muffled thumps from what we assumed to be Badshah's bedroom, and in a few minutes that large gentleman, clad in handsome blue pajamas, appeared. The charm and courtesy of the East showed itself, as it had on so many other occasions. Our reception was as warmly enthusiastic as it could have been even at a more civilized hour. We were taken to a comfortable room and, as we had taken the precaution of bringing a quart of whiskey, we were soon settled with full glasses in our hands discussing the next day's program. Shikarees, a riding elephant, and a mahout had been reserved for us for two days, and we were to start at 5:30 in the morning. Sri. Badshah promised the sight of elephants, Gaur, Sambar, Chital, Barking Deer, and numerous other lesser creatures. We were to discover that he was as good as his word. At 4:00 a.m., we turned in for an hour's sleep. Just as I climbed into bed, a Leopard coughed not far from the Rest House.

It seemed that I had hardly hit the pillow when I was awakened by the houseboy bearing "bed tea". Just before dawn, we scrambled up onto the gaddi, the platform-like seat, on the elephant's back, and the big beast rose from her kneeling position and began her slow and deliberate shuffling into the jungle.

The air was chill, but it was a fine morning with promise of sun and heat before many hours passed. The sun came up quickly and light stabbed down the hillsides awakening the diurnal creatures of the forest.

The first birds we saw were Red-vented Bulbuls, smoky-brown Cardinal-like birds with a conspicuous crimson patch under the tail. Then a thin nasal voice drew our attention to a little bird busily engaged in rustling up his morning meal on the moss-covered limb of a big Sal tree. This little bird was almost identical with the common European Nuthatch or the North American Whitebreasted; it was a strong deep reddish-brown below—the Chestnutbellied Nuthatch of India.

It seemed that we were moving slowly, but when I tried to use the binoculars I realized that the amble of the elephant was deceptively fast. A moment's glimpse was all I got of most of the birds I saw during the first hour, and many went unidentified.

We soon came to a small stream lined with bamboos. The elephant had to negotiate low but slippery mud banks on both sides as we crossed. It was remarkable how careful she was in climbing down the near bank. The forefoot was placed testingly on the mud. If a spot proved satisfactory the foot was stamped two or three times to make a firm, flat step. This was repeated with the other front foot a little farther down. As she progressed downward on a diagonal, the hind feet were placed carefully in the "steps" made by the forefeet. Two or three minutes were taken to effect the descent of the sloping, perhaps six-or-seven-foot-high terrace. No such precautions were taken on the opposite slope. She scrambled up the equally steep embankment in a rush that almost dumped us off the gaddi.

The bamboo thicket was a populous place. A herd of common Langurs—big, slender, whitish monkeys with long tails and black faces shielded by silvery eyebrows, the hairs of which stuck straight out like a visor—leaped and climbed at our approach. They were silent and quickly melted into the leafy canopy of the bamboo. The mahout halted the elephant; presently we could see a number of black faces watching us. Each langur seemed instantly aware of being detected, however, and one or two seconds of observation was all it allowed before disappearing with hardly a movement of the surrounding clusters of spear-shaped bamboo leaves.

192

A rush of noisy wingbeats and harsh double-noted cries heralded the approach of a flock of Blue-winged Parakeets. They arrived in the bamboos, twisting, turning, and dashing wildly about before settling. Then they proceeded to climb and clamber about, upside-down, hanging by one foot, and generally behaving like parakeets —handsome blue-green birds with pinkish-grey crown, back and breast, and a brilliant blue-green and black collar. This is the species known as the "Bababudan Parrot", frequently seen in the markets of Mysore and Calcutta and with the spurious reputation of being able to converse in Arabic.

An almost imperceptible pressure of the big splay foot of the mahout on the elephant's nape set us in motion again and disturbed a large animal that had been lying in the shelter of a stump. It looked like an overgrown rodent—less than two feet long and about a foot high in the middle of its back. Its head was small and pointed.

"What's that?" asked Ario.

"It's a Mouse-deer," I answered.

"Deer?" said Ario. "We've seen bigger rats in Trinidad."

"It's not a true deer," I explained. "A better name for it is Chevrotain, but it is an ungulate." The Pacas that we had seen in Trinidad were very similar in size. Certainly it was inferior in bulk to that big Canadian rodent, the Beaver. It had an overstuffed body, short in the withers and highest just in front of the well-padded rump. Its legs seemed too thin and delicate for its inflated torso. In general it looked like a fat bologna propped up on four swizzle sticks. It walked with a peculiar stiff-legged mincing gait on the very tips of its hooves, but it was attractively coloured. Its dark greyish-brown coat was grizzled with buff-yellow, and along its sides were streaks and spots of purest white. To our surprise, it suddenly bolted into the stream we had just crossed, swam half-way across, submerged, and disappeared!

As we reached level ground, two small thin men suddenly appeared as if out of thin air. The almost black skin of their faces, legs, and arms contrasted sharply with their loose, khaki garments. They conversed briefly in Tamil with the mahout, giving a fine display of gleaming white eyeballs and teeth. Our shikarees had been with us all the time, but they had moved with such stealth and silence that we had not been aware of their presence.

We had an opportunity now, in the stronger light, to get a look at our "chauffeur". He was about five feet tall, had a great shock of lustreless black hair, standing out at all angles from his head and face, and was wearing a kind of shift of some indeterminate shade of faded black. A more unprepossessing character would be hard to imagine, but as he remounted he flashed a smile revealing a set of the most perfectly formed, snowy white teeth I had ever seen. The important thing was that he was a first-rate mahout. The elephant responded instantly to his every subtle move. A good mahout and his elephant are almost a coalescence—anticipating each other's thoughts.

From the actions of the shikarees and the obvious pleasure of the mahout, we sensed that something worthy was about to unfold. The two trackers moved about thirty feet in front of the elephant, one to the left, the other to the right, and advanced swiftly forward. They were noting the flattened grass, a browsed shrub or other signs. Then I realized that the tantalizing bird whistles I had been hearing were, in fact, signals from these little hill people to the mahout.

After a quarter-mile, during which I saw little but a Blacknaped Hare and a Red Spurfowl, the shikarees halted, turned about, and headed toward us. As they passed us they silently gestured to the mahout. They melted into the forest behind us; there was silence save for the occasional gurgling snort from the elephant. Then we detected it: the unmistakable odour of oxen. The shikarees had done their work well. They had tracked down a herd of Gaur, and having guided us to it had retired to allow us to proceed alone.

We were in the midst of a Teak forest and, in spite of the anticipation of seeing one of the world's largest land animals, I found myself absorbed by the Teaks. Their leaves are as large as dinner plates—those of saplings and coppice shoots as much as three feet long and two and a half feet wide. They are an intense warm green, and the tree trunks, gracefully sinuous, are light yellowish-brown. The effect, as shafts of mid-morning sun pierced the leafy canopy above and tinged the lower foliage with gold, was enthralling. Teak is one of the few tropical trees that may be found in extensive, pure stands.

Moments later we came on a cow Gaur, her hide a shining plum colour, her nose rosy pink, and her legs from above the "knees" (in horseman's parlance) and hocks white as if she wore sox. She paid no

194

attention to our elephant, but to our chagrin the mahout paid as little to her and the elephant surged ahead. This we soon appreciated because as we entered a more open part of the Teak forest, we were plunged into the middle of the herd. A huge bull took my attention.

I had seen mounted specimens and photographs of Gaur, but neither had prepared me for such a beast as this. He stood a good eighteen hands (six feet) at the shoulder, his horns must have been more than thirty inches in length, greenish-yellow with black tips. His satin-like coat was so dark it looked black. Most impressive of all was the enormous ridge, caused by the great height of the spines of the anterior vertebrae that ran from his neck to the middle of his back and the strongly projecting brisket that looked like a butcher's cleaver. His weight must been a ton and a half. Even a big bull American Bison would have been dwarfed by him. There were about three dozen Gaur in the herd, six or seven mature bulls, an equal number of calves, and the rest cows and young bulls. Occasionally a bull would sound a deep reverberating bellow, and the cows *moo-ed* in typical bovine fashion. They were quite unconcerned by the presence of the elephant and we were able to go in among them.

There were distractions: once in the form of three majestic Sambar, one of them a massive stag whose three-tined antlers were well over three feet in length. Once it was five Chital, the superbly beautiful, white-spotted rufous deer of India. In my opinion its colour and form make it the most handsome of the deer family. One would think that such a brightly coloured animal would be conspicuous in the green forest, but this is not so. Unless it moves, few large animals are more difficult to see. The white spotting produces a cryptic pattern that effectively disrupts the body form. We also saw a Great Black Woodpecker that flounced heavily toward us, alighted on the bole of a Teak, and started hammering at the bark. This big fellow, larger than the Pileated Woodpecker of America, is jet black with scarlet crest and cheek patches, and white rump and belly. It was quite the largest woodpecker I had ever seen and, although I was surrounded by Gaur, I felt I would regret it if I didn't spend at least a few minutes watching him. His behaviour was very much like that of the Pileated. When he had found a spot on the Teak trees that promised food, he flicked off the bark with the same slanting blows and quick sidewise

195

prising of his big beak. Like the Pileated, he seemed to prefer working close to the ground. He had detected the tunnels of wood-boring ants or beetles about a foot and a half above the base of an old, deteriorating Teak. I later saw several other examples of his work at about the same height. Like the Pileated, he made rectangular rather than round holes.

A few moments later I drew the attention of the mahout to a movement in the lush grass that floored the Teak forest. He seemed amused and somewhat disdainful, but manoeuvered the elephant in that direction. The grass disturber proved to be a Hairy-nosed Porcupine. I felt slightly sheepish because I could imagine the contempt one of our Canadian bush-guides would have had for a tenderfoot who wanted to behold one of our porcupines after hiring the guide to show him bear or moose. The lumbering ground "Porky" proved to be a most interesting animal; when the elephant was close to him, he stood his ground, turned his back, and erected his formidable fifteen inch spines. He shook and rattled them vigorously, producing a loud, rustling clatter.

I have heard of people being accused of "advancing backward": here was a "critter" who not only could advance backward but could charge backward, inflicting painful and dangerous wounds on attacking dogs with its sharp quills. The elephant was commanded to halt, and the porcupine, still rattling his quills, meandered away.

No sooner had he disappeared and I was refocusing my attention on the Gaur than two Muntjacs, or Barking Deer, appeared in the clear, bounded through the herd of Gaur, and trotted right across our bow. Many times I have had the extraordinary experience of having travelled long distances, seeing hardly a sign of life, to come suddenly on an area that teemed with animals. This was one of them, and I wondered what had brought so many creatures together in this quiet glade. Was it, possibly, a salt lick?

I tried to communicate this question to the mahout by pantomine—with scooping fingers, digging hands, licking tongue, and chewing jaws. The result was almost calamitous: the mahout seemed to think I was hungry. I presume I *had* given a pretty fair imitation of the finger-scooping, two-handed feeding habits of the *panchamas*—the untouchables, or "outcastes". Anyway, with a fine show of consideration, he turned the elephant about and drove her

196

back in the direction from which we had entered the clearing. If I was hungry, then I must be taken back to the Rest House. This was the last thing I wanted, but it was only by elaborate gestures and great effort that I convinced him that I seldom bothered with lunch—that, in fact, the very idea of eating was rather abhorrent.

Such a rapid reversal of requests no doubt confused him to no end, but he just shook his head and guided the elephant back into the herd of Gaur. This time we were able to ride up to within a few feet of the master bull that I had admired so much before. At close range he was even more impressive. I thought I had never seen a more magnificent animal. I had already noticed his glowing coat (for all the world as if it had just been curried), his white sox, his pink nose, and his long greenish horns; now I was amazed to discover that his eyes were blue, as blue as those of a Siamese cat. He appeared to accept us as part of the elephant, an animal for which he apparently had no fear. This was puzzling, for surely he had gotten our scent, or was the elephant's even stronger?

We spent another hour among the Gaur. Ario used up three rolls of movie film, and I used up two thirty-sixes of 35 mm. We agreed that changing film in either the movie camera or the 35mm. camera on the back of that barcaroling elephant was a true aptitude test. We saw other animals in that sunlit, verdant space: crow-sized Malabar Grey Hornbills, Nilgiri Wood Pigeons, Purple Sunbirds, and Black-naped Blue Monarchs. A patch of bare rock served as a sunning spot for a big *agamid* lizard, named Sita's Lizard after Sita, the wife of Rama, god-hero of Hindu mythology. Since the distinguishing peculiarities of this lizard are its four instead of five toes on each foot, and the most gigantian dewlap conceivable, I wondered why it had been so named.

It was now past high noon, and the heat was becoming unbearable. Only a few wisps of cloud gave fleeting and feeble protection from the blistering sun, and our elephant had been on the march for seven hours. Now she rebelled. Her means of showing her displeasure were unorthodox but highly effective. Her trunk curled up until the nostril openings were directed squarely at the mahout and us. She gave an elephantine snort and enveloped us in an overpoweringly maladorous spray of aqueous vapour. Two servings convinced us that she had indeed worked hard, and that she had earned a bath and her

197

lunch back at the compound. As if to remind us of our thoughtlessness and inconsideration, she gave us two or three more samples from her atomizer on the way back.

That night, we had a choleric curry. South India is the true home of the curries: the name comes from the Tamil word *Kari,* a hot sauce. It was served fervently pungent, ardently acrid, peppery, passionately spiced, and above all irascibly scalding. I don't know what it tastes like. At the first bite, the peppers exploded rendering my taste buds impotent. From there on I ate for nourishment alone!

It seems remarkable that "hot" foods and hot countries go together. I suppose the custom had its origin in the covering up of the tainted flavour of "high" meats owing to the difficulty of retaining freshness in the heat. I had long before learned to deal with "hot" meals in Mexico where a Mexican friend explained that there were three kinds of chilis: *caliente,* hot; muchos *caliente,* very hot; and *imposible.*

Happiness is a Scream in the Night

A blood curdling scream ending in a gasping, choking gurgle . . . on a stiflingly hot night near a big sandalwood tree in South India . . . on a starlit, subzero night outside a window in Manitoba . . . on a dark winter's night close by a little log cabin twenty miles from the heart of downtown Toronto. . . .

It was an oppressively warm night on the road from Kotagiri to Mettupalaiyam in the State of Madras. It was so hot and humid that the customary heavy night-traffic was absent. (In India, those with produce to take to market habitually travel during the cooler hours of darkness.) Only a few two-wheeled oxcarts rumbled slowly along, without lights and with their occupants sprawled in fitful, jolting sleep in the rear of the carts. It was left to the oxen to do the steering. Ario Gatti, our driver Chinnaswami, and I stopped to stretch our legs and to eat the rice cakes that we had purchased earlier in the day in the town of Conoor. The sky to the east was being cleft rhythmically by ragged streaks of viciously furcate lightning. It had been a period of particularly bad storms, and only a few days before we had been delayed in Mysore by the shattered and twisted branches and trunks of trees that littered the road following a cyclonic storm. There was, of course, the grumbling of distant thunder. All in all, an appropriately Gothic setting for the events that were to follow. As we munched our rice cakes, I became aware of a stealthy scuffling in the branches of the great sandalwood tree under which we had parked the car. I was carrying my hunter's headlamp; so, I switched it on and trained its beam into the lower branches. A more comical sight than the one that met my eyes would be hard to imagine. Three rows of Bonnet Monkeys stared into the light in petrified amazement. They had ruddy-pink faces with deep-set, dark brown eyes under beetling brows, each face topped by a ludicrous centre-parted hairdo—some smoothed down as if with hair grease in typical "sheik" style of the 1920s, others with unruly swatches sticking stiffly out from the centre part. One female, clasping a tiny, big-headed, almost-naked baby to her bosom, suddenly came to the realization that behind the light were monkeys' most despised and hated relatives—human beings. The Macaque epithets she spouted before departing to the higher limbs of the tree with her precious bundle would have been the envy of a mule skinner. This outburst triggered off a maniacal chorus from the group, and a big old burgomaster raised his hackles, bared his long, inhuman teeth, swelled out his chest, and made first threatening and then obscene gestures at us. It is sad and strange that the animals most closely related to us phylogenetically should hate us with the greatest fervour. The din ended abruptly as I turned off the torch; it was replaced by scurrying sounds as the Bonnets climbed up into the crown of the sandalwood. While switching off my torch, I had lowered my head, and the fading beam swept across the bole of the tree, enough to reveal a slight movement. I snapped the light on again, and the beam transfixed an Indian Bloodsucker, a beautiful sand-coloured lizard nearly two feet long with a row of small regular spines running down its back from the nape to near the tip of its long whip tail. Even as I watched it, its head and the fore parts of the torso began to flush with rosy pink —when really excited, these parts become dark red, as if gorged with blood. This habit has given it its unwarranted and unlovely name of "bloodsucker"; of course it does not suck blood. Our stop was proving to be a rewarding one, and the swamp to the east of the road was echoing to a chorus of frogs. I kept the light on and swept its rays beneath the big sandalwood hoping to see some other form of Indian wildlife. Nothing presented itself, but the beam picked up two familiar objects: dark grey and shaped like short thick sausages. I recognized them as owl "pellets". When an owl captures a small vertebrate with hair or feathers, such as a rat, mouse or small bird, it swallows it whole or in large chunks. The digestive process divests it of all hair or feathers and bone, and "rolls" these into a cylindrical wad, firm and tightly packed. These wads of roughage are regurgitated and fall to the ground under the owl's favourite perch.

Owls are creatures of alluring witchery. Their soft, intricately-patterned feathers, noiseless flight, strange voices, and nocturnal habit wrap them in a cloak of mystical enchantment. They are so much more frequently heard than seen, and they are so *unlike* other birds that I am always anxious to make their acquaintance. Finding two big owl "pellets" that I judged to have been disgorged by a bird at least the size of a Great Horned Owl, I became very "owl-conscious". This was most fortunate because even as I played the torchlight over the branches above me, all of us were frozen in our respective postures by the most hideous shriek, horrid, long-drawn and ending in a bubbling, gurgling choke. It emanated from a stand of jungle about a hundred yards away.

"A woman is being murdered in the shola," sobbed Chinnaswami, near collapse. In the light of the torch, Ario's face was white, but he rushed to the car and snatched up the only "weapon" in sight—his tripod! He was already rushing off in the direction of the *shola,* followed somewhat reluctantly by the driver, before my owl-oriented mind fully realized their apprehension.

"Wait," I yelled. "It's an owl—a big *Bubo*! Get the camera and flash!" My companions hesitated, looked at me in disbelief, then took off again; but my thoughts had flashed back well over forty years to an

200

incident that I shall detail later—to the first time that I had heard the bloodcurdling screech of a big Horned Owl. I dashed back to the car, seized an Exacta with flash, and ran through the dark after my hurrying friends who were still certain that in those dark woods a foul deed had been perpetrated. Just as I caught up with them, a low, deep moaning *whooooo* reverberated from the *shola*. To Ario and Chinnaswami, it was a deathrattle; to me it was now definitely an owl. I gasped, "It's an Eagle-owl; we must try to get a picture." To North American nature-photographers such a proposal may sound ridiculous, but it must be remembered that India is populated by people who abhor the taking of life. As a generalized statement, an animal in India is not as likely to take alarm at the sight of a human as, to our shame, it would in most parts of North America. I was therefore confident that we could approach even a great owl closely enough to photograph it.

My colleagues were still dubious, but we all had one geographic objective and were proceeding with haste toward the spot from which the ghastly cry had come. We splashed through knee-deep swamp, fought our way through thorn-bedecked, clinging shrubbery, and finally reached the *shola*. Even as we entered the enveloping blackness of the tall trees, the shriek sounded again. We stopped in our tracks. We were now very close, and the awful scream was enough to provoke panic. At this range it seemed less agonized, more demoniacal; it was a cruel, malignant sound. Demoralizing. Even though I was sure of its author, I admit to having had the urge to flee to the car and be away from this bedevilled spot; but the naturalist prevailed.

"Look, you can't slit a woman's throat twice; its got to be an owl," I croaked inanely and with faulty logic. Could one not cut *two* women's throats once? Then the deep sad *whoooooo* sounded again and all fear vanished.

"It *is* an Eagle-owl," I cried joyfully. "Come on, let's get his picture." We worked slowly forward and I began to realize how hot it was—my shirt and trousers were drenched with perspiration. In addition, my boots were filled with swamp water, and I had the uneasy feeling that jungle leeches had attached themselves to my legs. I flashed the torch and illuminated Gatti's legs: he was wearing shorts, and I saw that already the thin trickles of blood were running down his calves. I said nothing as we couldn't do anything about it at the moment. At this point I noticed that Chinnaswami was no longer with us. Vaguely I thought that he had bolted for the car and might even have driven off. We pushed on and began to play the torchlight on the heavy tree-limbs around us. It wasn't long before we caught the flash of eye-shine, two glowing orbs about an inch in diameter as the eye lenses reflected the light of the torch. He was on a big leafy branch about fifteen feet from the ground. We could now see the upper half of a huge owl. It was unlike any other I had ever seen: it was larger than a Great Horned and its huge eyes were dark and lustrous, appearing totally black as it glared directly at us, and very different from the bright yellow irises of the Great Horned. Its feathery "ear" tufts were different as well: they drooped to the sides and were longer and more pointed than in the American bird. Its wings and back were rich chocolate brown mottled with buff and black, and its breast was heavily marked with coarse transverse barring. "Forest Eagle-owl *Bubo nipalensis*," I whispered and, while I held its gaze in the light of my torch, Ario quickly calculated the range and adjusted the camera flash. We got only one picture because the brilliance of the flash seemed as fearsome to *Bubo* as his screech had been to us. He launched forth from his perch, making a most unseemly racket for an owl, and flew off over the swamp in the direction of another *shola* a quarter of a mile away. Months later we had the satisfaction of looking at him again, but it was his silent image projected on a beaded screen.

At the car we found Chinnaswami pacing nervously about. He explained that he had felt it his responsibility to return to ensure that no harm came to the car or its contents. We were pleased enough at the outcome of the whole adventure to congratulate him on his wisdom and judgment—and indeed he had a point. The next few minutes were devoted to the task of removing jungle leeches by the somewhat droll process of sprinkling them with salt.

While thus occupied I explained to my companions how I had guessed the identity of the weird vocalist. I cannot remember the date, but I was about six years of age at the time and my parents, who had come to Canada from Ireland just before I was born, had moved from their home in downtown Winnipeg to a house on the western outskirts of the city. Deer Lodge was then "in the bush". It was a cold clear night in February, and the ground was covered by a thick blanket of snow. The last layer had fallen that evening and was as yet unsullied by footprints. It was that wonderful hour of late evening just before my brother and I were packed off to bed. There was a cheery fire in the enormous stone fireplace. All of us, father, mother, grandmother, Angus, and I were absorbing the warmth of the blaze before braving the chilly bedrooms upstairs.

With shocking abruptness, the peaceful quiet was shattered by a shriek like the one which I was to hear in India. It was naturally a totally new and nerve-wracking sound to all of us. My father quickly took down his shotgun, threw open the door, and rushed out. I think all but Granny followed him, not out of courage but rather from the lack of it. Nothing could be seen; the bare trees were stark and empty in the moonlight which, reflected upward from the new-fallen snow, cast an eerie light on the undersides of the treelimbs. The only movement was that of our vaporized breaths; the only sound the crunch of our own feet in the crisp snow. My father circled the house, criss-crossed back and forth through the trees and shrubs, looked everywhere and found nothing. As we re-entered the house, he muttered to my mother in a most disturbed voice that there weren't even tracks. Nothing had set foot anywhere near the house, and yet the sound had originated just outside the front window. We all trooped back in and Granny murmered something about the "banshee". Angus and I were permitted to sit up much later than usual that night. I'm not sure that my father went to bed at all.

The next morning we went out and looked again. We found nothing but our own footprints—except that I noticed a fat grey thing like a sausage embedded in the fresh snow under one of the big Bur Oaks on our front lawn.

About twenty years later, I heard it again. One weekend in January I had gone up to a small log cabin some twenty miles north of Toronto to do some sketching. That Saturday was a fine clear day, and I tramped about a good deal making sketches; so, it was late when I got back to the cabin. I had the Coleman lamp lighted, a fire going in the stove, and bacon and eggs cooking when I went out to draw fresh water from the pump for my coffee. The screech that came from the beech-maple woods surrounding the cabin almost made me drop the coffee pot. But this time I saw the culprit. A Great Horned Owl, *Bubo virginianus,* sat on a limb of a Sugar Maple within thirty feet of the cabin. He didn't repeat his horripilating effort but, having seen me, flew silently off.

It's strange how memory performs; it can launch itself on prodigious journeys across time and space, and at that moment I saw again, as clearly as in a photograph, the grey sausage-shaped object, which because of its warmth, had sunk into the snow under the Bur Oak on our lawn at Deer Lodge some twenty years before. . . .

The scream? It is happiness. It is a love song. It is *Liebesnacht*. It is ecstasy as expressed in the language of *Bubo*. If I should ever be so fortunate as to hear it again, it will not be a scream but a sound to be cherished along with the sad, dulcet cadence of the Tinamou or the long, smooth howl of the Timber Wolf.

Seeds of Sedition

Our collecting for the Indian exhibit had been completed with one exception. I had not obtained a cast of the trunk of a Teak tree. None of suitable size grew in the Injipara *shola* but there was a fine Teak forestation project some twenty miles from the town of Valparai, down on the Ghat road. Roger Hands wrote a chit to the forest ranger at the reserve explaining in detail why we wished to make a rubber mould from one of his trees and that no harm could result from the operation. He told him that I would be at the ranger station the following morning. Accordingly, I equipped myself with the materials I would need and set off in the Consul driven by Chinnaswami. The temperature as we left Injipara was 85°F./.30°C., and it promised to be hotter still down in the Teak forest a thousand feet lower.

We were warmly received by the ranger, an old friend of Roger's, and were soon discussing the project over a cup of tea. Eventually I suggested that we go out and select the appropriate tree.

His face fell. "I would be most pleased to let you work on one of our trees, but I have no authority to allow you to enter the Teak Reserve. You must get permission from the head ranger at Waterfall, *isn't it?*" Because the Ghat road ran right through the preserve, which was guarded only by a somewhat neglected three-strand wire fence, it seemed a little ridiculous. But, as I was anxious to conform to regulations, I thanked him for the tea and courtesy, climbed back into the Consul, and directed Chinnaswami to proceed to Waterfall, twelve miles farther down the Ghat road.

The head ranger, a charming gentleman, received me in a cool, Teak-log house at Waterfall. Once more I explained my need. The ranger was fascinated by my description of the technique and discussed it fully over a cup of tea.

"It is with the utmost regret," he said finally, "that it is not within my power to give you permission to enter the forest to perform this important task, *isn't it?* However, you will readily get this from the Chief Forest Officer at Pollachi; then return here, and we will give you every assistance, *isn't it?*"

Pollachi lay at the foot of the Ghat road, on the flat dusty lands of the Madras plain, twenty-three miles away. The temperature had soared to over 100°F./38°C. in the shade when we drove into the crowded streets of Pollachi. They were jammed with people, dogs, sheep, sacred cows, chickens, vegetable carts and stalls, sadhus (holymen), beggars, bicycles, rickshaws, oxcarts, and even a few cars. A feculent smell permeated everything. We found the Forestry office; were told the Chief was out and asked if we would care for a nice cup of tea while someone was dispatched to find him.

It was some little time before the messenger returned, no doubt having taken the opportunity to spend some minutes gossiping with his cronies. His report was that the Chief was at the police station. We piled into the car and, after some difficulty, wherein crowds of people surrounded the car each pointing in a different direction, we found that imposing edifice. The constable who challenged my right to enter spoke only Tamil; so, I called in Chinnaswami. There was a long and heated conversation after which I learned that there was no such person as a Chief Forest Officer in Pollachi. I asked to see the Kotwal of Police. This gentleman soon appeared, shook hands, *namastied,* and ushered me into his office. He offered me tea, which I accepted (wishing it were iced). Once again I was forced to go through the lengthy explanation of my purpose. The Kotwal, or Chief, his big belly shaking, laughed heartily.

"Your silly man has misunderstood the constable," he roared. "At this moment there is, indeed, no Chief Forest Officer in Pollachi, but he was here this morning in this very office, sitting in the chair that you now occupy; he has gone to Udamalpet, however, in order to obtain more evidence for the prosecution of a most important case and will not be back in Pollachi until tomorrow, *isn't it?*"

"I see," I said, "and if I were to go to Udamalpet, do you think I might be able to see him?" (I almost added *"Isn't it?"*)

"Yes, yes. By now he should be in the Forestry office there."

When the facetiae had been fulfilled, the witticisms and pleasantries exchanged, I staggered out to the car muttering to myself, "I'll wager that the serious case that has taken the Chief Forest Officer to Udamalpet is one leading to an indictment against some ignorant slob who had inadvertently, but illegally, set foot within the boundries of a Teak forest." I joined Chinnaswami who had retreated to the car. I suspected that like many people he felt uneasy in the presence of the law, though from what I had seen of him I doubted very much if he had ever had a brush with it.

"He's in Udamalpet, Chinnaswami; where the hell is that?"

"It's just seventeen miles, sahib; good road, we'll be there in half an hour."

We might have been there in half an hour had it not been that we had to stop several times while I "de-tea-d" behind a big sandalwood or tamarind tree. It wasn't a bad road, but the dust was appalling, the heat intense, as it can be only on the plains of India, surging against us, filling the car, sifting through our clothes until eyes were smarting, lips cracking, and every mucous membrane tingling and prickling. You could even smell it. Every dead and decaying thing, vegetable and animal—and there were plenty as we passed Pollachi market—sent up great billowing swells of stink. Whitebacked and Long-billed Vultures soared about or sat satiated in gaunt, dessicated trees. It was a relief eventually to be free of Pollachi; even though there was no respite from the blistering heat, at least the air was sweeter.

There were fabulous things to be seen on the road to Udamalpet:

206

flocks of Pied and Common Mynahs, Brown Shrikes on the hydro wires, and Angleheaded Agamid Lizards racing about on the trunks of Tulip trees with their crowns ablaze with cup-sized blossoms of intense orange-red. But I hadn't much heart for it; I was too hot, too tired, and too frustrated. Time was running short—not only for this day, but also for my stay in South India. In less than a week I had to turn in my gun permit to the Calcutta Police. In person. So I had to be there.

Udamalpet was a shimmering mirage as we approached it. A small town of tumble-down shacks, many with mud walls, it was crawling, creeping, and seething with people and animals. Innumerable chickens, ducks, peacocks and pigeons, dogs, and cattle added to the strange orderly confusion of multitudinous people. It seemed there was no place to go in Udamalpet, yet everyone seemed to be going somewhere, on foot, on bicycle, on every conceivable form of cart, on donkey back, on water buffalo, and even legless people travelling on knees or propelled on rumps by arms rowing like oars. The smell? It was an Augean stable, needing the attention of a Hercules.

We found the Forest Office, and were ushered into a clinically bare room, on the ceiling of which two, big, old-fashioned fans slowly revolved. The chief looked very much as though he had just lowered his feet from the desk top and was trying hard to get some of the sleep from his eyes; I sympathized with and envied him. I suspected that he was in Udamalpet because this office seemed cooler than the one in Pollachi.

"How fortunate that you have just arrived in time for tea." It would not be polite to do more than state my business until the tea arrived. Then, while sipping, we discussed many things—all the details of our work in India, our collecting methods, and in particular our "so very clever" technique of collecting a tree, which he somehow likened to the old English saying of "eating your cake and having it, too". I hoped that Chinnaswami had found friends and was not sitting in that roasting car. We were getting along so famously and with such joviality that I felt sure that nothing stood in my way of securing what had now become an obsession—a mould of a Teak tree.

Finally, the tea was finished and a sheaf of papers shuffled and scanned. With sinking heart I knew that they had nothing to do with

207

the present problem, and that he was putting off his decision. A long pause.

"So you wish to enter the Teak forest and make a rubber casting of one of the trees; and you assure me that this will in no way harm the tree?"

I assured him that the casting liquid would only clean the tree; the rubber would remove all the dust and loose dirt, and that he would have the cleanest Teak tree in all Asia.

He sighed, "I wish it were within my power to grant so reasonable a request and for such a pleasantly ingenious and noble purpose, but regretfully I must tell you that I have not the authority to grant you permission to enter the Teak forest. I suggest you apply for a permit from the Collector at Coimbatore. Upon receipt of this, I shall be glad to give you a letter to the ranger instructing him to allow you to cover the tree of your selection with rubber, and also to assign one or more of his men to assist you."

Inwardly seething, I arose, put on the best smile I could muster (it must have been a sickly one), thanked him for his hospitality and assistance, and especially for the tea, and stumbled out to the car and to the heat.

Chinnaswami looked at me in disbelief when I said "We've to go to Coimbatore, Chinnaswami, to see the Collector."

Coimbatore was equally as far on the other side of Pollachi as Udamalpet was on this. Again we drove off in the dusty, swirling heat. Even Chinnaswami seemed ready to shed some of the military-style khaki shikar, or hunting uniform, that, as a Tea Estates driver, he was so proud to wear. The collar of his shirt was opened; the cap, British army style, red banded like a general's, was lifted several times, but always replaced after a quick mop with a kerchief. It created too good an impression to be laid aside because of the heat. I'm sure he was often mistaken for an Indian general.

Through smarting eyes I could see gorgeous Indian Rollers, their cobalt and cerulean wings flashing against the intolerable glare of sun on pale, sandy red earth. There were Paddy birds, Black Ibises, Kestrels, Yellow-wattled Lapwings, Pied Kingfishers, Black Drongos, Bee-eaters, and Hoopoes. For once I was satisfied to see them from the car and did not ask Chinnaswami to stop. Once, he looked at me with some concern as we passed two Egyptian Vultures—"Pharoah's chickens"—perched on a dead tree close to the road without even a comment from me.

The road was clogged with vehicles, mostly bullock carts or big-wheeled hayricks drawn by water buffaloes. Rapid progress was not possible; Chinnaswami obeyed Indian highway law and blasted his raucous horn each time he approached one, whether he were overtaking or simply passing an approaching one.

With the heat and the dust and the noise, I was nearly "bushed" when we crawled into Coimbatore. I felt a mess as I climbed the wooden steps up to the Collector's office. My khaki shirt was limp and dark with perspiration. I had beaten off as much of the red dust as I could, but it still clung in muddy patches to the wrinkles in my sodden shirt and trousers. A hell of a sight to come asking favours of the Collector.

A dhoti-clad clerk told me the Collector was engaged and bade me take a seat. I had a lengthy wait in the outer room, and it was then, with moisture running down my back and mopping my face with an already sopping handkerchief, that the seeds of sedition began to sprout in my mind. There must be other ways of getting the mould of a teak tree without this damned craven appeal to authority. As the seedlings grew I formulated a plan. Then I snipped them in the bud. I knew the Collector; we were not exactly old friends, but he had personally issued me a few permits and licences including one entitling me to buy booze. He would surely grant my request, and everything would be done legally and with helpful cooperation. That was the way ROM officials liked their representatives to work.

Finally, I was ushered in. Once again the cordial greeting. "It is a pleasure to once again meet my Canadian friend, please be seated." He was a big, heavy man, one who should have suffered in this heat, but his collar was crisp and white, his tie in place, trousers neatly pressed, and he wore a jacket. He took in my dishevelled appearance at a glance. I felt uncomfortable.

"I will call for tea," he boomed.

Now I had lived for over a month among tea bushes. Every morning before six o'clock I had been awakened by a house boy bearing "bed tea". On the estate, I was seldom without the aromatic and refreshing aroma of tea in my nostrils; the smell of tea bushes (not unlike roses), the smell of fermenting leaves in the factory, of toasting tea, and of the great piles of black tea in the warehouse. And, of course of brewing tea. Today I had had bed tea, breakfast tea, tea at the ranger's cabin, tea at Waterfall, tea at Pollachi, and tea at Udamalpet. At the risk of giving offence, I felt justified in declining with thanks another cup. Instead, I smoked a cigarette while the Collector sipped his tea.

I apologized for my appearance and recounted the story of the day, trying to keep the edge of bitterness from my voice.

In the end it was the same sad story. It would be necessary to get permission from the deputy minister of forests in Madras.

"I will be glad to communicate your request to him, to attest to your good intentions and character. We should have a reply in a week, *isn't it?*"

Through my weary brain ran the thought, "And he'll have to ask Nehru, *isn't it?*" The seditious seeds began to germinate again. This time there was no staying them. They grew like Jack's beanstalk and began to blossom. I could almost see them bearing fruit.

"No, no," I expostulated. "I couldn't put anyone to any more trouble. Everyone has been so kind and considerate. I don't wish to press the matter further." Everyone *had* been kind and considerate, but it had been like shovelling smoke or nailing jelly to the wall.

I finally made my departure and climbed into the Consul's oven.

"Injipara, Chinnaswami," I said.

"You didn't get permission?" he asked.

"No," I replied, "but night must fall."

"Yes, Sahib," said Chinnaswami. "There will be no moon tomorrow, what time shall I pick you up?"

It was a relief to see the green hills, to pass the great dam at the foot of the Ghat road with its shimmering lake, the gaunt, drowned trees about its margin decorated with Indian Darters, Pygmy Cormorants, and Brahminy Kites. It was heaven to start the long, tortuous climb up the Ghat road to greenery and coolness.

But our misadventures were not over. We were barely a quarter of the way up the Ghat when the fog rolled in. Traversing the narrow winding road with its scores of hairpin turns, passing oxcarts, pedestrians, cars, bicycles, and enormous buses and transport trucks is an experience at the best of times, but in a dense fog it was excruciating.

It required constant vigilance from every eye we possessed, and a speed as low as the car could maintain.

Even so, we had a dozen near misses. Several times, we had to stop and work our way, a few inches at a time, around the big buses that very nearly filled the entire narrow road. On these occasions the bus passengers and I would dismount and everybody shouted instructions in Tamil, Hindi, and English to the drivers.

It didn't help much when, on one of these episodes, the bus passengers, with great white-toothed grins, pointed out where some vehicle recently had crashed through the low stone retaining wall and plunged down hundreds of feet into the jungle below.

We finally made it back to Injipara. Our eyes, first from the heat and dust, then from the strain of peering through the mist, had developed the appearance of peeled purple grapes. Thank heaven, we were too late for afternoon tea.

I will not disclose how it got there, but the trunk of a big Teak tree, constructed from a mould made in India, now stands on the south side of our Indian diorama.

From small seditious seeds mighty Teak trees can be grown.

A Snow-Facing Room

Calcutta. All of our collections, packed in a dozen big crates, were in the hands of our broker, and shipping had been arranged. My gun permits had been surrendered. I was now just a tourist. I had no guns, that would excite consternation. The Bengal police had no further interest in me. There had been several days of endless altercation and debate with customs, the zoological survey, the police. I almost despaired at times but, with the able assistance of Mr. Roy of Brooke-Bond, it all came to an end eventually.

Audrey joined me in Calcutta a few days later. She had been travelling about in Egypt and North India during much of the time I had been working in the south. Now that we were just tourists, we determined to have another go at reaching the country bordering on the "roof of the world"—the Himalayan region bordering on Tibet—and to which we had been previously denied entry.

There were problems and obstacles to be overcome, but eventually we had our return tickets on Indian Air Lines from Calcutta to Bagdogra. The travel agency, preening itself, proudly announced that it had succeeded, despite great odds, in securing for us a "snow-facing room" in the Mount Everest "Luxury" hotel in Darjeeling. The windows of one's room must face the mountains so that a glance outside in the morning will reveal the great snow-clad Kanchenjunga and associated peaks. All we needed now were police permits to enter the militarized border zone—war with China still threatened. We were assured that these would be forthcoming upon application to the Calcutta police the following Monday.

At that moment, a man named Lee Oswald was preparing to fire a shot that would be heard around the world. It even had its impact on two Canadians in Calcutta. On the Monday, the day of the funeral of John F. Kennedy, even the police station in Calcutta was closed out of respect. Our plane was scheduled to leave at 6:00 a.m. Tuesday, and there was no possibility of being aboard it equipped with police permits.

We caught the plane anyway, and in mid-morning arrived at Bagdogra airport. Because it was a militarized zone, there was a kind of internal customs and immigration procedure to go through. I explained our situation to the local police and soon found myself involved with the Indian army. The captain was most considerate. He offered his condolences (Canada evidently was a part of the United States to him), and explained that it would be necessary for us to drive to Siliguri, eight miles to the east, to obtain our permits from the authorities there. A car driven by a young Nepali corporal was placed at our disposal, free of charge, and we drove off in sweltering heat for Siliguri. It is strange how a short trip with an unknown outcome at the other end can seem interminable.

On our arrival we parked in half shade. It was still extremely hot. The corporal who, I suspect, thought it all a lot of nonsense, said,

"You and *memsahib* wait here; I will look after everything for you."

He took our passports and application papers and entered the government building. It was probably not more than an hour, but in the heat it seemed like half a day before he emerged and, with a small smile, he said, "It is all arranged, you and *memsahib* can go up to Darjeeling this afternoon."

The trip back to Bagdogra was too fast. There were birds to be seen on those fence posts and wires that went whipping by. Siliguri to Bagdogra was accomplished in what seemed only minutes.

I tried to recompense the corporal, but he refused. "Thank you," he said, "but it was part of my duty. I was assigned the job and did it to the best of my ability." I hope his ability has been recognized.

There must be very few drives that a zoologist can take that equal the one from Bagdogra to Darjeeling. One starts down on the hot dusty plains, the watersheds of the Ganges and Brahmaputra. After some miles of this, one is with shocking precipitance plunged into the tropical rain forest: gigantic trees with flaring buttressed trunks, covered with vines and lianas; giant straight bamboos; wild bananas and screw pines. Everywhere the great cut-leaved *Rhapidophora* vines twine about and drape the trees. Ferns are unbelievably luxuriant, big *Cleichenias* festooning all the slopes and banks. A cutbank here does not long remain an ugly scar. The lush growth of ferns quickly conceals it.

This moist foothills forest gradually gives way (from about four thousand feet) to a more temperate or subtropical aspect. It is still a dense tall forest, but is made up largely of oaks and tree rhododendrons. About six thousand feet, Silver Firs, magnolias, maples, birch, and small bamboos make their appearance.

Still higher, above Darjeeling, near the eight-thousand-foot level, one enters the coniferous forest of hemlocks, spruce, Blue Pine, Silver Fir, and junipers, still with a dense undergrowth of shrubby rhododendrons. My enjoyment of the changing forests was greatly enhanced because I had been briefed by the gentle and charming Mr. F. Ludlow of the British Museum, the leading authority on the botany of the eastern Himalayan region.

But it was not the ecological changes that constituted the most exciting feature of the trip, which could be made either by car or by narrow-gauge railroad. The road and the railway tracks crossed each other innumerable times, often with dense forest surrounding the crossing and reducing visibility to close to zero. Indian logic also decreed that car and train should leave Bagdogra at approximately the same time and should travel at approximately the same speed. Owing to the varying grades and the routes taken up the tortuous mountainside by road and rail, it happened that sometimes we arrived first at the crossing and sometimes the train. Approaching crossings, the car driver honked his horn, the train blew its whistle, but neither appreciably slackened speed. Several times, as we approached a crossing, we either saw the caboose of the train a few yards beyond it or the engine bearing down upon us.

We arrived at the Mount Everest Hotel, perched high above Gandhi Road and with no obstruction between its northern exposure and the Himalayas. We were taken to our room. It was small and rather primitive, but we congratulated ourselves that when the sky cleared we would be able to see the mountains from our window.

We went down to dinner, then took a long walk exploring the shops of Darjeeling. When we returned to the hotel, we found the manager, in his overcoat, sitting behind the desk. He seemed in a hurry to give us our key. A few pleasantries, and he said goodnight and went out onto the street. It took some little time, but it finally dawned on us that we were the only guests in the whole big hotel —and that the manager and all his staff had gone home to where it was warm. We were alone in this gigantic cold barn. So much for a "snow-facing room"—we could have had our choice of twenty-six of them!

In our room, a small wood fire had been kindled in the fireplace, yet the room was cold. There was no hot water; there wasn't much light. Our biggest thrill was to find two hot water bottles in the bed. When we weren't laughing, our teeth chattered. We had expected the "luxury" hotel to be lively.

I woke in the morning, thoroughly chilled, climbed out of bed, and went to close the window. I looked out. Nothing but mist. "Damn," I thought. "It's possible to be here a week and not see the mountains."

My eyes travelled up—mist; still higher—more mist. Then, with my neck craned back at 45°, I saw the mountains. I had never seen, or dreamt of seeing, mountains so high in the sky. You didn't look out

214

on them, you looked *up* at them. Dominating everything was the immense peak of Kanchenjunga.

"Audrey," I said, "come and see this."

Her teeth chattering, she came to the window.

"What? I don't see anything but fog."

"Up there!" I said, pointing at a preposterous angle through the window pane, "The big one is Kanchenjunga, and away off there to the west is Everest."

I don't recall that we said much, but I know we stood at the window for a long time, long enough to realize that we had better get into some warm clothing fast.

Over the next few days, we were captivated on many occasions by the magnetism of the mountains, but I never failed to be amazed at the head-tilt that was necessary to look at them.

During this time we explored on foot and by car the town and the surrounding countryside. The town was colourful with its hosts of refugees from Tibet; herdsmen in quilted garments, fur boots, and fut hats with ear flaps; monks in saffron or red-brown robes and shaved heads, reeking of rancid butter and grease; women with strings of beads and bracelets of lapis lazuli and turquoise matrix over dark and worn rags. Blonde Audrey was a centre of attraction! She was stranger to the women of Tibet than they were to her. She had to be examined, her hair gently touched and marvelled at, her white skin exclaimed about.

There was the market place with its stalls of brightly-coloured fruits and vegetables laid out in neat rows as if to create the finest colour effect. More rows and mounds adorned the streets, many of exotic fruits and vegetables, and even little piles of sunflower and other seeds. Each little bunch was carefully counted out and advertised as "ten for one naye paise"—a twelfth of a cent. There were the shops, piled high with semi-precious stones, leather goods, temple bells of brass, and cheap, crude souvenirs. There were visits to the monasteries: the beautiful new one in Darjeeling with its four tall sentinels of odd-shaped bunch-topped Silver Firs, as if pruned by a topiarist, and the much older and quainter one near Kalimpong where we were allowed to examine the scrolls.

I was seeing birds, of course: Ravens, Yellowbilled Blue Magpies, Himalayan Nutcrackers, Spotted Forktails, Himalayan Rubythroat,

215

Snow Pigeons, Hill Partridges, and Himalayan Griffons. Early one morning before the mist cleared from the terraced slopes of the valleys, a Lammergeyer sailed majestically across the face of Kanchenjunga, a most gratifying sight; here indeed in the great craggy mountains, fit home only for the gods and the Abominable Snowman, there was surely Lebensraum for this greatest of the vultures, now rare or extirpated from its formerly extensive range from Spain, through Africa and Europe, to eastern Asia.

Our last night in Darjeeling was frosty. There was a hint of sleeting snow in the air, and we hadn't adequate clothing. We sat out on the wide verandah watching the changing colours of the snow on Kanchenjunga and the other titans. From pure shining white they changed to pale mauve, to rose pink, and finally to blazing orange, when all else was steeped in blackness. There was an abrupt finale as the massive peaks disappeared in blackness, as sudden and absolute as the blowing out of a candle.

We awakened early. If it had been cold the night before, the room was now frigid. The fire had died. Even the hot-water bottles were cold to the touch. The taps in the bathroom produced only ice water. Washing and shaving was martyrdom.

There came a knock on the door. A Nepali entered with "bed tea".

"Your car will be leaving soon, sahib and memsahib; the porters will take down your bags if they are ready."

Our companions in the car on the trip down were an Indian gentleman and a Burmese prince. There was a brief stop at a town appropriately named Ghoom.

"I know a good place here," said the prince. "It's clean; may I stand you and your wife a cup of coffee?"

The place was dark and dingy, the besmirched and befogged windows effectively kept out the light. The tables of bare wood were greasy and dead flies lined the windowsills; the coffee was strong and hot, however, and our companion cheerful and entertaining.

Our second stop was at Kurseong, a colourful town nineteen miles from Darjeeling. It is in one of the heavy rain areas of north Bengal, averaging about 180 inches a year. Audrey had developed a headache, and we went in search of a drugstore. A Nepalese druggest waited on us. Yes, he had acetylsalicylic acid tablets. From behind a mound of dried sea horses, pickled skates, grasshoppers, chili peppers, and dessicated leeches, he extracted Bayer Aspirin in a thin phial, wrapped in paper that was twisted at the ends. We looked about the store. There were sulfa drugs, brand-name mouthwashes, toothpaste, linaments, ointments, a good looking prescription department; also there were powdered scorpions, dried mushrooms, and pulverized Rhinoceros horn for an aphrodisiac. It was without doubt the most intriguing drugstore we had ever been in. If you wanted modern super drugs, they had them: penicillin, terramycine, whatever. But also they had the age-old Indian and Chinese herbs and faunal medicines, the medicines of the mountain people. We might have browsed in that store for a couple of hours had it not been for the waiting car.

The trip up to Darjeeling had been exciting with its game of tag with the train, and on the steep grades at least it had been in slow motion. Going down, however, both car and train took full advantage of gravity. We speeded around hairpin turns and darted across the railway crossings. The train was equalling our speed, its whistle blowing incessantly. For a while it was exhilarating. Then came the near miss. The car shot out of the jungle, the tracks at right angles dead ahead and equidistant from the crossing, the train under full stream. For a second it seemed there was no possibility of avoiding collision. Our driver put on an extra spurt, and we sped across the tracks just as the train thundered by behind us.

Past the crossing, both car and train sounded horn and whistle and jammed on their brakes. Not enough to come to a stop, just enough to scramble everything and everybody in both vehicles. Then on again at full speed to continue the *Danse Macabre*.

"We are playing Russian Roulette," said the Burmese prince, retrieving his black fez from the floor of the car.

"You'll never be closer to heaven, nor I to hell than that without actually achieving them," I said to Audrey. "I don't think that the train missed our rear end by more than six inches."

The Indian gentleman smiled wanly, then laughed. He was a gentle, kindly man no doubt more fatalistically prepared to meet death than the rest of us. It is likely that he had lived with death in one form or another all of his life. This is not to say that the Indian does not mourn or grieve as we do. It is simply that he is more resigned to the inevitable than we are.

217

The near miss spurred our driver; he overtook the train and before long outdistanced it. We could hear its plaintive whistle far behind. It was one of those high-pitched Old World train whistles, disconsolate at the loss of its playmate. It sounded like a young child whose older and bigger companions had run off and left it. But we were relieved when we arrived at Bagdogra without it.

Indian Lorikeets, awakening in Guava Tree,
Valparai, India

NINE

At Long Last, An Africa Expedition

Ever since I was a small boy reading *Chums* and the *Boys' Own Annual,* I had had a great desire to go "On safari to darkest Africa". And eventually getting there was indeed "Not as the Crow Flies". My work had taken me off in almost every other direction. Determination and desire, however, finally paid off. In 1968 I was rewarded with a three-month trip to that paradise for naturalists—the one Carl Akeley called "Brightest Africa".

In 1967, we had completed a biogroup of Ellesmere Island based on my experience there nearly thirty years before. The Museum now had the Arctic tundra, the Asian Monsoon forest, and the Galápagos Islands represented by dioramas. When I suggested to Dr. Peter Swann that we should attempt to gather the material for a grasslands group and that Kenya in East Africa was the logical choice, he agreed and found us the money. At the suggestion of our Curator of Mammals, Dr. R.L. Peterson, I got in touch with Mr. John G. Williams of Nairobi.

Williams was planning a personal trip to the Budongo Forest in western Uganda. Here was a marvellous opportunity: I arranged to accompany him on this expedition to collect the materials for an African Tropical Rain Forest exhibit, and then to travel to Kenya to gather the specimens for the Grasslands exhibit.

221

The Budongo Forest

The sound of morning. Flights of White-casqued and White-thighed Hornbills shout and squawk like gangs of railway section-hands as they troop toward a breakfast of figs. Flocks of croaking Green Pigeons, squeeking sunbirds, chattering kingfishers, and the turbulent, blustering yells of Chimpanzees pleasurably uproot and annihilate sleep.

During the heat of the day the forest is surprisingly quiet. Many creatures are abroad, but most go about their business in relative silence. There is the occasional outburst of Chimpanzee vociferation and tumult. The birds sing in a detached and desultory way. Cicadas harp endlessly on one inharmonious theme.

> Even among insects, in this world,
> Some are good at singing,
> Some are bad.
>
> *Issa.*

But it is only at dusk that the equatorial rain forest truly comes alive: bats of many kinds take to the wing; the mighty orchestration of the forest is then heard. At dusk there is a "tuning up" as at a symphony concert. Then the concert begins; and one begins to acquire that certain awe of the rain forest. The age-old forest: its music seems timeless, changeless, and enduring.

If one is near water, the greatest sound will be that of the fantastic chorus of a dozen species of little *Hyperolius* tree frogs, augmented by the violins and cellos, the zithers and sitars of a hundred different

222

kinds of stridulating insects. The nocturnal birds, nightjars and owls, add their persistent and repetitive contribution. Some sound as if they had learned their music from a correspondence school, but at least they have timing and rhythm.

It should be mentioned that there is the ubiquitous, irritable whining dissonance of mosquitoes which often, through multiplicity and proximity, drowns out all the more melodious and pleasing sounds. One cannot stop the sound of mosquitoes. The roar of frogs can be silenced by tossing a stone into their pond. A yell will quiet a nightjar or owl and even many insects, but I know of no way to hush a horde of hungry "mozzies". Truthfully, the song of a mosquito is not an unpleasant sound. We reject it because of its implications. Who knows—if they didn't sting they might even lull us to sleep with their music. But in the Budongo with the prevalence of *Anopheles,* one can only be grateful to the developers of efficient anti-malarial pills.

There are many other creatures abroad in the dark, many of which are usually silent. A powerful flashlight played about through the treetops or along the edges of tracks will seldom fail to reflect the shine from the eyes of night animals such as Potto; Demidoff's Galago; African Civet; Large-spotted Genet; Marsh, Whitetailed, and Percival's Dwarf Mongooses; Red, Blue, and Bush Duikers; Bushbuck; Scalytailed Flying Squirrel; Bunyoro Rabbit, and of course, the dangerous Leopard. Nearly all these can be vocal, but only the chattering of the Galago adds much to the night's euphony.

But the big sound of the darkened forest comes from a small mammal. One could travel the Budongo by day for months and never be aware of the thousands of rabbit-sized animals, which look like big Guinea Pigs and live up in the tall trees. These are the nocturnal Tree Hyraxes. When night descends they become active.

Activity to a Tree Hyrax seems to constitute eating and screaming. It is a vegetarian, and if it were as accomplished at the first suggested activity as it is at the second, I would despair for the continued existence of vegetation in the Ugandan forests. For such a small animal, its cry is immense, and it reiterates interminably. The cry is a startled scream, as if someone had been jabbed, stabbed or grabbed in a tender part. To the uninitiated the scream could be terrifying, coming as it does from the darkened forest. Once the identity of the sound has been established, it is exceedingly funny. The thought of

223

dozens of big "Guinea Pigs" sitting up in the trees and "yelling like crazy" was always amusing. I suppose to Tree Hyraxes—especially the females—it is great music or eloquent oratory. I imagine Mozart's "Eine Kleine Nachtmusik" would be as repulsive and frightening to them as their screams are to us.

The African rain forest is not a place for aimless wandering about at night. A very short distance from where we had been working one day, a poacher's snare intended for duiker caught a Leopard. The snares and pit-traps of the poachers are in themselves a hazard.

One can meet African Buffalo on a narrow, rutted track through the deep bush. Once, two bulls, blinded by the headlights, charged directly at our car. Swerving at the last moment, they brushed against its side, rocking it, and then crashed off into the forest. With me at the time were John Williams and Rob Glen. Their only comment was: "Seemed quite red, didn't they? Probably hybrids between the little red Congo Buffaloes and the big black eastern ones." It would take something more to rattle these two veterans of the African bush.

Another night we encountered a big herd of cow buffaloes on a track only a mile or two from the Masindi-Butiaba road. They were docile and retreated before us, but at a leisurely pace. We herded the whole gang of them right out onto the main road. Paul Geraghty, my companion on this expedition, who had remained at Don Baggeley's Rest House that night, had as yet not seen African Buffalo. Rob said, "I hope we can steer them right into Don's compound; Paul would like to see them!" I'm sure Don Baggeley wouldn't have wanted to see them—not thirty buffaloes in his beautifully kept flower garden, munching his Mexican Sunflowers. Anyway, they soon turned off the main road.

There were wild African Elephants in the forest: great silent beasts whose presence one might not detect until too late unless one heard and recognized the digestive rumblings of their stomachs. Almost daily we came on fresh signs indicating where the big pachyderms had pulled up shrubs or broken down tree branches in their browsing. Even more frequently we came upon their droppings on the tracks through the forest. Not once in our month's sojourn in the Budongo, however, did we see an elephant. They were much more elusive than

224

the elephants of the open bush and woodlands or of the dry thornbrush country.

Night brings one consolation to the traveller in the forest. The *siafu,* the Driver, or Safari, Ants, suspend their fierce devotion to killing and establish temporary bivouacs in sheltered places. During the day, when they are on the march, they travel in long columns, killing and eating everything they can capture and overcome. Pity the poor duiker caught in a snare and unable to flee. Although I never saw them in such enormous swarms as *Echiton,* the Army Ants of South America—columns a dozen feet or more across, and with vanguard and rear lost in infinity—they were encountered frequently enough and in such numbers that a few million one way or the other didn't matter much. The *siafu* columns I encountered in the Budongo were seldom more than a couple of inches wide. This portion of the swarm was composed of workers only, usually carrying pupae. On either flank, up to two feet from the column, roamed the big soldiers, about an inch long, half of which is head and great murderous jaws. They were ready to attack anything alive or even freshly dead. Once they fasten their enormous pincers into flesh they never release them even if the body is torn away from the head. The people of the Budongo, with typical human ingenuity, have turned this characteristic to their advantage: they use the ants to suture wounds. Once the jaws of the living ant have drawn together the flesh and skin, the head is snipped off still clinging firmly like a surgeon's clip.

We are perhaps a little too frightened of Driver Ants. It must be grim when they invade a chicken farm or horse corral, but it is not difficult for the traveller to escape them though he may first have suffered a few punishing bites. Perhaps it is not their vast numbers, their preoccupation with killing or their size or painful bites that intimidate. Perhaps it is their total indifference, their insensitiveness, their unfeeling, stolid obstinacy to persist in their purpose regardless of the obstacles we may put in their path. Douse the trail with gasoline and fire, scorch a hundred thousand, and there will be more to circumnavigate the blaze and keep on the way. Dig a water moat and they will bridge it with their own bodies and drive on. Perhaps it is this lack of perception or cognizance of danger that frightens us—they are blind!

225

There are many kinds of ants in the tropical rain forest. Hundreds of kinds. There is no doubt that there are more ants than all other kinds of animals added together. We think of ants as living in anthills in the ground. In the tropics they are particularly numerous in the trees, some kinds living 160 feet above the ground. The most tormenting ones are the *Polyrachis* ants, which attach their little oval, hamburger-sized mud nests to the undersides of leaves. The entomologist Paulian found that one tree in five harboured colonies of these ants. In parts of the Budongo, I'm sure it was four out of five, and they are not inactive at night.

One evening I shot a Pell's Tomb Bat, which fell into the forest near the road. I couldn't search for it in the dark without touching or brushing against trees and saplings, even though I carried a torch. Every jarred sapling sent down showers of sharply biting *Polyrachis*. By the time I found the bat and was able to retreat, I was so covered with ants that I had to strip off and brush them away a score at a time.

There were other ants in the forest whose fascinating habits outweighed any irritation their bites might occasion. Among these are the *Oecophyllids*, which are found in the foliage of the trees and shrubs on the forest edge. These ants construct nests of leaves stitched together with a silk-like fibre. The adults are incapable of producing the fibre, but the larvae can, and are used by the adults as shuttles for sewing the leaves together.

One morning as we drove along the Masindi-Butiaba road, we came upon dozens of the Budongo people on the road and the roadside. They were gathering termites for food. Baskets, bags, cloths with the corners tied together, every kind of container was being filled with termites. The children were gorging themselves on the spot. It was the annual swarming of the winged first reproductive caste. Each one of the millions of insects had had four clear, iridescent wings an inch-and-a-quarter long. They had swarmed along a mile or more of the road where they had shed their wings. That mile of road was like a shimmering mirage as the sunlight reflected off myriads of abandoned pennons. Only a few cars and trucks had preceded us; yet the road was already greasy with crushed bodies. Crested Guinea Fowl and Scaly Francolins were stuffing themselves. Woodland and Pygmy Kingfishers swooped down from roadside perches. For the people and some of the forest animals, it was an epicurean bonanza.

226

The Budongo abounded in birds, from the massive monkey-eating Crowned Hawk Eagle to diminutive barbets known as tinker-birds. Splendid Glossy Starlings flew through the tree tops, their wings making loud susurrous sounds—louder than the sound produced by the wingbeats of any passerine bird of my experience. Great Blue, Ross's, and Black-billed Turacos ran through the branches like squirrels, brandishing their garish wings and croaking, squawking, and cawing. African Grey Parrots flew high above the trees seeking rendezvous with a distant fig tree. Without any effort we recorded over two hundred kinds of birds in one month in the Budongo.

If the forest has its gorgeous birds it also has more than its share of venomous snakes. On none of my other expeditions have I seen so many poisonous reptiles. It is true that I didn't find very many of them myself, but one way or another I encountered Gaboon Viper, Rhinoceros Viper, Jameson's Mamba, Blacklipped Cobra, Puff Adder, Boomslang, and Blanding's Tree Snake as well as a number of lesser but still formidable rear-fangs.

It was a snake that gave me one of my few opportunities to practise one-upmanship on Glen and Williams. As I sat on the edge of my bed one morning, yawning, I saw something moving out from under my bed and creeping along the floor. It was a Night Adder, one of the deadliest of the smaller vipers of Africa. I remembered the episode of the Buffalo at night. Too often I had been impressed or excited; my Nairobi friends remained blasé. I have never had any great fear of venomous snakes—though I thoroughly respect them. I had handled rattlers, fer-de-lance, bushmasters, kraits, cobras, lanceheads, coral snakes, and others in the field and in the lab. I knew that my companions had collected a Night Adder the day before; it had escaped.

Keeping a weather eye on the reptile's whereabouts, I shaved, dressed, picked up my notebook and pen, and strolled into the bedroom of Rob and John. "Good morning," I said. "Sleep well?" After greetings and solicitations had been exchanged I asked, "Anyone mislaid a Night Adder recently?"

"Why?"

"Because one woke me up this morning stomping around under my bed."

They exploded from under the sheets. Rob grabbed an empty snake bag.

"Where is it?"

"Last I saw of him, he was in the bathroom beside the toilet. Its sides are pretty smooth and slippery. He may want a 'leg up'!"

I went into the living-room and started writing yesterday's notes. There was a flurry of activity in the bathroom and Rob emerged with a full snake bag.

It was one of the few times I went "one up" on Rob.

Monkeys were plentiful in the forest, and almost daily we saw one or more of the common species: Black and White Colobus, Redtailed and Blue Monkeys, and the Blackfaced Vervet as well as Olive Baboons. More often one heard only the swishing of branches and saw the movement of leaves as a troop made off through the most dense levels of the forest.

My work in the Budongo Forest required the collecting of the flora of the treetops: the ferns, orchids, and other epiphytes that grow on the sunlit upper limbs of the big trees. I also needed a cast of one of the higher mahogany branches.

Big mahoganies were being felled daily in one sector of the forest. Through the co-operation of the manager of the Budongo Sawmills I was permitted to work on one of the newly-felled trees in the area. I made casts of the limbs and collected the leaves, lichens, lianas, and air plants that I needed.

For ten days I made almost daily trips into the cutting tract. It was a disheartening experience. The big mahoganies were being cut down systematically, each prostrated giant creating a hiatus in the forest as disfiguring as the gap left by an extracted front tooth in a human smile. The big trees literally exploded when they hit the ground. Limbs flew in every direction, and I saw big trunks snap into from three to eight pieces. Their tremendous weight crushed smaller trees like matchsticks. Lianas were torn loose from their grip on other trees and came away whipping the air like live wires.

It was not only the lumber trees that were being destroyed; the figs, the *muzirus* with theiir damson-like fruits, and other species classified by the lumbermen as "worthless" were being poisoned so that they would die, rot, and fall to make way for a new growth of "desirable" species—for a harvest to be reaped in fifty to a hundred

228

years time. Many of the food trees of the Chimpanzees, Hornbills, Turacos, Giant Forest Squirrels, Green Pigeons, and innumerable other creatures belonged in the "worthless" category.

Thus was the ecology of a cradle of evolution being eroded and destroyed. So it was that I learned of the mortality of the forest—not changeless and enduring but vulnerable and transitory—at the hands of man.

Scuppered by a Bikini

Many of our finest birds have been so reduced in numbers that they no longer constitute spectacles observable by the average birdwatcher. The great flights of Whooping Cranes across the western prairies will never be seen again. The horn-like beeping of vast flocks of migrating Trumpeter Swans is no longer heard across the continent—only in restricted areas of the far west. North America's longest-winged bird, the California Condor, is doomed. Pesticides have all but finished the Bald Eagle, the Osprey, and the Peregrine Falcon throughout nearly all their ranges; they are also seriously depleting the numbers of Pelicans and Gulls.

Around the world it is the same sad story. Man has no room for his neighbours and the largest and most handsome go first. We have not yet succeeded in eliminating all of them though, and there are many amazing bird spectacles that can still be observed. It was the extravaganza at Lake Nakuru in Kenya that started me thinking about some of the other grand bird phenomena that I had witnessed. Which was the most thrilling?

Hordes of upwardly spiralling Sandhill Cranes, the highest flocks

229

already reaching toward the vanishing point, seen above the tall converging spires of eighty-foot White Spruces, and the air filled with the wild stormy melody of their voices, near Snag in the Yukon. . . .

Stately flights of Openbill and Painted Storks coming in to roost at Vedanthangal in Madras, some silhouetted against, others illuminated brilliant orange-pink by, a tremendous ovate orb of cadmium-red setting sun. . . .

The pageant of a thousand garishly ornate Mandarin Ducks frolicking on Shinabazu Pond on a dull December day in Japan. . . .

Skeins of Eider Ducks, bead necklaces flung across the sky, flighting above and between pale, opalescent icebergs off the glacier-lined coast of Melville Bay, Greenland. . . .

Scarlet Ibises, made doubly radiant by the red-slewed spectrum of sunset, their flocks coming in like fiery rockets and reflected in the still, dark waters of the Caroni Swamp in Trinidad. . . .

Droves of Black-necked Ibises, punctuated by Egrets and Spoonbills, blaring white against the rich green of mangroves, skimming lightly as in a Japanese print over crocodile-infested shallows at eventide in the Sundarbans. . . .

Flock after flock of Canada Geese, flying in near-perfect V-formation—the symphony of their untamed voices raising "goose-flesh" in the watcher and the joy of returning spring. . . .

The lone Lammergeyer, soaring effortlessly against the backdrop of the mighty Himalayas. . . .

Oxpeckers creeping about the head and body of a giant Black Rhinoceros, deticking him. . . .

A Secretary bird in courtship display at Amboseli. . . .

Crowned Cranes dancing at Naivasha. . . .

An old familiar Redtail soaring above a farm woodlot against blue sky and fleecy cloud in southern Ontario. . . .

Before I witnessed "the most fabulous bird spectacle in the World", I had passed sixty-one winters and fifty-five summers. (The discrepancy can be explained: I had spent more of our summers amid snow and ice in Arctic regions than I had of our winters in the tropics.)

Lake Nakuru is an alkaline, or soda, lake lying in the Great Rift

Valley about ninety-five miles north of Nairobi, in Kenya. It is a small lake, less than eight miles long and four wide, covering in all an area of about twenty-four square miles. Its physical vegetational features, as befits an alkaline lake, are not particularly attractive. It has bare parched shorelines, caked with soda deposits and, for most of its margin, is bordered by broad belts of rather uninspiring Pa grass *(Sporobolus)* and sedges *(Cyperus).* Near the entrance gates, however—the lake and its surroundings are a Kenyan National Park—there are extensive stands of graceful "Fever trees", *Acacia xanthophloea.* These large relatives of the familiar plains country *acacias,* with tawny-orange bark, umbrella-like crowns, and fine feathery foliage, prefer areas near water. It followed that early African explorers frequently camped under them because of the certainty of water and shade. Naturally, areas with water in the arid portions of Africa were also favoured camping grounds for *Anopheles,* the malarial mosquito. In those early days, it was not known that *Anopheles* carried the malarial parasite, but it was soon deduced that those who camped beneath the sheltering shade of *Acacia xanthophloea* very often contracted malaria. In the days of the belief in "marsh miasma"—malaria means literally "bad air"—the association was made between emanations from the tree and the fever. For years, until the discoveries of Alphonse Laveran (1845-1922) and Sir Ronald Ross (1857-1932) in the late nineteenth century, the beautiful and innocent tree was shunned, and even today it carries the opprobrious name "Fever tree". Botanists, with greater sympathy, but with perhaps less imagination, call it the "Yellow-barked Acacia".

Beyond the lake on its eastern rim rises the rugged and tattered escarpment known as the Baboon Rocks—exciting to me as the home of a pair of giant, black Verreaux's Eagles.

What sets Lake Nakuru apart from every other lake in the world is the easy accessibility to close range observation of from one to two million flamingos.

My introduction to the flamingos of Lake Nakuru and "the most fabulous bird spectacle in the world" could hardly have been improved upon. A fairly stiff breeze was blowing and the water, instead of reflecting pale blue-sky colour, was rich oil-green, the perfect foil for pink flamingos. Pink against blue, palish blue, is not a colour combination an artist would choose, but pink against warm translucent green, its complement, was artistic perfection.

To say there was a flock of flamingos, a throng, a multitude or a swarm would be an understatement: there was a congestion of flamingos, a vast pink broadloom of flamingos, so densely packed that it was almost impossible to see singles for the mass. The halation from the almost solid crush of birds under the bright sun blurred and dazzled the eyes and stunned the senses. They were of two species: the rosy pink and crimson Lesser Flamingos, and the taller, white and light scarlet Greater Flamingos. The small Lessers outnumbered their big relatives by perhaps two thousand or more to one. That still meant there were about a thousand of the Greaters!

The fresh breeze was keeping the birds active, spreading and flapping their wings and lifting from the water in groups of a dozen to several hundred. As they spread their wings in their running, wing-flapping take-off, they revealed the bright colour of their wing coverts that resembled a crimson scarf or shawl across their backs. At times there were several thousand in the air at once, and though they flew only half a mile or so before realighting, they invariably formed up into some sort of rough formation, usually a coarse or ragged V or in Indian file. Their wings were long and adequate for the body size, but the long necks and legs, stretched straight out fore and aft, made them appear relatively short and small.

In flight the head is carried high, bent abruptly upward from the neck. This habit, combined with the curious configuration of the beak, presented a singularly bizarre appearance. The upward posturing of the head and beak was more pronounced in the Lesser—more so than in the Greater or in the American Flamingos, which I had seen some years before.

It is hard to describe their noise. The closest I can come to putting it in words is to say that it is something like the "honking" of geese. It is perhaps closest to the cries of some of the grey geese of the Old World. It lacks the deep resonance of the big Canada Goose, but is lower and richer than the "small-dog bark" of the Blues and Snows. There were too many calling at once and too much conversational gabble and cackle from the feeding hordes to hear a single voice clearly, but I got the impression that it was a two-syllabled, *honk-honk*. Assuredly, their vocalization has, en masse, the same

232

thrilling quality of wildness, of wilderness as the descant of wild geese.

The two species were almost invariably segregated. The Lesser, feeding on microscopic plant-life and blue-green algae, packed the shallow water near the shore. The Greaters, in small groups, were usually on the periphery where their long legs (ten inches longer than the smaller birds') and long necks permitted them to sieve the muddy bottom for their non-vegetarian diet of insect larvae, shrimps, and other small crustaceans. Because of its diet, the Greater Flamingo is not confined to soda lakes, and I had previously seen them in large numbers on the fresh-water lake near Point Calimere on the Coromandel coast in South India.

More remarkable even than the species segregation was the "generation gap". The immature Lesser Flamingos—easily distinguished by their white rather than rosy plumage and lack of the crimson back plumes of the adult—invariably formed the shoreward margin of the flocks. I was not able to discover why. Do they eat different food or are they forced to poorer feeding grounds by the adults? Out beyond the jam of feeding birds, in the deeper water of mid-lake swam rafts of flamingos. Their resemblance to pink swans was surprisingly precise.

It was not all flamingos: in the grass along the lake margin were Sacred Ibises, Blacksmith Plover, Kittlitz's Sand Plover, Egyptian Geese, and Yellow-billed Storks. Wading in the shallow water among the flamingos were Avocets and Black-winged Stilts, Ruffs and Marsh Sandpipers. Twenty Cape Widgeon were pirouetting in their mating dance, and out on the lake a big line of White Pelicans, behaving just like their American White Pelican relatives (though they are distinct species), was driving a school of some kind of alkaline-loving fish ahead of it into the shallow water where the carnage would take place. Behind us in the Pa grass a Secretary Bird, running with spread wings, caught a Cane Rat, and several solemn Marabous stood, each clutching the shaft of one leg with the foot of the other. In half a day, we recorded forty-two species of water birds; yet, we had spent nearly all our time watching flamingos.

It was with considerable reluctance that I left Nakuru that evening; I would dearly have enjoyed another two or three days on the shores of that lake. I promised myself that when Audrey joined me in Nairobi later in the month I would arrange another visit.

John Williams had planned a drive of about fifty miles that night to the Safariland Club on Lake Naivasha so that we might spend most of the next day on the launch touring about the lake. We would then push on to Nairobi to get on with our work. He told me that he really couldn't decide which of the two lakes he preferred. Head swimming from the sight of the flamingos, I found it hard to comprehend that any lake in the vicinity *without* flamingos could be competition to Nakuru. And flamingos just do not inhabit Lake Naivasha.

We arrived at Safariland long after dark, having paused numerous times to observe zebra, ostrich, and other animals. As we drove through the gates, several Spring Hares (giant rodents—dog-sized and with long hind legs) leaped through the beam of the headlights and bounded along the road in front of us like kangaroos.

Early next morning we boarded the launch and set out for Crescent Island Sanctuary. The contrast between lakes Nakuru and Naivasha—only fifty miles apart—was unbelievable. Naivasha is a sweet-water lake; thus, its shores support a rich vegetation. Papyrus abounded, its graceful feathery plumes imparting a soft, luscious margin in strong contrast to the bare harshness of bitter Nakuru. There were huge areas of cat-tails, their seeding spikes narrow and several times longer than the familiar Canadian species; every quiet bay was choked with bluish-pink water lilies.

I soon came to share John Williams's dilemma. From every clump of vegetation rose herons—Snowy, Yellow-billed, and Greater Egrets; Purple, Goliath, Grey, and Black-headed Herons; Squacco Herons, Greenbacked Herons, and Cattle Egrets. There were Hadada and Glossy Ibises; Long-tailed Cormorants and African Darters; Great-crested and Little Grebes; Moorhens, Red-knobbed Coots, big African Purple Gallinules, Lily-trotters, and Little Bitterns. The papyrus beds and cat-tails abounded with Black Crakes. Of ducks we saw African Pochards, Yellow-billed and Red-billed Ducks, Hottentot Teal, Knob-billed Geese, and the pert little African counterpart of our Ruddy—the Maccoa Duck. There were Grey-headed Gulls and White-winged Black Terns. Fishing Eagles perched on dead, drowned trees and squealed.

It was a maelstrom of birds. A dozen at least were in the air about us at any given moment: Herons and ibises flapped by, gulls and terns investigated the launch. What a richness of avian food must

234

exist in Naivasha. Perhaps the abundance of little *Hyperolius* tree frogs and their multitudinous tadpoles contributed largely to the heron larder.

Some birds obviously are not particular about what they eat or where they eat it. Common to both lakes were the Yellowbilled and Maribou Storks, Sacred Ibises, Pinkbacked and White Pelicans, Avocets, Blackwinged Stilts, and Egyptian Geese. But there were no flamingos and no Cape Widgeon.

I didn't keep an accurate list, but afterward, from recollection, I totted up the score. We outdid Nakuru by at least ten kinds of waterbirds.

A few days after Audrey arrived in Nairobi, John Williams drove us up to Lake Nakuru. Nairobi had been experiencing those "Scotch mist" days—dull, dark, and drizzly. Once we got down into the Great Rift Valley, however, the sun was shining, and although it was not hot it was pleasantly warm.

"It should be a great day for photography," said John. "I hope the flamingos will be there as they were the last time." I hoped so too, not only for Audrey's sake, but because I was laden with cameras and film. I approached the lake confident that I would get truly good photos of flamingos. I had no idea that I was to be sabotaged by a bikini.

There they were, one and a half, two million of them, packed in close to the shore. Can anyone distinguish between one and two million at a glance?

The excitement and the confusion of the first visit was forsaken. I felt calm. This would be a cold, calculating recording of the great spectacle of Nakuru. I prepared the camera; there would be no wild shooting today. It would be serene and purposeful.

We rolled closer.

"Whoosh." Suddenly the air was filled with flamingos. They had taken wing in alarm, in panic.

"Good God," I yelled, "what did that? A Marabou Stork or was it the Verreaux's Eagles from Baboon Rock?"

"No!" said John. "It was that damned woman."

A tourist's car had stopped a little ahead of us, and a shapely girl in a bikini had leaped out and, frolicking like a movie starlet, had run down to the shore to scare up the flamingos. Her long, light brown hair flying out behind her, she then ran along the beach with exaggerated grace, conscious of her lovely body, waving her arms and exploding all the flamingos into wild flight. Scuppered by a bikini!

The flamingos rose in great ruby clouds, and as fast as their wings could carry them, they flew to the inaccessable opposite side of the lake. It was the most beautiful sight that I have ever *not* enjoyed.

I didn't say a word—I couldn't.

The only compensation was the almost instantaneous appearance of a Park Warden who, in obvious anger, stopped his car and raced out after her. He escorted her back to her car, put her into it, and convoyed the car out toward the exit gates.

She and her companion had been expelled from the Park. All visitors on entering are cautioned against disturbing or closely approaching the birds. They are asked to respect the rights of others who follow them.

The day was ruined. It was one of those calm days when the birds found it comfortable to stay where they were. They settled down in an immense rosy blanket at the far end of the lake, and stayed there. A few hundred did come back, and I photographed them, but it was ashes in the mouth. I had wanted the *big* flock.

Atmosphere of Africa

East Africa—whirlwinds leaping across the dusty plains of Amboseli as the dawn sun agitates the cold night-air. Some mere twenty-foot "dust devils", others awesomely tall, dark whirling chimneys threatening to grow into tornados. Their powdery-fine dust enveloping herds of zebra, which emerge still calmly feeding, but now a pale clay colour, their stripes all but invisible. The gloomy, foreboding Budongo Forest, its thousand naves echoing to the hooting of troops of Chimpanzees and the thunderclaps of violent flash storms. The tranquil Victoria Nile fringed with beds of graceful feathery papyrus and enormous crocodiles. Old belligerent tusker elephants challenging for, and invariably achieving, right-of-way on the brick-red murram roads of Tsavo. Pale, delicate-looking, but immensely hardy thorn bushes pioneering the fresh lava slopes of the volcanic cones of Shitani. The delightfully cool oasis below Mzima Springs, its pellucid waters revealing every detail of swimming hippos. The chimerical world of giant heaths and groundsels and Hygenea trees vestured in ten-foot, swaying strands of yellow lichen high in the Aberdares. A stealthy leopard in Nairobi Park with the id of Kipling's cat "that walked by himself, by his wild lone, and all places were alike to him". Testy young bull elephants jousting, the evening air of Kilaguni resounding to the crash of ivory. The leggy elegance of gorgeously patterned giraffes in the lush undulating woodlands of Manyara. Vast Lake Edward, its Kazinga channel choked with snorting, wallowing hippos, its banks spattered with Pink-backed and White Pelicans, with Egyptian Geese and Water Dikkops and Yellow-billed and Marabou Storks. Lammergeyers soaring effortlessly on the convection currents rising up the sheer, rust-coloured cliffs of Hell's Gate. The snow-clad crests of the Ruwenzoris—the Mountains of the Moon—towering above fulvous, moisture-saturated cloud. Lean, near-naked Masai carrying staves and lion spears and driving their rabble of cattle, which stir up billowing clouds of choking dust. A Black Rhino charging the Land Rover. A glimpse of Kilimanjaro at sunset.

The big old "tusker" stood by the roadside stuffing himself with morning glories. He pulled up the whole plant with his trunk, beat off the dust against his chest and sides, and conveyed it to his mouth. While we watched he ate four, ten or twelve-foot long vines—leaves, white flowers, stems, roots everything.

We edged forward in the Peugeot station-wagon. When we were about forty yards away he stopped consuming morning glories and laid his ears back like an angry cat. He walked to the edge of the road and faced us. We backed up thirty yards. He looked at us for a few minutes and then ambled off to the bed of morning glories. He pulled

237

one up, beat the red dust off on his forelegs and stuffed it into his mouth. He was about twenty yards from the road. We gingerly edged forward again, but when we got close he whirled and raced out to the roadside. We backed up, this time about fifty yards.

The routine was repeated several times.

"He just isn't going to let us by," said John Williams. "And he's far too big to argue with." John turned the car around and we found another road to our destination. When last seen the old bull was stuffing his mouth with morning glories.

It wasn't a rare or isolated occurrence in vast Tsavo National Park in Kenya. Each time it was an old, lone bull. None actually charged the car, but each played a game with us. It was as if the big, petulant brute got pleasure out of tantalizing us. Invariably he would walk off just far enough that we thought we had a chance to sneak by; but every time we tried, he ambulated quickly back and stood eyeing us. The head was held low with its tusks in direct line with us. There was no denying he meant business. Anyway, only a fool would call the bluff of a six-ton elephant.

Whether these solitary bulls have been ousted by the herd or are hermits by crotchety choice is a good question. I suspect the latter because there was no sign of apathy or decrepitude about any of them.

The silence with which elephants can travel through the forest is astonishing. It is best demonstrated at a water hole where they come to drink in the late afternoon or evening. A five- or six-ton animal, twelve feet high at the shoulder, will suddenly just "be there" at the water's edge. There has been no sound, no warning. They are just rather quiet animals that take great care where they place their feet.

Except from bigger and stronger specimens of their own kind, I never saw an elephant back away from any animal—except one. That was from a big bull Black Rhinoceros at the waterhole at Kilaguni in Tsavo Park. He emerged from the shadows of the thorn scrub one evening and approached the waterhole to drink. There were several elephants at the water's edge on the opposite side of the pool. The rhino had no sooner lowered his head to the water than one of the elephants objected. He was a young hothead, spoiling for a brawl. He went around the waterhole at a trot and stopped a few feet short of the rhino who had turned to face him. The elephant's ears were fanned and held high, his trunk was curled in behind the tusks he was

238

waving to and fro. His tail stuck out almost straight behind with a shallow S-curve in it. He was an elephant that meant business. He took a few more shuffling steps, gave out an irritable squeal and shook his big head. The rhino stood his ground and lowered his head until the massive nose-horn pointed squarely at the elephant. There was a discordant din made up of snorts, squeals, screeches, and trumpeting, much of it made by the rhino; then the elephant slowly backed up a few steps. The rhino having stared down his opponent, followed up his advantage with a short, light-footed charge. The elephant turned and shuffled off to a respectable distance. He still watched the now-drinking rhino, and several times vocally expressed his displeasure, but he didn't resume his physical challenge.

The ferocity of rhinos has been, I think, greatly exaggerated. They are very quick and restless in their movements and capable of a smart trot. They often seem a bit flighty and rattlepated, whisking around on a whim and trotting off like a light-footed fat man in running shoes. I had a rhino attack only once and that was hardly a charge with genuine intent. The Land Rover easily pulled out of the line of his rush and he stopped right on the spot where the car had been and looked the other way. He was puzzled. He looked as if he thought he had had a hallucination—there was no Land Rover there. He quickly forgot about it and with a toss of his head trotted back to rejoin his mate. I grew to like rhinos; I felt a certain sympathy for them. (I can be quite as rattlepated as they are.)

It was giraffes that truly won my affection as no other animal has quite done. Start with one of the most grotesquely shaped and gorgeously coloured and patterned animals in the world. Also the tallest. Add a gracefully waving neck and long slender legs moving in dream-like, slow-motion ballet steps, the front feet falling almost in line, the hind ones straddling. The giraffe is a pacer—the legs on the same side work in unison. It seems to move faster than the leg action would allow; as if a giraffe running west has its apparent speed aided by a slow motion camera panning toward the east. There is almost a time-lapse movement; yet, the animal seems to flaunt rapidly by as in a fantasy.

I was fortunate enough one day to witness two separate combats engaged in by male Masai Giraffes in Nairobi National Park, combats normally aimed at winning or holding territorial domination and the possession of females. We had had a long spell of dark, cool, cloudy weather, but this day broke fine and clear and turned warm. All the animals in the park seemed in buoyant good spirits as if exhilarated by the emergence of the sun. The baboons were even bolder than usual, leaping on the car hood and peering in through the windshield. The wildebeest were frisky and skittish, prancing and curvetting, kicking up their heels and pursuing each other at their utmost speed. A female ostrich, crouching low with wings outspread and elbows raised high above her back, enticed a male off into the acacias. The zebras' behaviour was scandalous!

The duelling of giraffes was, like every other giraffe action, graceful and refined. There were four males paired off into two sets of antagonists about thirty feet apart. "Neck wrestling" was their method of fighting. Wrap your index fingers loosely about each other, imagine them to be six or seven-foot long giraffe necks and you have a fair approximation. On occasion a long neck would be inclined sideways, almost in a semi-circle, sometimes wrapped around the front of, sometimes the back of, an opponent's neck. Only rarely was there a buffeting blow, but there was no doubt a good deal of muscular exertion involved. It was reminiscent of the combat wrestling of Red Rattlesnakes or even the pub game played by men in which the elbows are placed on the table, right hands locked, and pressure exerted to see who can put the other down. Eventually, all four desisted and browsed together in harmony among the acacias. I concluded that they were young males merely playing at or practising fighting in preparation for the day when it would be of serious consequence.

Whatever, it was one of the loveliest sights I've ever seen, so gracious that I half wished it could have been courtship between the sexes—necking—rather than brawls between males.

Nature is like a gigantic variety show, she has her fine singers and actors, the stars, but she also presents, on occasion, the comedians. My favourite African comic was the Wart Hog. The thing about "wart-piggies" is that they don't have to *do* anything to be funny, except just being there. Their disproportionately huge, ugly heads, the ragged mane of coarse hair on the shoulder hump, the white "mutton-chop" sideburns combined with dainty, little feet make one think of the outlandishly dressed "top bananas" of the burlesque of

240

earlier days. But it is when he runs that the Wart Hog becomes a real wag. He trots off with rapid little mincing steps, albeit pitter-pattering as lightly as a cat, with his ridiculous, thin little tail stuck straight up like a tiny flag pole. His "flag" is a few stiff hairs that project horizontally from the tail-tip. I always think of a slim-handled Japanese back-scratcher, the kind with the carved hand on the end.

Zebras impressed me as dumb horses—not that this is bad, because on earlier pack-train trips I had learned not to care too much for smart horses. A horse with a mind of his own can be a bother and a nuisance. So, I liked the stupid zebras as soon as I saw them. Many years ago, we ran an animal-popularity contest at the Royal Ontario Museum among the school children. To our surprise, it wasn't the lion who won nor the deer; it wasn't the rabbit or the fluffy owl. It was the zebra. True, it was in the days when horses drew milk and bread wagons, and I attributed the zebra's success to it being a familiar animal in clown's clothing—in harlequin stripes, just the thing to appeal to a child's humour. It was probably the zebra's stubborn stupidity that saved it from domestication and disappearance from the wild scene and preserved it for what it should be—a stunningly beautiful component of the African grasslands landscape.

My conversations with game wardens and hunters in East Africa led me to the conclusion that the African Buffalo is the most re-spected and dreaded of the "big five" (buffalo, elephant, rhino, lion, leopard). Yet, under normal circumstances it is the one least likely to inspire fear. In Queen Elizabeth National Park in southwestern Uganda we had an uneasy moment as a big herd of Buffalo broke from the bushes and raced toward the stationary Land Rover. Edward, our guide, didn't budge. The herd, obviously impelled only by curiosity, came to a standstill at about one hundred feet and stared at us with typical uncomprehending bovine expressions—a herd of cows in a pasture field. How long they would have remained gaping I don't know, for we wearied and drove away.

Next to the giraffe, I was impressed by the Cheetah. There is something gallant and sporting in its lung-bursting chase of a gazelle—the Cheetah's sides and rib-cage heaving after every kill run down in fair pursuit; not dry-gulched from lurking ambush as with the Leopard. Yet, the Leopard, by his wile and cunning and fierce

241

adaptability to rain forest, thorn-brush country, and open woodland will likely survive for many decades. The Cheetah is already rare and vanishing.

But when I think of Africa, my mind conjures up the dry thorn-brush country, dotted with parasol-topped acacias and Whistling Thorn, with the beauteous, statuesque necks of giraffes towering above them.

Guess Who's
Coming to Lunch

Most of our alfresco luncheons in East Africa were a failure. There were too many interruptions or disturbances of one kind or another. Once it was a Gabar Goshawk at the Hippo Pools in Nairobi National Park. It was a big female and she had the poor timing to arrive just as I had the ham and cheese between two pieces of French bread. By the time I got through examining her with the binoculars, I was involved with a Nubian Woodpecker, a fine species between a Hairy and a Downy, or a Great Spotted and Lesser Spotted in size—olive-grey with scarlet crown and golden-yellow tail. I never did find that sandwich again.

Another time it was a pair of D'Arnaud's Barbets. They chose the very moment that I was about to bite into the cold roast beef to start singing. Their song is one that cannot be ignored. The pair faces each other and starts a weird song that John Williams writes as *doo, do, dee, dok.* First it is antiphonal, then in duet. Heads are thrown back, beaks widely opened. The performance is a masterpiece of timing and amusing, too. I had to go over to see and listen to it. On the way back I got stopped by Von der Decken's Hornbills.

I had a sandwich in the car.

Even the lunches in well-run Kilaguni Lodge in Tsavo got all distracted and befuddled by the arrival of numbers of Superb Starlings and Redbilled and Whiteheaded Buffalo Weavers. They landed cheekily on the tables and proceeded to help themselves to our lunches. They seemed very partial to butter especially the starlings, and dabbed greedily at the saucers full of butter pats. The rib-tickler came when they wiped their beaks on the backs of the chairs. Thus alerted, Audrey and I noticed many greasy chair backs and soon learned to sit up straight and well forward at subsequent meals. We couldn't help chuckling at the consternation of fat men and dowagers who wondered how they got butter on their necks, their collars or their pearls.

One day, high in the Aberdare mountains, it was baboons who came to luncheon. We were going to have a picnic lunch at the most scenic spot opposite Queen's Cave Falls. I suppose the impressiveness of the straight drop of the falls, the giant groundsels and heaths on the abutting slopes, the wild gladioli, the Martial Eagle in the sky, all relaxed our vigilance a bit too long. We tarried a while before going back to the car. A window had been left open. A dozen Olive Baboons, big dogs, females, and big-headed, big-eared youngsters had invaded the car. A big dog baboon can be an ugly and dangerous opponent; so, we made a concerted charge by our entire force, shouting and yelling as loud as we could. We routed them, but not before the biggest "dog" had made off with a detective novel in his mouth.

Another time, John Williams took Audrey and me into Nairobi Park. We planned to have our picnic lunch under the big acacia, down on the flat rocks near Hippo Pools. We had a fine old cheese, some excellent sliced cooked ham, a loaf of French bread, some apple tarts, and a thermos flask of tea. It was going to be a luncheon to remember.

It was.

We had no sooner laid everything out on the big table-like rock—the food, the knives, forks, spoons, plates, and cups—and settled ourselves down to eat and to discuss the observations of the forenoon when *they* appeared. They came down the trees, through the grass; they came through the thorn scrub; they vaulted the stream on stepping-stone boulders. They surrounded us. They were Blackfaced Vervets, small yellowish-grey monkeys, with black faces that were bordered on both sides and above the close-set beady eyes with tufts of white hair. Audrey and I were enchanted; John, who knew better, was umbrageous. He bellowed, threw sticks, charged them. To no avail. They were too quick, too agile, too nimble. One had the cheese, one the bread. We got back the cheese; John chased the big male with the bread. Fortunately the loaf was too long and awkward for the vervet. He stumbled enough so that John caught him and grabbed the bread. A tug-of-war followed. John won.

The rest of the luncheon was consumed in a state of siege. Vervets sat, stood or wandered about, trying to look unconcerned, then darted in on a daring raid, to be yelled at, chased, and flung at with sticks and stones. In spite of the utmost vigilance, they stole half the cheese and spilled the tea. One small ball of greased lightning raced up on our blind side and snatched an apple tart right out of Audrey's hand just as she was about to take a bite of it. The luncheon degenerated into a shambles. We packed everything up, surrounded by the most innocuous and innocent looking group of monkeys ever seen.

The height of interjacence occurred one day on the Magadi road. Starting from Nairobi we had crossed the seven-thousand-foot southern end of the Ngong hills, dropping rapidly down the eastern wall of the Great Rift Valley to the hot plains five thousand feet below. We passed Olorgassailie, the site of the prehistoric cultures of hand-axe people, which had been developed into a natural Museum-National Park by Dr. Louis S. B. Leakey.

Our objective on this day was to collect as many of the specimens as we could for the ROM's grasslands exhibit. We began to hunt near Lake Magadi, and soon had some Helmeted Guinea Fowl, Yellow-necked Spurfowl, Namaqua Doves, and other needed species. By mid-day, it had become extremely hot and we sought out a luncheon site under the partial shade of some acacia trees near a waterhole. We hoped from this point we might see enough wildlife to make the meal more than just restorative. We looked out on open plains with lofty outcrops of rock, of rounded hill, and dense semi-desert scrub-thickets—"all those bushes have thorns," I thought.

One moment, we were sitting there on the ground, talking, enjoying the food and the accomplishment of the morning; the next we were surrounded by Masai. Tall, thin, lissom, with no great muscular development but nonetheless well-built. Long-limbed, big hands and feet. Their features were almost Caucasian with well-developed bridges to their noses and with finely cut nostrils; only a slight tendency toward prognathism distinguished their features. Their ears had been deformed by piercing the lobes and extending them into long loops like leathery string. Their hair had been twisted and plaited, probably interwoven with strips of leather or straw, matted and coated with red ochre and mutton fat or cow dung and gathered into four broadbased queues, one at the back, one over the forehead and one over each ear. Their bodies, too, had been coated with grease and red ochre. They were adorned with long pendulous earrings, necklaces, armbands, calf-bands and anklets of iron wire, seeds, trade beads, bird feathers, and common nails. Slung over one shoulder and exposing their entire nudity as they moved about was a cloak or cape of orange-ochre or terra-cotta calico.

As they appeared, boldly but soundlessly from all sides, they spat. They spat to the right and to the left. They spat within inches of our feet. One, whom I afterward learned was a head man, spat the four points of the compass.

Most of them were carrying lion *assegai* six to seven feet long, the extremely long narrow spear portion of which occupied about half of their length. Others had short broad-tipped *simes,* a kind of sword, and shillelagh-like knobkerries.

I admit to having felt quite uneasy, but decided to take my cue from Rob Glen who spoke fluent Swahili and passable Masai. After all, we had one shotgun between the lot of us and it was in the car, thirty feet away.

Rob said, "Spit", and suited his action to the word. My mouth felt too dry. I took a big swig of tea and spouted out a voluminous expectoration. This was greeted by a cackle of laughter from the Masai. I thought of my stupidity with the goat-rancher in Mexico years ago. "Tonto Norteamericano, I've done it again," I thought. But it passed off without notice. "Keep spitting," said Rob. "Its their way of saying welcome."

Rob spoke to the head man or elder and a lengthy conversation followed. It seemed to consist of a brief query, succeeded by an equally brief reply and a long series of *ums, aiys, aas* and *n'yas,* all enunciated as we would say *uh-huh*. At the conclusion, the elder took a small cigar-sized cylinder, I think a section of bamboo, from a fold in his cape, removed a plug from its end and poured a pinch of coarse dark snuff-like powder, which I suspect was tobacco mixed with potash, into Rob's hand. Rob tucked a fingertipful into the space between his lower lip and front teeth and extended the remainder to the elder. This ritual seemed to be repeated several times at the end of which we were evidently accepted as friends—or at least as customers, for it soon became apparent that the Masai had goods to sell.

At this point Rob offered some of our lunch. It had been my understanding that these men—warriors of the pastoral Masai—ate nothing but cattle blood mixed with milk. Chunks of French bread, good cheddar cheese, and fine sliced ham were accepted and eagerly consumed. How times have changed. After that I never saw a Masai, at Magadi, Amboseli or Ngorongoro refuse my proffered bread, cheese, cookies, apples, or whatever!

All the while, swarms of flies clustered about their eyes and lips, the Masai making little or no effort to brush them off. These were flies that looked similar to house flies and, as a natural consequence of the Masai's enormous rabble of cattle, are superbly abundant. Soon, we had flies buzzing about us and attempting to alight at the corners of our eyes to drink. I abandoned any semblance of politeness or stoicism. I brushed and swatted them away. I had seen too many Masai children, along the roadside, with their eyes bunged up and with flies feeding on the moisture—probably with chronic ophthalmia, a disease that eventually leads to cataracts and blindness, and is spread from one to another of the Masai by the millions of flies that are attracted by their cattle and the inescapable dung.

We finally made our escape, pursued by the Masai whom Rob said had thought better about the price paid for spears and fly swishers by some of our party.

I had admired the Masai. I admired their fierce integrity, their refusal to be brain-washed, their refusal to be indoctrinated by advancing "civilization". I had been disappointed that their capes had looked so faded and drab. Then I learned the truth and I didn't like what I learned. The facts of life are usually sordid. The government of Kenya had denied the Masai the dyes that they had used for ages to make colourful their sublime and distinctive robes.

246

The Lion Who
Wasn't Afraid

I had been in Africa for more than six weeks and hadn't seen a lion, in fact had begun to despair of ever seeing one. I had encountered much rarer animals—Chimpanzee, Serval, Neumann's Genet, Stuhlman's Elephant Shrew, Honey Badger, Giant Forest Hog, Percival's Dwarf Mongoose, Pell's Tomb Bat, and Chanler's Mountain Reedbuck, but no lion. I had, by day, actually had a good view of a Tree Hyrax. Everybody *hears* them at night, but they are seldom seen. The thought of returning to Canada and being forced to acknowledge to my colleagues that I didn't see a lion in Africa was unthinkable.

It is true that I had other things to look for, to study, and to collect, and that I had spent much of my time in lion-less Budongo Forest. I had been in Nairobi National Park four times, however, and in other lion-inhabited areas and had anticipated that I would surely encounter a lion, even fortuitously, in that time. I began to chide my hosts that I didn't believe lions still existed other than in California zoos.

It was on my fifth visit to Nairobi National Park that Daphne Ball put an end to that. She spotted a young male lazily sunning himself in tall Red Oatgrass. He may not have been much of a lion, but he was my first and, as it turned out, he proved to be the ice-breaker. From then on we just couldn't miss seeing lions. In another six weeks, I would be telling a National Park ranger in Uganda not to bother looking for lions, that I would much prefer to see more of Topi, Uganda Kob, and Bush Pig; yet, he led me to my finest experience with lions.

It was in Queen Elizabeth National Park and the Chief Game Warden had assigned a ranger and a Land Rover to Audrey and me. The ranger, a big burly but very quiet man, was named Edward. One day when I was out alone with Edward, he took me to a swampy place where at least a hundred hippos lay snoozing in thick mud. Edward seldom spoke. On this occasion he just pointed. At first, all I could see was a flock of Cattle Egrets perched on what appeared to be a large area of mud flat. For a second I was puzzled—what was so remarkable about four dozen Cattle Egrets? Then I became aware of the strange conformation of the mud. It was composed entirely of low, slightly-rounded hippopotamus-sized mounds each of which sported an eye and an ear. They were packed in like plums in a basket and had wallowed in so thoroughly that the only unmuddied parts were the eyeballs and insides of the ears! I laughed; it really was one of the most amusing sights I had ever witnessed in nature. I was sorry that Audrey had missed it.

The following day, after having had fair luck with Uganda Kob, Topi, Defassa Waterbuck, elephant, and buffalo and a good view of a Crowned Hawk-Eagle as well as many other birds, Edward made a lengthy detour that puzzled us a bit. We travelled through parts of the Park unknown to me and even took off across country, Edward driving faster than I had ever known him to do. Just before dark, we arrived at the hippo wallow, which he had approached by a short cut. Flashing one of his rare handsome smiles, Edward proudly pointed them out to Audrey. She wasn't going to miss anything if Edward could help it.

Late the next afternoon Edward announced that he wanted to show us some lions. Now, we had, over the past three weeks in Kenya and Tanzania, seen lions, lions of almost every description: large, small, spotted, fat, and lean. We had even seen lions dozing fifteen feet up in big acacia trees at Lake Manyara. I therefore told Edward not to waste too much time or go to too much trouble over it. But with silent, dogged determination he persisted in driving over quite bumpy savannah country, circling about, and scanning every patch of thorn bush. He drove right through a herd of elephants and when I said, "Isn't that a bit dangerous, Edward?" He replied, "Oh, no. I know the elephants in this herd." The search continued. We decided to "give him his head". After all, he had known what he was doing when he took Audrey back to the hippo mud-bath, and whatever kind of lion he was pursuing must be something special or he wouldn't be insisting.

At last he gave a small grunt of satisfaction and wheeled the Land Rover toward a patch of scrubby brush. In its shade reposed the remnants of a lion kill—a big mature African Buffalo. Its internals and most of its flesh were gone and there was little left but the dark and bloody skeleton. Gnawing idly at the carcass were two lionesses. Others lay on their backs in the flattened grass about it. One was lying on her back with all four limbs extended about as far apart as possible, her neck stretched out so that the top of her head and nose touched the ground. As we drove closer, we could see between the almost-bare ribs of the buffalo something moving about in the body cavity. It was a small cub that had climbed inside and was enjoying a snack of short ribs.

Then Edward, in his imperturable way, pointed his massive arm to the right. Lions! The grass was full of lions. Replete on buffalo beef, they sprawled in every conceivable position. I think every comfortable, flexuous, resting attitude assumed by the common domestic cat was represented in this "sprawl of lions". Some had heads or forelegs or even hind legs cradled on the bellies of others. Frisky cubs wrestled each other or their mother's tail. They were surfeited and content now, but the scene at that buffalo carcass an hour or two earlier must have resembled a rummage sale in a bargain basement—for they were all females, except for a few yearling males and presumably some cubs.

We stood up with our heads and shoulders through the roof-hatch of the Land Rover. We counted nineteen lions and there were undoubtedly more because the presence of one or two of those we counted was betrayed only by a twitching tail or the yawning stretch of a forearm and paw. The only missing element was an adult, maned male. I suspect that if any males were associated with this huge pride, which I doubt, they were hiding and dozing a good safe way off from all those youngsters.

Larger groups have been recorded, but not very often, and we were glad that we had not been able to dissuade Edward. Although it was already a bit dark for photography, I shot some film anyway. Edward had both the courtesy and the courage to shut off the motor, and I started taking pictures with the lens wide open and at exposure speeds I had never attempted, hand held, before. I didn't know it at the time but I was actually getting some of my best lion shots.

I conveyed my thanks to Edward wordlessly: one doesn't talk too much or too loudly when you are in the centre of a pride of nineteen or more lions, all within eighty feet. He silently acknowledged my thanks, started the motor, and then instead of retreating, drove slowly and carefully right up to the largest sleeping, dozing, and "burping" group. I popped up through the hatch again and finished the roll of film. We had lions to the right of us, to the left of us, in front of and behind us, some of them not ten feet away. I thought of the long years during which I had dreamed of seeing just *one* wild African Lion. This was beyond any expectations.

We stayed until it was almost dark. Just sitting there, looking, enjoying, drinking in the whole delightful experience. Then Edward drove away, carefully avoiding lion tails. I'm sure much of his concern was not to disturb or frighten the lions.

I was greatly impressed by the multiformity of the lion. There is greater individual diversity in facial bone and limb structure and possibly in temperament than in any other wild cat I know. I believe they even challenge the house cat in this respect. It is particularly noticeable in adult males. Some have an insolent, common expression, others are true patricians.

It was in the caldera of Ngorongoro in Tanzania that I met the lion I christened "Bert Lahr". He was an enormous beast with a great heavy head, and the darkest and most luxuriant mane that I had ever seen on any lion, not excluding those in zoos or museums. But his face was *funny*! He reminded me of the "cowardly Lion" played by Bert Lahr in the motion picture *The Wizard of Oz*. It was evidently the result of extremely well-developed masseter and buccinator muscles, and his upper lips, from which sprouted an exuberant growth of pale vibrissae, were extravagantly puffy. His eyes were small, set close together and squinty. When we were near him, he looked at us with an air of inquiring good humour, for all the world like an overgrown puppy. I have seen the same kind of expression on the face of a dog inviting a boy to play. But there could be no cowardice anywhere in his five hundred pounds of spring-steel muscle. Hence, he couldn't be the "cowardly Lion"; he had to be "Bert Lahr". He had a way with females that I envied. Three beautiful lionesses lay near him in the grass. He rumbled, growled, and bit lovingly at the ear or nose of one—the others showed no indication of irritation or jealousy. Once something that I couldn't see approached through the tall grass and he leaped up with lashing tail and gave forth with a bellowing growl of the magnitude and authority peculiar to his kind. He stood for a moment, then allowed his angry tail to relax and lay down by one of his wives. Whatever had had the temerity to intrude also had the good sense to heed the warning and look for another area of operation. I suspect that it was a jackal.

At the other end of the scale was a big male at Lake Manyara in Tanzania. We discovered him under the shade of some acacias. He was old, his blunted canines were dark orange-yellow with age, his straggly thorn-torn mane was orange-red, his eyes a cruel pale green, and his hide bore innummerable scars. That long rip on his back—a gouge from the horn of buffalo or waterbuck? The broad, rounded scar on his shoulder where the hair now refused to grow—the kick of a terrified giraffe? Those short, deep scars on his nose and muzzle? Any one of many things could have left those mementoes, but I preferred to think they were the lesions resulting from cuffs given him by recalcitrant mates. But I had to change my opinion as I became aware of his lioness standing not far away. She was young, as evidenced by her still strongly spotted legs, but she was mature. Tall, lean, and heavily muscled, she was a superb specimen. It was a bit of a shocker to discover the ugly old boy had a young and beautiful wife. But it was a stunner when in a moment or two, a second and equally young and equally handsome lioness emerged from the thorn bushes and joined them. Two young and beautiful wives!

The patriarch was angry. I believe he was crotchety from the heat and the flies. He became truly upset when we drove right up to him. He was of course, totally within his rights. A tourist attempting to take a picture of me in a deck chair in the privacy of my own garden would have been greeted, very probably, by an even more bellicose reaction. But being humans, the lords of creation, we pressed on until at last I was taking portraits of his outraged face at about twelve feet. The Tanzanian ranger remarked, "He's quick-tempered, you see he has red hair." This unexpected remark struck our funny bones and we laughed. That did it. It was as if the old warrior could stand

251

anything but ridicule. He charged, snarling viciously, cuffed the side of the Land Rover, and then apparently considering that we had been sufficiently chastised, turned and walked deliberately off into thicker brush, his tail lashing like that of an angry tom cat. For a moment it appeared that one of his loyal mates was about to take up the combat, but she thought better of it and both lionesses followed "old redhead" into the trees.

It was in Ngorongoro Crater, though, that I found the Lion I had been looking for. We had left behind the bone-chilling equatorial cold of the ten-thousand-foot rim of the great crater and were now driving across the close-cropped grass of the crater floor, two thousand feet lower. We had been seeing Eland, Spotted Hyaenas, dainty Bat-eared Foxes, Defassa Waterbuck, Masai Giraffe, and of course lions, and there were thousands of wildebeest and zebras outlined against the blue-scraped rim of the amphitheatre. Suddenly, a great dark blob on the plains caused me to sing out, "Buffalo at 2:00 o'clock."

As we drove across the grassland toward the object it soon became evident that it was no buffalo but the dark mane of an enormous lion. He was the most magnificient one that I had seen. Here indeed was a lion entitled to the term "noble". He made it easy to understand the awe and admiration in which lions have been held since the beginning of recorded time. He was young enough to have retained a few faint spots on his hind limbs; old enough to exhibit a few battle scars on his muzzle. A lion in the prime of life. His long face had an aristocratic expression. His powerful lower jaw had a protruding goatee of purest white. His mane, long and luxuriant, was dark tawny with an almost black blaze rising up from the centre of his forehead, and was rich, dark brown where it fell around his shoulders.

"Bert Lahr" had been funny, the "Redhead" had been ill-tempered. This one was what you expected of the "King of Beasts". He was not, perhaps, quite as large or heavy as "Bert Lahr" or some of the other lions we had met, but he was still a giant. It was, rather, the proud nobility of his carriage, the symmetry and fine proportion of his head, and the quiet unruffled dignity that appealed. He scarcely looked at us as we drove up. One felt that it must have been some of his lordly ancestors who had inspired the great paintings and sculptures of the "ideal" lion. He had obviously eaten well and, as there was a stiff breeze blowing, he was not being bothered by flies. This, perhaps, explains his placidity. I had ample opportunity to photograph him in a variety of relaxed lion postures. He gave me full face, three-quarter views, and his "John Barrymore"—left and right. He licked his paws, his lips, and his nose. He growled a little, snarled a little, more I think from a full stomach and a touch of flatulence than from annoyance at us. Finally, he yawned prodigiously, lay down, and went to sleep.

All the while, four wildebeest were standing less than forty yards behind him. They stood and stared at him in what seemed like an uncomprehending manner, but they must have known instinctively that he and his pride had fed and that there was no danger, at least until sundown, because instead of bolting in typical, skittish wildebeest fashion, they resumed feeding, grazing casually, and even moving a little closer.

I took one more picture of his massive dozing head and left him in peace. As we drove off I had a sensation of inward warmth and satisfaction. We had approached to within twenty feet of the king of beasts.

And he had not been afraid.

Epilogue

A museum is an extraordinary place, very unlike most organizations with which one can be associated. It is staffed largely by accumulators, gatherers with a difference. They collect not for their own private holdings but to add to the treasures of a public repository. Strangely enough, they lack none of the private collector's ardour, indeed their zeal would be difficult to surpass.

In the history of any individual, institution or state, the early struggling years are perhaps the "finest hours". This, I think, is especially true of an establishment conceived and dedicated to the stimulation and advancement of the cultural atmosphere of a community. Aspiration, passion and opportunism are at their optimum when directed toward as yet unattained ideals. There is indeed "zest in quest".

In the late summer and autumn the life sciences side of the old Royal Ontario Museum became agog with excitement as the field parties began to return with their collections. New species and new knowledge were being added to the storehouse and we all shared the exhilaration of it. The important acquisitions, of course, were the large general collections that filled the gaping holes in our awareness of the distribution and ecology of our common animals, but the excitement often lay in the discovery of the unexpected. One year it would be the finding of Yellowcheeked Voles and the resolving of their habitat requirements in the province; another year perhaps Sharptailed Sparrows breeding on the margins of James bay. Then the palaeontologists would bring in their summer's work—two dinosaurs new to science! The staff's curiosity and elation were tempered only by the knowledge that it might well be a year before they could be uncrated, removed first from their protective wrappings, then from the matrix they were found in and exposed to our eager gaze. Species new to the collections were always milestones. Each represented a niche filled and added to our conjoint pride in the growing collections of the Museum. (I vividly remember my first—a Kittlitz's Murrelet collected from a skiff after two misses on the billowing waves of the Gulf of Alaska.)

Those concerned with "The Works of Man Through All the Years" were equally zealous and the great collections for which the institution is now renowned grew at an astonishing rate.

Behind the objects in the Museum are the people, most of them long departed, who acquired them, by hard work, sometimes at risk of life and limb, usually with determination, perseverence and with a kind of fanatic pride in their institution.

It was my special privilege to be initiated into the small team of fiercely persistent acquisitors of that period so there is probably an element of nostalgia and introspection in my recollections. The Royal Ontario Museum goes on, with new stimulating challenges, new exciting responsibilities, new broader horizons. Collecting continues to be important but also there is a growing need for refined research, an increased demand for publication and dissemination of knowledge and an important role as the unbiased supplier of proven data on the all important subjects of conservation, resource use and survival.

But it remains that a museum's first and basic function is that of a receptacle of history in the form of specimens and artifacts and their provenance. And so it is that my frequent lone rambles through the galleries and collection rooms are not solo ones. In front of a showcase housing Chinese porcelain figurines I seem to hear a hearty voice proclaim, "Aren't they marvellous! Have you heard how I got them?" The skeleton of a big duckbilled dinosaur invokes another voice that tells of the prospecting for, the discovery, the field preparation and the transportation by horse and wagon of the great bones of the Badlands. Before a tray of specimens of many gorgeous Birds of Paradise in the "Bird-Room" I fancy I smell the smoke of Peg-Top cigars. And so it goes. As I look at the gallery mounts of the big bison, the caribou and the lions, at the scintillating gemstones in Mineralogy, anthropomorphic masks and totems from the west coast, a Grecian urn, tropical lepidoptera, Eskimo sealskins and ivories, faces emerge and loom in a shadowy montage; voices return and reverberate through the high ceilinged chambers.

The ghosts of the giants walk the halls of the Museum.

Five people read my manuscript in its early, floundering stages and urged me to persevere. My thanks to Mr. C. Fred Bodsworth, Mr. John A. Livingston, Mr. Anker Odum, Mr. E. B. S. Logier, and Dr. W. B. Scott for their advice and encouragement.

Mr. Julian Mulock went over the nearly final stage and contributed many useful suggestions.

My gratitude to Mr. Peter Buerschaper, staunch and valued colleague whose friendship has helped me through rough times of which he may or may not have been aware.

For all those cheerful souls who shared the joys and hardships of the expeditions I have fond and nostalgic recollections.

Lastly, I acknowledge my indebtedness to a multitude of wild creatures; their beauty of form and colour; the melody of their voices and their very wildness have given me a fuller and richer life.

T. M. Shortt

All illustrations by Terry Shortt